TUNISIA

SAIS African Studies Library

General Editor
I. William Zartman

TUNISIA

The Political Economy of Reform

edited by
I. William Zartman

Lynne Rienner Publishers • Boulder & London

Published in the United States of America in 1991 by
Lynne Rienner Publishers, Inc.
1800 30th Street, Boulder, Colorado 80301

and in the United Kingdom by
Lynne Rienner Publishers, Inc.
3 Henrietta Street, Covent Garden, London WC2E 8LU

Library of Congress Cataloging-in-Publication Data
Tunisia : the political economy of reform / edited by I. William
  Zartman.
  (SAIS African studies library)
  Includes bibliographical references and index.
  ISBN 1-55587-230-1
  1. Tunisia—Economic policy. 2. Tunisia—Economic
conditions—1956- 3. Tunisia—Politics and government. 4. Tunisia—
Social conditions. 5. Tunisia—Foreign relations. I. Zartman,
I. William. II. Series.
HC820.T865 1990
338.9611—dc20   90-45574
                                                           CIP

British Cataloguing in Publication Data
A Cataloguing in Publication record for this book
is available from the British Library.

Printed and bound in the United States of America

The paper used in this publication meets the requirements
of the American National Standard for Permanence of
Paper for Printed Library Materials Z39.48-1984.

To Jeanne Jeffers Mrad
for her untiring and enthusiastic efforts in building
Tunisian-U.S. academic cooperation and understanding

Contents

Tables and Figures

■ **Tables**

■ Figures

Acknowledgments

T his study is the result of a conference on the political economy of contemporary Tunisia, organized by the African Studies Program of the Johns Hopkins University Nitze School of Advanced International Studies (SAIS) in Washington, April 1989. The conference was part of SAIS's annual African Country Day Program, which each year features a collective investigation of a selected African country. We are grateful to the Joint Committee on the Near and Middle East of the Social Science Research Council for support for this project, to the Ford and Rockefeller foundations for their support of this program, and to the Tunisian ambassador, Abdelaziz Hamzaoui, for his gracious assistance. We are also grateful to SAIS and to the Center for Maghrib Studies in Tunis (CEMAT) of the American Institute for Maghrib Studies (AIMS) for their help. We are particularly thankful to Theresa Taylor Simmons for her skillful administration of the program and to Douglas Bayley for the processing of this volume.

I. William Zartman

Tunisia

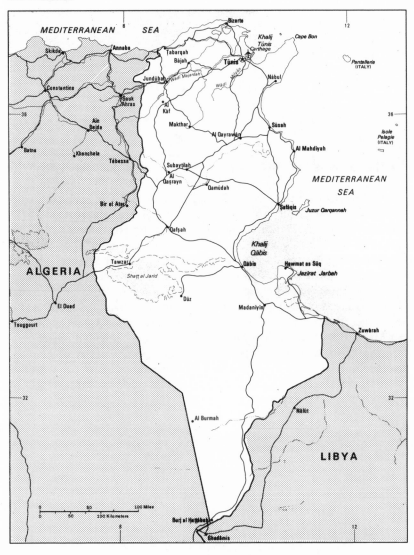

Introduction

I. William Zartman

Tunisia is typical of many countries in the late 1980s undergoing intensive reform. Societies as diverse as the Soviet Union, China, South Africa, Algeria, and Mexico—and many other countries struggling with structural adjustment in combination with political change—are all going through a similar experience in their own ways. *Reform* is a distinct process with its own dynamics and its own literature (Huntington 1969, ch. 6; Hirschman 1963; Coulton 1986). Clearly something short of revolution, it is nonetheless not the only alternative and is different in its aims and outcomes from stagnation, reaction, and simply muddling through. Reform is a broad policy approach or project of accelerated and purposeful change in social, economic, and political arenas within and through established state institutions. New leaders dedicated to change use their positions to resolve—rather than simply manage—past problems on the agenda and in the process make some changes in the nature of the agenda itself and the social base of power as well. This is the idea. Whether the individual case in history fits all the defining characteristics of the phenomenon or not is part of the eternal problem of fitting concepts to reality, or (for the politician) of turning intentions into accomplishments.

Reform is a state response to a rising cry from the body politic for a resolution of urgent issues. That cry is probably not universal, of course, since there are likely to be many who benefit from the current state of affairs or who fear changes that resolve. But it is loud enough to pose a crisis or crises in state–society relations and to legitimize and support the efforts of the reformers. As a particularly concentrated moment of both government activity and social pressure (Bentley 1935), a time of reform is a time of intensive interaction between state and society. Yet the body politic—or segments of it—may not like the particular reforms enacted as a response, so that the reformers often find themselves caught between pressures to do something and opposition to what they do. Unless the reformers are able to

1

build up a base of support for their reform measures that takes over the legitimization and support functions of the original demand for change, the crisis will return—often in renewed strength because of the disappointed expectations. Thus, reformers are called by crisis, but they need both to resolve the urgent issues of the agenda and to build an ongoing base of societal support.

The crisis in Tunisia toward the end of the 1980s was manyfold (Camau 1987), its issues fitting nicely into the classical triple division of the public agenda—political, economic, and social. The political crisis was most apparent, although it, too, had multiple layers. Basically, it was a crisis in the legitimacy of the Bourguibist state. The crisis was topped by the question as to life president Habib Bourguiba himself, the founder of the state, who had outlived his charisma, routinized his revolution, and handed over his legal-rational order to cronies, thus destroying the three classic sources of his legitimacy (Gerth and Mills 1958, ch. 4). But Bourguiba was only the most visible part of the problem, just as he was only half of the legitimization of the state. The other part was his party, the Socialist Destourian (Constitutional) Party (PSD), Tunisia's nationalist-movement-turned-single-party. In its heyday (lasting into the early 1970s) it had been both a great coalition of Tunisian social forces and a vanguard of the Tunisian polity (Micaud, Brown, and Moore 1964; Moore 1965); but by the 1980s it had become ingrown and ossified. Tunisians were increasingly alienated by the single-party system and looked for its natural evolution into a multiparty system with some choice. Without any consensus on the answer, Tunisians questioned both the individuals who governed them and the system within with they governed.

It would be satisfying to be able to present organizational or public opinion evidence for this crisis, but crises usually elude such elegant data even in the best organized and best polled societies. Evidence is clear, nonetheless. It comes on the personal level from private expressions of disaffection toward the personalized regime and its increasingly embarrassing media portrayals. It comes, on the organizational level, negatively from the absence of support for the PSD and for the state's directives (as in the striking inability of the party to win support for the decision to eliminate bread subsidies in January 1984) and positively from the rise in the following of the Movement of the Islamic Way (MTI) with its alternative project for governance and its outspoken challenge to Bourguiba's legitimacy.[1]

The economic crisis was also multidimensional. Its internationally visible manifestation was the weakening position of Tunisia in the world economic system after decades of impressive domestic economic growth, putting the country among others requiring structural adjustment before they could qualify for a standby agreement from the World Bank. But the recent history of growth posed distributional questions that were even more pressing on the domestic level. The economic miracle of Prime Minister Hedi Nouira, former governor of the Bank of Tunis, in the 1970s brought a greater span of class divisions than Tunisia had ever seen. Conspicuous consumption among nouveaux riches made them offensive to both lower classes recently promoted to an improved but very vulnerable position and to middle-class youth educated for unemployment. Socialism, in the party name and the Tunisian practice, was discredited by its imperfect implementation; and private enterprise was preferred above all because bureaucratic control was not.

The January 1984 bread riots were again the dramatic evidence of the economic crisis on the domestic level, just as the World Bank reports were evidence on the international level. Economics, unlike politics and society, produces constant data by which performance can be judged; Tunisia's trade balance, hard currency reserves, budgetary balance, and employment rates all underscored the need for economic reform.

The social crisis was also highly visible but of a different order from the other two. Arguably, Bourguiba, like Ataturk in Turkey, deserves most credit for his secular modernization of society, with its centerpiece, the Code of Personal Status of 1956 (Micaud, Brown, and Moore 1964, 147ff; Camau 1987, ch. 13), which radically changed women's social position. Along with this came a personal attitude on the part of Bourguiba that could only be qualified as antireligious, not just secularist, and could only be seen in Tunisia as anti-Islamic. From the beginning, many Tunisians were offended by this attitude, while supporting the secular modernization measures. Until the late 1970s and the rise of Islamic fundamentalism in the Muslim world, no one could or dared organize the feelings of opposition; but when social offense was reinforced by political alienation and economic discontent, mobilization of dissatisfaction became possible.

In this arena, however, the crisis came from the opposition, not from the condition. Exacerbated residual protest against earlier secularizing reform, not the disintegration of the original reform program, was the urgent issue. It, too, raised its own ramifications. The Bourguibist state never was very concerned about individual rights in the face of collective progress (Zartman 1963, 70); but the confrontation between state and Islamicists raised human rights issues in the late 1980s, just when human rights in general were receiving another surge of international attention. Like the Islamicists, the human rights advocates became spokesmen for broader feelings of political crisis and swung into action during the outbursts of economic discontent. Thus, political, economic, and social agenda were linked together in many ways at the end of the decade, often resulting in strange bedfellows but also generating conflicting attitudes of loyalty and opposition toward the regime.

A study made as late as mid-1987 would have highlighted these contradictions and the incoherence of Tunisian polity, society, and economy

(Camau 1987). But the sudden removal of Bourguiba on November 7 in a situation supersaturated with oppositions crystallized support behind the new president, General Zine Labidine ben Ali. The state and the president were relegitimized, economic confidence and even performance were restored (with a little help from the rain), and the silent majority behind the social accomplishments of the old regime came to the fore. Seizing on the momentary support, ben Ali swung into action as a reformer to deal in depth with the crises of the times. His third anniversary provides a good opportunity to take stock of that effort and evaluate the concerted reform program.

Ben Ali's accession to the presidency did not clear the agenda, but it did clarify the three crises. By lancing the abscess of succession, it showed the political issue to be not simply personalism but an entire political project—single-partyism versus multipartyism. By the same act, it showed the Islamicists to be not simply an antipersonalist expression but the expression of an entire counterproject for society—Islamicism versus secularism. Even on the economic front, where the confrontation between two economic projects—state socialism versus structural adjustment (private enterprise)—was already posed and decided (with a little help from the World Bank) at the end of the old regime, the debate and the need for implementing reforms continued under the new.

Unlike the act of accession (which commanded a large majority of support after the fact), the many acts of reform aroused different and competing social pressures. Often these were *for* general change but *against* specific change that disturbed vested interests, opened new risks, and enlisted no organized support groups. Multiparty competition, free and fair elections, civil liberties, and national consensus were all aspects of political reform that aroused conflicting socioeconomic (as well as political) pressures. These measures responded to a broad-based cry from society; but once enacted, they left the reform regime with an emerging coalition of urban business and intellectuals and rural notables and organizers as support, with urban and potentially even rural underclasses as the basis of opposition (see Part 1). Subsidies, parastatals, bank controls, and agricultural development projects were all subjects of economic reform running between shifting sociopolitical pressures (see Part 2). Although hard to enact, these reforms responded to pressures from every segment of society except for the bureaucracy; yet the insufficiency of their effects produced neither a new and coherent social base for the regime nor an enthusiastic great coalition. Personal status, tourism and holidays, Islamic symbols and values, and religious expression and representation were the key ingredients of the social agenda also involving political and economic pressures. After an initial government effort to steal the agenda from the opposition, the antireformists have been able to throw the government on the defensive, forcing it to chose between losing either its secularist supporters or its religious supporters (see Part 3). Similar pressures and reforms are visible in foreign relations (see Part 4).

This book analyzes reform in Tunisia in the first two years of the ben Ali regime as both a program of the new ruler and his team and as a focus of social pressures. It seeks to explain the course of events, in terms of both accomplishments and limitations and thus develop a fuller picture of both state and society in motion.

■ **Note**

1. This book will use the name "Movement of the Islamic Way" as a translation of "harakat al-ittajah al-islami" instead of the more usual Islamic Tendency Movement taken from the French, but will keep the initials MTI.

PART 1
POLITICAL REFORM

1

The Conduct of Political Reform: The Path Toward Democracy

I. William Zartman

Tunisia at the end of the 1980s represents a striking case of transition toward democracy. The opportunities, intentions, and decisions are all clear and present. Observers had long predicted a multiparty evolution for Tunisia; there was pluralism in its past from the early years of Independence, and an attempt—eventually flawed—had been made to open up the political system at the beginning of the decade. Pluralist, competitive democracy was the major plank in the platform of the new president, Zine Labidine ben Ali, from his first proclamation of November 7, 1987 onward. His first eighteen months were punctuated by careful decisions establishing the rules for the democratic opening, which finally occurred in the general elections of April 1989, followed by the municipal elections of May 1990. But other pressures and participants were also involved, working in the opposite direction. Some, such as the Islamic movement, widely perceived as a threat, restricted the process by threatening to overwhelm it. Others, notably the leadership of the old single party, subverted the process by utilizing it.

The following story is an analysis of how these competing and cooperating forces shaped the drive to political reform, leaving its future impact ambiguous. It is a structural analysis, because the structure of the situation dominated the unfolding of events. But it did not determine them. It only narrowed choices and established the context for decisions. The evolution of politics—and the movement of the Tunisian polity along the path of reform—was ultimately a matter of choice of more or less skilled, more or less committed individuals. Human actions are not determined, either by structure or by analysis. Within structures, choice is a matter of perception and will.[1]

9

■ **Criteria**

Works on transitions from authoritarian rule toward democracy have identified a certain number of elements in the process—not to be taken in any strict sense of order but as progressing, overlapping, and reinforcing each other until an end is achieved (Rustow 1970; O'Donnell and Schmitter 1986; Binnendijk 1987). These are defined as the opening and undermining of the authoritarian order, the establishment of new pacts and of the rules of the new game, the restructuring of civil society and public space, and the organization of participation and elections. The essential nature of the process is to turn politics from a private to a public process and therefore to organize and reconstitute the components of that shift. Included in that process must be the establishment of safeguards that politics not be reprivatized, that is, that public participation in politics not end with the selection of leaders, who then proceed to do politics privately.

But what happens if politics is already public in ideology and organization, although without competition—if participation and election are already present, but within the framework of a monopolistic structure—if the history of the polity itself has produced a belief system branding all opposition treasonous and providing consensus around a past program—if the people who are skilled and interested in doing politics are already doing it in the old order, leaving those outside radical and inexperienced in democratic competition?

This is the situation one meets in single-party regimes. Here the problems are not the same as in military authoritarian regimes, and the transition is more difficult. Single parties tend to come from (quasi-) revolutionary origins with pretensions to ideological justification and purport to incarnate the nation; as mass movements, they can often claim a broad social basis and a glorious moment in the nation's history. Unlike the military, the single party does not withdraw when it makes the democratic transition; it remains in place and to take on the competition. Previously, competition was viewed as subversive; and the party was highly experienced in making sure that none appeared. If any dared appear, the party knew how to ensure that it could not claim any victories. Now, opposition suddenly is legitimate, although the limits to its exercise remain to be established and tested. The opposition must distinguish itself from the single party—as indeed must the new democratic result—but without destroying or denying many of the accomplishments of the previous system. Yet neither new parties nor old, neither government nor opposition, know what loyal opposition is or how it is expected to act. The shift from single-party to multiparty rule is a traumatic moment in a nation's history.

There are identifiable conditions that can focus the trauma on the old party system and facilitate the transition to the new, although they are not always unambiguous in their effects. A thoroughly discredited single party can leave the field open to newcomers, but it may also undertake internal reforms and combine a new image with old skills and expertise to block the competition. A new leader may make it easier to open up the political system, but he also has to worry about his own legitimacy and authority and perhaps lack of experience. The old leader could make the transition more easily; but, like an outgoing military dictator, he must look on the transition as the crowning act of his regime. There are no perfect conditions, where all the interests point in the same direction; and the tensions of conflicting structural imperatives form the obstacles of the course.

It has sometimes been suggested that a single-party polity is so unnatural that its persistence—rather than its collapse—is what needs to be explained (Zartman 1967). Since politics is by definition conflict—optimally operating nonviolently and within consensual rules—a single-party can persist only if it contains pluralistic competition within its own rules and organization or if it skillfully manages the sources of pluralism so as to tame them within the single-party framework. In one case it becomes civil society, in the other it stands between civil society and unusually wise central leadership. Otherwise, it is merely the appendage of authoritarian rule—a historic facade, a ministry of mobilization, or a club of cronies. Thus, it is most likely that once a polity has passed through the "funnel phase" of politics dominated by a single, overriding issue such as independence or revolutionary restructuring, the single party will fall apart under the pressure of ideological, personal, regional, social, or generational differences. Such explanations are still accurate in analyzing the problems of the single party, but they do not address the problem of effectuating a transition.

The more the single party—in whatever role it has operated—is threatened by one or more of these sources of division, the more it will seek to fight back and preserve its existence against the threat. In the process it may well change its role, healthily or unhealthily for the polity; that is, it may move from a ministry of mobilization to a democratically competing party or from an effectively coopting body to an authoritarian facade. To pose the problem in these terms is not to reify a collective entity; it is to recognize a structural imperative operating on the entity's leaders and followers. The point is that the single party does not simply fall apart or retire. It continues to play during the transition and in playing continues to defend its existence and its predominance in the polity. Its purposes, by its nature and structural position, are almost never the purposes of transition to democracy, so that the effectiveness of that transition to its announced goal depends on the skills and resources of opposing forces. The single party has long prevented democracy in its own name, and it can still undermine the transition to democracy by playing by its rules. Hence, this particular case—more than the more usual one of transition from authoritarian rule—poses the question of the sustainability of political reform: How long does it take under what optimal conditions to reform a political system from monopoly to meaningful competition?

■ Background

The Socialist Destourian (Constitutional) Party (PSD) had long been a textbook case of single-party rule, with all its strengths and weaknesses; and Tunisia had been cited as a place where a functioning single party could—and would—break up into a multiparty system as a normal stage of its evolution (Micaud, Brown, and Moore 1964; Moore 1965; Rudebeck 1969). Indeed, when the nationalist movement came to power at Independence in 1956, it had to establish its monopoly of power over competing factions and, especially, to undo an attempt by the General Union of Tunisian Workers (UGTT) under Ahmed ben Salah to set up a separate Socialist party. But the single-party system grew rigid along with its formerly charismatic leader, Habib Bourguiba, who had frozen it in the mid-1970s at the same time as he had himself made life president. In the early 1980s President Bourguiba, through his prime minister Mohammed Mzali, tried both to revive the PSD and to hold competitive multiparty elections. The liberal Democratic Socialist movement (MDS) of Ahmed Mestiri, the Tunisian Communist party (PCT) of Mohammed Harmel, and the socialist People's Unity movement (MUP) of ben Salah participated alongside the PSD (Slim 1982). But once the multiparty vote was cast, in 1981, Bourguiba, Mzali, and their interior minister Driss Guiga could not bring themselves to announce the real results and usher in the multiparty era; and the figures were falsified. The bread price riots of January 1984 showed the incapacity both of the party to mobilize popular support for policy and of the president to steer a firm course. More and more sharply engaged in a battle over the social and political program for Tunisian society with the Movement of the Islamic Way (MTI), which benefited from the rising current of Islamic values and also from the absence of any other means of expressing disillusionment with the sclerotic regime, Bourguiba led his country toward a collapse of civil order (Burgat 1988; Vatin 1982; Camau, Amrain, and Achour 1981; Hermassi 1984; Souriau et al. 1981). On November 7, 1987 he was replaced in a "constitutional coup" by his prime minister, ben Ali (cf. Vandewalle 1987, 1988).

There were three triggers to the accession of ben Ali. The first was Bourguiba's deteriorating physical—and hence mental—condition, as exemplified by the accelerating personnel shuffles. The same day he raised ben Ali from interior minister to prime minister, October 2, 1987, Bourguiba revoked the appointment of a party director made three days before;

the new director, Mahjoub ben Ali (no relation), then served only two weeks before being replaced in turn by Hamed Karoui. Then again, at the end of the month, Bourguiba reversed himself on the appointment of two secretaries of state for planning and finance, accusing those around him of lying and trickery. Personnel instability was becoming more and more frequent, making governance impossible.

The second, and more proximate, cause grew out of the ongoing trial of Islamic fundamentalists—members of the banned MTI and others. The state security court had handed down its verdict—judged "clement" by the defense and the opposition—on September 27. The appeals court rejected the appeal, and Bourguiba refused clemency for the two Islamicists under death sentence, who were then executed on October 8. A week later one of the accused condemned to death in absentia was captured, and Bourguiba used the occasion to demand a retrial of other fundamentalists who had received lesser sentences. When ben Ali pointed out the illegality as well as the civic danger of this course, he was ordered to reopen the trial by Monday, November 9 or lose his position. Bourguiba had set his own date for succession.

The third trigger is still partially unclarified. At the beginning of November, incidental arrests brought to light a plot by the militant wing of the MTI to assassinate top political figures, including Bourguiba and ben Ali, if the fundamentalists' trials were reopened. The assassinations were to take place on November 8. Subsequently, seventy-three members of the plot were arrested and remained in prison without trial in Tunis for two years. (The plot is also discussed in Chapter 11.)

The accession to power of ben Ali occurred on the night of November 6–7, 1987, when he assembled seven doctors and received from the procurator-general their statement of Bourguiba's "absolute incapacity" to govern. A new government was named with Hedi Baccouche (former party director, who drafted the declaration of November 7) as prime minister and Habib ben Ammar (commander of the National Guard, who conducted the takeover of the presidential palace) as interior minister. The "constitutional coup" was announced with a stirring declaration of a reform program, known as the Principles of November 7.

Ben Ali is in many ways the opposite of Bourguiba: an unassuming not a galvanizing speaker; a listener, not an autocrat; a bureaucrat from military intelligence, not a founding father of a party; and a man with a sense of the separation of state and party and of civil liberties for citizens. He faced two broad challenges: to assure his own position within the troubled political and social context of Tunisia and to bring about a transition to democracy as his program. The two are related but are not coincident. The new president had to "regularize" the temporary legitimization conferred by his seizure of power with an institutionalized legitimization by plebescite. He had to impose his own political direction on both a *system* that though glad to be free of its senescent leader, was used to having a deux ex machina emerge from the clouds at crucial moments to save it from itself and on a corrupt *party machine* that even though skilled and experienced, was, with the former president, the cause of political alienation within the body politic. Coming to office the way he did, ben Ali had no rivals to contend with; nor was there any agency that could remove him. At the same time, he had to get a respectable vote in his plebescite and ongoing popular support and bureaucratic cooperation for his reforms. The threat he faced was not a loss of office but a loss of authority over groups and people around him, who might run off with pieces of his power and hem in his ability to lead the program he wanted.

His political reform program was transition to democracy, but the competitive components were not readily at hand. The PSD needed to be restructured and revitalized but at the same time was obliged to move over and make room for others as well. The MTI had to be tamed, reduced, and made to play by democratic rules while accepting the modernizing accomplishments of the previous regime; licensing the hitherto subversive fundamentalist movement posed the key question of the limits of democratic pluralism and loyal opposition. Criteria had to be established for licensing other parties as well. The appropriate time, level, and form of elections also had to be decided; but before that, a new constitution with guarantees and procedures was needed for multiparty democracy. But the new elections dare not be merely the occasion to throw the rascals out, to mortgage the new democracy to the old single party, or to set up the fundamentalists' revenge. The wrong results could discredit the whole democratization process, but (as every politician knows) "right results" are not easy to produce freely.

Ben Ali's dilemma has been that he has not been entirely free himself from the forces that he has sought to tame. Although he is a popular figure with a knack for not saying the wrong thing, he has never felt strong enough to take on the party directly and never had any sure counterparties to balance the Destourian machine. Unlike Mikhail Gorbachev, he could not bring himself to make the "ultimate escape: jumping free of his place atop the . . . Party before that institution falls of its own dying weight . . . by neutralizing what remains of the old guard and modernizing its program, and simultaneously build[ing] up the presidency and elected legislature as stable power centers" (Keller 1990). "No presents!" party leaders kept on repeating at every stage of their engagement in the democratization process. Because of the interests of the party and the habits of the bureaucracy, ben Ali was not in control of the credibility of his processes. But if he would play a stronger role, relying on his decisiveness and popularity, he could easily fall into the autocratic mold left by his predecessor. Observers were quick to identify symptoms of the reappearance of the neo-Bourguibist personality cult, just as they were ready to recognize the unchanging dominance of the single party.

Caught between the shadow of Bourguiba and the machine of the Destour, ben Ali and his transition to democracy walked a narrow path.

Ben Ali's initial legitimacy derived entirely from the way he came to power. The fact that he broke the inability of the political system to rid itself of an eighty-five-year-old embarrassment was a mark of his decisiveness and courage; the act of ousting the supreme combatant was a test of political muscle equal to a coup or a campaign (Burling 1974, 258). The constitution gave formal sanction to that act, but the prime minister had a chance to succeed only because the man of action took the gamble of declaring and enforcing the incapacity. Faced with an earlier temptation to do the same thing, Mzali was to have said, "I didn't have the guts."

In addition, ben Ali came to power with a mixed reputation of firmness and humanity. Although his initial appointment to the government as interior minister earlier in 1987 brought public concern over the first entry of a military man into the cabinet in a state where the military has been kept under tight control, Ben Ali soon became known as the person who argued for clemency and legality in dealing with the fundamentalists. From the beginning, his entry was given a mixed welcome, and it is likely that he mended his fences early with the liberal opposition (Gharbi 1987; cf. Vandewalle 1987). Yet from the moment of his first radio announcement at 6 A.M. on November 7, ben Ali was most careful to preserve all that was positive in the reputation of Bourguiba and to pay his deepest respects to Bourguiba's primary role in building the state.

■ Decisions Toward Democracy

The move toward democracy involved ongoing and overlapping decisions on a number of aspects of the reform process. Not all of them were made by the government, nor was the government a single and unified decisionmaking agency. The president, (including his advisors) and the former single party were two centers of decision; but crucial roles were also played by other agencies (including the MDS and other opposition party leaderships) and also by the more pluralistic leadership of the fundamentalists. There were twelve steps toward competitive multiparty elections and the establishment of a new political system in Tunisia—major decision points surrounded by lesser ones at crucial junctures in defined areas of political activity where a choice among alternatives was available and a fateful path chosen. In overlapping sequence, they were the decisions to liberalize political activity, discourage a new presidential party, conduct several by-elections, revive the PSD under presidential direction, coopt opposition members, make the president of the country the president of the revived PSD, schedule general and presidential elections, authorize competing secular parties, formalize political consensus in a National Pact, maintain a winner-take-all electoral law, reject a common front, and register a vote creating a hobbled two-party system. These decisions generally cluster into five areas of activity: (1) the legal rules of politics, (2) the institutions of pluralism, (3) the institutions of consensus, (4) the relations between the reformer and the polity, and (5) the electoral judgments of the polity.

The accession was accompanied by a number of immediate measures of *liberalization*, which translated the spirit of the new regime but also relieved the worst grievances of the Bourguiba regime. Despite the potential danger that past and present opposition figures and forces might pose to the new regime, the new prime minister announced on the morrow of the coup that opponents abroad could return to Tunisia; the new interior minister added a week later that they would nonetheless have to take care of judgments outstanding against them. Various opposition leaders, including ben Salah, Guiga, and Tahar Belkhodja, returned, most of them receiving presidential clemency. In general, they were has-beens, too involved with the old regime—despite their exiles and sentences—to pose any threat to the new order. Ben Ali also expanded his contacts with the local opposition parties from the beginning; both he and the prime minister met Secretary-General Mestiri of the MDS, Secretary-General Harmel of the PCT, and Secretary-General Mohammed Belhaj Amor of the Party of Popular Unity (PUP) at the end of November and the beginning of December.

At the same time the president inaugurated a series of pardons and amnesties that emptied the prisons of political prisoners. He began by freeing all students conscripted in the army for having participated in the university riots of the previous year and amnestied 2,487 political and criminal prisoners, excepting only 90 fundamentalist agitators sentenced in September and 73 fundamentalist plotters of the November countercoup. The death sentences given in the September trials were commuted to life imprisonment, the trials stopped, and the security court abolished by law at the end of the year. In March another 2,044 prisoners were pardoned, and two capital sentences were commuted to life at hard labor; in July another 32 prisoners were pardoned; and in November the last 88 political prisoners were released (as certified by the Tunisian Human Rights League) along with 2,031 others. A general amnesty law signed in July 1989 restored civil rights to 5,416 former political prisoners. Liberalization measures also continued in other domains, as in the revision of the 1975 press code and the reduction of requirements for the authorization of associations, both passed in July 1988. These liberalization decisions were not mere atmospherics; they were evidence of a basic change in the nature of the political system, opening it up to pluralism of opinion and debate without incrimination.

Presidential partnership was a major issue to be decided. As PSD president, Bourguiba had combined the two sources of legitimacy in independent Tunisia—charismatic leadership and nationalist movement. Ben Ali wanted to be president of all Tunisians and was concerned that a too-close party affiliation would be a drag on his popularity. In response, his party advisors argued the case of the U.S. president, titular head of his party and president of all citizens. At the time of his prime ministership, ben Ali had felt uncomfortable with a party role, since he had had no past as a party man and wanted to be relieved of the inherent concomitant of government leadership, the secretary-generalship of the PSD. Bourguiba had refused his request. From the moment that ben Ali took over the presidency he was torn between his role as president of all Tunisians and president of the party. During the budget debate in December 1987, he was pressed on this question by PSD deputies, to whom he had delivered (through Baccouche) the message that he was indeed president of the party as well as president of the country. Yet the question was not resolved in any of the players' minds.

The most important decision on the subject was taken later in the same month, when ben Ali agreed with his prime minister and other party advisors not to encourage the formation of the November 7 Clubs that were springing up around the country nor to unite those that were formed into a national organization. This decision represents a major lost opportunity in ben Ali's campaign to restructure the polity and was accompanied by a decision to focus the reform efforts on the party instead. Crucial as it was, the decision was natural, since ben Ali had no party experience and relied for advice in the matter on the very people whose past and future was associated with the party.

Party renewal was a compelling topic of early attention. Although the PSD was discredited by the end of Bourguiba's reign, after November 7 the party rallied immediately to ben Ali's support, distanced itself from the old order, and remained part of the ongoing legal order. The most natural but crucial decision was made on November 9, when ben Ali assumed the chairmanship of the party's Political Bureau and reduced it from twenty to twelve members, only four of them carryovers. A contrary decision would have left a center of power open to a potential competitor, although it would also have demoted the importance of the summit itself. Instead, the president took over the party, enabling the party to begin its takeover of the president. At the end of December, the Political Bureau called a meeting of the Central Committee for late February. On the agenda were measures to democratize and strengthen the party for an extraordinary Party Congress in July, in preparation for the democratization of the country through early general elections. The ambiguity of the reform was symbolized by the new name that the Central Committee adopted for the old PSD: the Democratic Constitutionalist (Destourian) Rally (RCD). The historic word *Destourian* was kept only in Arabic; *party* became the broader and looser *rally*; and *socialist* was traded in for *democratic*.

Organizationally, the Political Bureau was to reform party structures by appointing federal committees, which in turn would propose a slate of new names to the president, who would appoint section committees from among them, which would in turn recruit new members into the party. The operation was completed in April; 80 percent of the section committee members were new to the committees, but only 20 percent of the members (i.e., a quarter of the 80 percent) were new to the party. The cells, sections and federations were then to elect their delegates to the Party Congress at the end of July 1988. At that time, a new Central Committee was constituted, with only 75 of its members elected from local cells and 125 (plus ben Ali) appointed by the Political Bureau; 22 had been members of the 1986 Central Committee. As early as May, presidential advisors were admitting that the remaking, or democratization, of the party was not likely to be as complete as hoped.

Reform, therefore, meant reviving the party by bringing in former party men and civic personalities from other political organizations and from non-political life. The process, though limited, was so successful that it left little room for the revival of other parties, which alone would make it meaningful. Although figures are not available, opposition and potential partner parties indicated that they had real difficulties in swelling their ranks. Politically minded Tunisians, encouraged to support the efforts of ben Ali to revive the Tunisian polity, joined the RCD, following the example of the president.

Two sets of *by-elections* mandated by existing legislation set warning lights on the channel leading to party reform and pluralization. The decisions were in the hands of the voters, filtered through the local administrators' decisions about their own role in elections on the threshold of the new regime. On December 20, municipal elections in Ksar Hellal saw the PSD defeated for the first time by an Independent slate composed of breakaway Destourian members (Chaieb 1987). On January 24, 1988, by-elections were held for parliamentary seats vacated by Bourguiba's closest lieutenants in Tunis, Zaghouan, and Gafsa and two seats in Monastir. The PSD learned the previous month's lesson: it won all, but it took machine intervention in Gafsa to assure that the Ksar Hellal experience was not repeated (al-Nasiri 1988); although ben Ali gave personal help and assurances to the Independent candidate (who then got 31 percent of the vote), the president was obliged to admit that "there were irregularities here and there." The experiences of December and January confirmed the fears about the new broom and the old machine in the minds of both the public and the party.

Once party revival—rather than renewal—was accomplished, the second act of *presidential partisanship* could be played out. The 1988 Party Congress at the end of July—named the Congress of Salvation in order to avoid the choice between *XIII* and *I (New Series)*—culminated this reform of the organization established by the former president. After some real hesitation as to whether his desire to be president of all Tunisians allowed him to become president of the party and with a lot of justifying reference to the U.S. party-presidential system, ben Ali decided to accept the party presidency and thus, automatically, its label as candidate for the national presidency. The Political Bureau was reduced to seven men, consisting of ben Ali, Hedi Baccouche, Abderrahim Zouari, Ahmed Kallal, Ammar, and, as new members, Habib Echeikh, and Ismail Khelil—all ben Ali's men. All but Ammar and Echeikh (the military men) and Khelil (the economic technician) were members of the 1986 Central Committee. Zouari was chosen as the new secretary-general, in effect the party director. From the Central Committee, six new functional committees under assistant secretaries-general were chosen to make functional studies on policy as well as to run internal party activities. The president had agreed to tie his personal legitimizing plebescite to his candidacy as party leader.

Ben Ali's lingering notions of "president of all Tunisians" began to be translated in the spring of 1988 into the notion of a "presidential majority" into which he would *coopt opposition* figures to counterbalance his growing attachment to the predominant party. While most of the members of his close entourage were former PSD activists—or at least military or economic technicians within Bourguiba's establishment—a few important recruits came from opposition sources. Unfortunately for new recruiting, these were rare under the pervasive Bourguibist regime. Since the subjection of the labor movement, the only remaining source of independent political thought was the Tunisian League for Human Rights (LTDH), whose leadership overlapped with the MDS and also included nonpartisan faculty members from the university.

The first notable addition from the LTDH–MDS was Hamouda ben Slama, personally solicited by the president to run as a then-PSD candidate in the January 1988 legislative by-elections, where he won handily. The next round of cooptations came when ben Ali's new government was announced, just before the extraordinary Party Congress (so as to prevent the congress from being dominated by delegations' jockeying for new government positions). Dr. Sadok Zmerli, president of the LTDH, was appointed health minister; and Habib Boulares, a former PSD minister who had followed the liberals into exile in the 1970s but then was serving as ambassador to Egypt, was returned to the position of minister of culture. When the National Pact was drawn up, Professor Mohammed Charfi, the new president of the LTDH, was chosen to chair the drafting committee in September; and in November, Professor Dali Jazi, another officer of the LTDH and also of the MDS, was appointed ambassador to Vienna, a move that tore apart the leadership of the MDS. In the second governmental revisions, immediately following the April 1989 elections, both Charfi and Jazi received ministries—Education and Health respectively (Zmerli not having proven to be an effective administrator). These latter members remained outside the party but visible evidence of a larger "presidential majority"; whereas ben Slama and Boulares became members of the new party Political Bureau in April 1989. By that time, a number of professors from the Law School and other parts of the university were brought into the party apparatus; and the RCD prided itself in having some eight hundred party members among the faculty, a figure unheard of in Bourguiba's day. In addition, a few notable members of the president's entourage remained close to ben Ali but outside the party, strengthening the presidency but ultimately undermining the independence of the opposition.

The next important subject of decisions involved the type and date of *elections*. "No power," said the president to the National Assembly in a remarkably binding and sweeping statement, "which does not rest on the sovereignty of the people, concretized by the free and direct election of its leaders, can claim legitimacy" (*La Presse*, July 26, 1988). Three levels of elections were involved: presidential, parliamentary, and municipal. The latter were normally scheduled for May 1990, and the parliamentary elections for November 1991; early parliamentary elections could not be held later than a year before their regularly scheduled date. Party and presidential advisors argued for another round of by-elections after January 1988 to test the nation's pulse in the absence of public opinion polls. For reasons difficult to understand, ben Ali was hesitant to set an early date for the presidential election that he needed for his legitimization; and party leaders were torn between fears of sweeping the general elections because of the habits and effectiveness of the party machine and being roundly trounced by a public vigorously seizing the opportunity to wield a new broom and sweep clean. Since, despite ben Ali's fears, there was no one who could lead a credible campaign against the president, the presidential election should best be paired with the parliamentary elections, where competition and campaigning would be possible, rather than left to stand alone. In the summer of 1988 there was some discussion among presidential advisors in favor of advancing the municipal elections and using them to test the nation's pulse.

The president's entourage was very troubled about the lack of information about the state of mind of the Tunisian electorate, since political polling had never been permitted. The December–January by-elections had only confirmed their fears, but the turn of the year marked the nadir of the PSD's fortunes; things had presumably changed since then, but no one was sure in which direction. Only the PCT took part in the earlier by-elections and then not under its party label; the other parties, MDS in the lead, refused to participate in any partial elections and called for early general elections instead. The PSD—now renamed RCD—did not want elections until it had got its own house in order in its extraordinary Party Congress. Up to that point, it was still most likely that the presidential elections would be paired with partial parliamentary elections and scheduled for November 7, 1988, as announced by the president at the end of July. At the same time as the Congress of Salvation, a new constitutional law was promulgated providing for early dissolution and election of the assembly sometime in 1988 or 1989.

Part of the liberalization measures was the *law authorizing political parties*, passed by the National Assembly at the end of April 1988. Reversing the former procedures, authorization was now to be granted unless the government objected (with reasons given) within a period of two months. A number of parties, old and new, lined up to be recognized—not only the PCT and MDS but also the PUP and then some new bodies of uncertain importance, such as the small Progressive Socialist Rally (RSP) of Nejib Chebbi (aspiring to be a labor party), the Arab socialist Democratic Unity Union (UDU) of Abderrahim Tlili, and the personal following of liberal lawyer Mounir Beji, called the Social Party of Progress (PSP) (see *Réalités*, March 31, 1989). The real problem (which remained unresolved, however) was the matter of the MTI, now reorganizing as the Renaissance party (Hizb al-Nahda). The presidency had maintained a dialogue with the fundamentalist leaders ever since November 7, carried out by Dr. ben Slama and then Moncer Rouissi, leading to the movement's reorganization and to increasingly moderate statements by Rachid Ghannouchi (Mezoughi 1988). Officially pardoned by the president in mid-May 1988, Ghannouchi immediately declared the support of the Islamicists for ben Ali's "program of national salvation" and two months later declared his willingness to participate in national politics within the confines of legality. But the government was still unsure that the movement was willing and able to play by democratic rules, and the movement did not apply for recognition as a party throughout 1988.

In addition to the more procedural questions of types and dates of elections, there was also the substantive question of *programmatic consensus*, or the acceptable extent of pluralism and the limits of the political system—the same question that had plagued the previous regime as it faced the prospect of pluralism in 1981. To avoid calling into question the accomplishments of the first quarter-century of Independence, parties running in the 1981 elections were to subscribe to a National Charter drawn up by the PSD; but Bourguiba was still frightened by the prospect of a programmatic opposition, and the election results were falsified. The new 1988 law authorizing political parties prohibited parties based on "religion, language, race or region" and required acceptance of the principles of "human rights and the accomplishments of the nation." On the anniversary of Independence in March 1988, ben Ali stressed the irrevocability of the Personal Status Code and other modernizing reforms of the previous regime. Still, that was not enough.

Attracted by the experience with national charters in Algeria and Spain and especially Nasser's Egypt, ben Ali in April decided to establish a

National Pact that would serve as the instrument of consensus for the forthcoming elections. Its main target was the MTI, with which there were ongoing discussions about the conditions under which the party might be authorized. In September, representatives of business, labor, national organizations, and political parties, including an unofficial representative of the unrecognized MTI, met to debate ben Ali's proposed document and then make editorial changes in the National Pact in a drafting committee dominated by the RCD (Anderson 1990). At the signing ceremony of the National Pact on the first anniversary of November 7, the president announced elections for April, at first on the ninth, then, because of Ramadan, moved up to the second. Only then was it decided to submit the entire assembly to reelection (as the opposition was demanding), without benefit of any preliminary "public opinion polls." In the interim, other important procedural questions—notably the revisions of the voters' rolls and the preparation of candidatures—needed to be handled. Extending the legal provisions, ben Ali decreed two voters' registration periods and held them open longer than the prescribed time. In their turn, the parties scoured their membership for candidatures, testing particularly the renewed structures of the RCD.

The *electoral system* was the subject of a major debate in the National Assembly and the media at the year's end. Opposition parties pressed for a system of proportional representation, against the RCD insistence on the maintenance of the list system with the possibility of cross-voting. In fact, the provision for cross-voting is generally agreed to be unworkable, reducing the system to a winner-take-all vote for competing party lists. With electoral districts the size of provinces (except for Tunis and Gabes, where the provinces [*gouvernorats*] were split in two by the districting finally announced at the end of February), there was no way for minor parties to win seats in the assembly. But French political figures visiting Tunisia at the time emphasized the role of proportional representation in favoring "extremist parties"; and since the government's fears were in fact focused on the danger of fundamentalist extremists (and perhaps communists as well) at the time, it opted for maintenance of the current system, with elaborate justifications solicited from as many quarters as possible.

The dilemma of the old machine versus the new broom still hung over the proceedings, compounded by the question whether there would be a fundamentalist party or not. The MTI registered its request for authorization of the Renaissance (al-Nahda) party on February 7, too late to require a response before the elections but early enough to place the issue squarely before the government and the public. A way of squaring the procedural and substantive questions would be to run a *common list* of candidates from all the parties of the National Pact, a tactic reminiscent of the early days of Independence under Bourguiba. The advantages were clear: a presidential majority, a gentlemanly consensus, an absence of bitter campaigning, and above all freedom from the surprises that stem from the absence of opinion polls—no new brooms and the machine working for all. The disadvantages were equally clear: no tests and no choice and a need to decide on a distribution of seats (and hence of potential losses) acceptable to all.

The notion of the common list, proposed by the president, was discussed in the RCD politburo meetings of January 31 and February 7 and presented to the Central Committee meeting on February 10–11 for its acceptance. The representatives of the National Pact parties were then convoked on February 13; in a cleverly worded proposition by Prime Minister Baccouche, they were offered the principle of a common list, leaving it to them to work out the proportions of an unannounced number of seats among themselves. The representatives of the Renaissance group accepted immediately; the others asked to consult their national organs and return with an answer in a week. During the period, the smaller parties—the PUP, RSP, PSP, and PCT—all pronounced in favor, for a common list would guarantee them a seat that they would find unlikely to win otherwise.

The key player in the crucial decision on the common list was Mestiri's MDS. The party was favored by ben Ali as the cornerstone of the loyal opposition, and he took measures to reinforce its position and that of Mestiri. Despite the contrary opinion of the ten members of his political bureau, Mestiri swung the decision against acceptance of a common list— even threatening resignation—for a complicated array of reasons. Fundamentally, the common list was antithetical to choice; and democracy means choice, with all its consequences. Beyond that, Mestiri was still thinking in 1981 terms of the 30 percent of the vote that had been taken away from him and in mid-1980s terms of his position as intermediary between the government and the Islamicists. He expected special consideration as a result. Instead, he could not even run or vote because of his previous sentence under Bourguiba; and his civic rights were not restored by ben Ali until the end of the candidacy period. Believing his party could run alone and win, Mestiri refused the common list and entered the contest on an electoral system through which he could not possibly win.

The presidential and parliamentary *elections of April 2, 1989* were the culmination of the first round of Tunisian democratic reform. The government announced its entry into the democratic era with understandable pride and enthusiasm, since Tunisia had its first free and fair, nonviolent, competitive multiparty elections. But the claims were somewhat premature and the results ambiguous. The elections gave Tunisia a de facto two-party system without a second party formally constituted and with an opposition of uncertain loyalty. The reinvigorated dominant party, the RCD, won all the seats by the winner-take-all electoral system retained from the old regime. The largest opposition force was the Independents, who stood for the still-unauthorized MTI, or Renaissance party. The election was characterized by normal and inevitable pressures and practices by both the RCD and the MTI such as are often found in machine politics, but it was also criticized by the MDS and MTI for outright falsification of results. As a result of these complications, Tunisia hobbled into the democratic era with less clarity than would have been desirable.

In the vote of April 2, the results were a cause of general surprise. The RCD's total vote of 80 percent was an embarrassing success. The 3.76 percent of the MDS (roughly the same as the falsified figure of 1981) was surprisingly small, although observers reminded themselves afterward that the party was viewed as a younger brother of the RCD and not a real alternative for those who wanted a meaningful protest vote. The overall 14.5 percent of the various Independent lists was surprisingly high, and was even higher (19 percent) when calculated for those districts alone where the Independents ran candidates or (up to 60 percent) for certain lower-class urban voting districts where they did best. Yet to the Independents themselves it was disappointingly low. The only nonsurprise was the nearly unanimous vote of support (99.27 percent) for ben Ali as the only presidential candidate, larger than any vote Bourguiba ever received. However, even behind that figure was the larger sign of dissatisfaction or at least lethargy: of the 4 million potential voters, only 2.7 million registered and 2.1 million voted. The president was plebescited, and the RCD won; but there remains also a tremendous potential for dissatisfaction and challenge, either against or within the new democracy.

The other result of the election was only a disquieting side. The MDS and the Independents launched vigorous challenges against the announced results, in the face of a repeated claim by the government that the elections were "fair and transparent." Already in the registration of candidatures, the Constitutional Court ruled in favor of two challenges by Independents over invalidated lists. The government has maintained that the Interior Ministry is distinct from the ruling party and that the commission will not hesitate to rule justly; and ben Ali has attached his prestige to this pledge. The MDS withdrew its poll watchers from the polling places in the middle of the afternoon on charges that voter intimidation was so strong that continued presence would only lead to violence. Yet when the violations cited are examined against the MDS results, they would only have raised the total by a percentage point or so. The Independents' claims are more serious. Independents were as active in pressuring and organizing voters as were RCD militants. Unlike the MDS, Independent poll watchers stayed at their posts throughout election day; and when the count was completed, they passed the totals to waiting motorcyclists who sped the figures to collection points on the federation and then to provincial level. Their figures differ widely from the official ones, with allegedly supporting information. In this matter—and against an experienced party machine—proof is hard to come by. Yet the Renaissance party people felt robbed of a rightful outcome, and they threatened drastic measures when their complaint was rejected by the Constitutional Commission in May. Similar threats accompanied the government's rejection of the party's application at the beginning of June on a technicality, even though it left the way open for further prolongation of the tractations that had marked government–fundamentalist relations since 1987 (see Ghannouchi 1989).

■ Conclusions

President ben Ali's political reforms had their effect. Enhanced civil liberties, a pluralized political system, and competitive, nonviolent elections were their undeniable result. To say that these accomplishments were only the beginning or that the transition has moved only from a single party to a dominant party rule without reaching its goal of a fully competitive multiparty system is not to deny the progress of the first round of reforms. Nor is it to say that that progress guarantees the success of subsequent steps. Of the elements identified earlier as comprising the process of transition from authoritarian to democratic regimes, significant, if incomplete, progress has been made on all four counts. The authoritarian order has been undermined and opened to a far greater liberty of political expression and action than ever before. New pacts and rules of the game have been carefully established, supported by a broad consensus and enforced by public authority. Public space, always large in Tunisia, has been expanded, as much by the action of the Islamicists and the civil libertarians as by the new government and also by the restoration of professional organizations to their client groups. Participation and elections have been openly organized.

On the other hand, the temptation to return to closed politics increases when hard choices are imposed on government by socioeconomic stagnation and when—as in 1990—public opinion feels that the political honeymoon of the new regime is over. The new pacts and rules of the game are threatening to become their own undoing, as a significant segment of opinion, aggressively organized, clamors for legalization but is suspected of seeking to undermine the open society that would give it voice. Public space and participation still have much room for expansion; the labor union needs to find its political and professional feet, and the nonvoting half of the population needs to be brought into the political system. These are the challenges of the coming rounds of political reform, needed to complete the first step.

Reforms do not leave the reformer unchanged. The agents of reform in the coming rounds have been profoundly affected by the results of the first step—probably the greatest testimony to their success. Four characteristics are noteworthy: the legal dominant party system, the potential open space, the still-unauthorized opposition, and the uncontested presidency.

The legal dominant party system has given new life to the Destourian movement by providing it with an occasion to revive and relegitimize itself. Around it gravitate a number of tiny parties whose weakness is recognized in their own self-characterization as "parties of support, not parties of opposition." Little in their programs or their clienteles promises growth in their future, and they are likely to remain small satellites of the RCD, their continued existence protected only by their position as guarantors of the multiparty quality of the system. Change in this constellation depends not on the growth of one of these tiny parties but on the breakup of the unity of the dominant party. Ben Ali's accession and the RCD revival unnaturally prolonged its existence as a great coalition, but there are presently visible and theoretically identifiable strains on its broad unity.

As in the 1970s, there are inchoate divisions between liberals and conservatives, identified in terms of the organization of politics, often opposing presidential advisors in the Palace at Carthage to party leaders in the party headquarters overlooking the Casbah of Tunisia. Some of this division was found in the split between ben Ali and Baccouche, resulting in the dismissal of the prime minister in September 1989; but another dimension of the same dispute was ideological, over the extent of privatization (*Jeune Afrique*, October 9, 1989, 20). A third source of internal stress lies in the nature of the RCD as Uncle Sasha's Store, expected to provide all things to all people but in reality under considerable strain to act at the same time as the party of business, the party of labor, and the party of farmers. When the demands of its diverse social base break out in direct contradiction with each other, reinforcing the organization and ideological divisions, the RCD will be ready for political mitosis and Tunisia will have a real multiparty system.

There still is unoccupied political space in Tunisia, which potentially can provide the other source of multipartyism besides an RCD split. Since Independence, the Tunisian political system has been straining to give birth to a labor party with a socialist program, an eventuality that has been carefully foreclosed by PSD (and then RCD) strategists, who fear that a labor party would run off with the bulk of their voters and operate against their economic, as well as political, interests. At the end of the 1980s socialism was a discredited programmatic option, and all hope seemed to lie in privatization; in the 1990s the limitations of privatization are certain to appear clear, and the degree of balance within a mixed economy will be the subject of intense debate. A huge nonvoting segment of the population plus some of those already activated by the Islamicists is the prize to be captured. How such a party will come into being is less clear, especially since its natural parent, the UGTT, is only finding its own way. But the opportunity is so clear that politics is likely to find a way of taking it up. For it to do so, however, new individuals will have to emerge as leaders; and the current RCD leadership will have to remain true to its own pacts and rules of the game under real challenge.

The natural evolution of this system has been hijacked by the unauthorized Islamicist opposition, in part because the establishment is uncertain about the extent of its own reforms for a pluralistic polity. The MTI, or al-Nahda, picked up the new pacts and rules of the game and pledged to play by them. But they also provoked a crisis in one of the three areas of governance in Tunisia by calling into question the entire social program of the Bourguibist state. The ben Ali regime was fearful of the challenge they posed, and the president spent as much time after the elections as before emphasizing his notion of democracy based on an exclusive, not an inclusive, consensus (*Jeune Afrique*, July 12, 34–35; October 23, 40–41; November 20–23; December 4, 38–39—all 1989). Within his entourage, a small group argued for recognition, which would help the Islamicists moderate by forcing them to compete openly for the political middle, pull them away from their extremist fringe, and keep them under public scrutiny. Another group, including the "conservatives" associated with the RCD and the parliament, feared that authorization would legitimize the Islamicist option, felt embarrassed to take stands on issues that Renaissance party members might raise, and suspected that the extremists were powerful and the moderates wily in the movement. Aggressive attacks by Islamicist leaders against the minister of education, Charfi in October (*Jeune Afrique*, October 16, 1989, 16–17) and the strong showing of the Islamicist student organization, the General Tunisian Union of Students (UGTE), reinforced the conservatives' argument in early 1990, as the country headed toward municipal elections. Many scenarios are possible: heightened confrontation born of poor economic conditions, leading the country back to the civil strife and defensive government response of 1987 (the Bourguibist option); continued indecision in which the Renaissance party functions as a group of Independents, with the elections of 1989 and 1990 as their high watermark (the Egyptian option); legalization of a Renaissance party weakened by the doctrinaire rifts and cleavages that riddle any religious movement (the Algerian option); or legalization of the party that goes on to destroy the political system (the Sudanese option). The two middle options appear the most likely, in part because of the general awareness of the dangers of the other extremes. Eventually, all opposition parties boycotted the municipal elections of 1990, hiding their weakness behind a weak complaint of not being consulted; the Islamicists ran a few independents, since their party was still unrecognized; and the RCD won another false victory over an absent opposition.

Political reform in Tunisia, as in much of the Arab and African world (Senegal aside), reached from the second level of elites on downward but does not countenance competitive pluralism at the very top. Democracy will not come to Tunisia until there is open competition and choice for the presidency, not because the current incumbent is defective but because nothing desacralizes a human being and personalizes public accountability like a good political campaign. Nothing guarantees that a political campaign remain "good," focusing on accountability rather than on the seamier sides of desacralization (as the U.S. public knows); but the ultimate maturity of the political system can only be achieved and maintained by exercise. By the constitutional amendment adopted in July 1988, ben Ali is limited to three terms, ending in 2004, unless another constitutional amendment is passed; opposition could come from either another party's candidate or from an Independent, provided that sufficient nominating signatures are available. Such eventualities are a long way off.

Political reform has been the program of the new ben Ali regime and has been carried out to the point where it must above all face its own challenges. Reform has both reinvigorated the country's dominant and historic political movement and provided the opening for an unexpectedly serious challenge from outside the reformist consensus. It is to the credit of the country that some of the important decisions of the reformist movement have come from the body politic (society), not from its decisionmakers (state). Now the polity must take up the opportunity offered to it and grow larger than the RCD, fill up the unused political space, contribute supportive participation to the task of governance, and impose ongoing accountability on the governors. The success of state reform comes when society itself takes up the movement.

■ Note

1. I am grateful to the Joint Committee on the Near and Middle East of the Social Science Research Council and the American Council of Learned Societies for its support for the research for this project and to the Center for Maghrib Studies In Tunis (CEMAT) of the American Institute for Maghrib Studies (AIMS)—and particularly to its director, Jeanne Mrad—for assistance. I am thankful to my many friends and contacts in Tunis for their time and help in my research, including Moncer Rouissi, Abderrahim Zouari, Ahmed Mestiri, Frej Chaieb, Azzouz Larbi, Azzouz Rebai, Abdelqader Zghal, Habib Slim, al-Baki Hermassi, Amor Chadli, Mohammed Sayah, Hamouda ben Slama, Dali Jazi, and Mohammed Charfi, among others.

2

Clientelism and Reform in ben Ali's Tunisia

Susan Waltz

There has been no shortage of adulation for Zine Labidine ben Ali and Tunisia's second republic, within and without the country. "An Opening in Tunisia," a "State of Grace"—so the Western press continues to sing a year and a half after ben Ali's 1987 bloodless coup. At home, references abound to the Miracle of November 7. The "miracle" is a twofold one: first, the Tunisian polity not only survived intact but survived without scars the presidential succession it had both dreamed of and dreaded for so many years; second, Tunisia has taken important steps toward instituting its version of a liberal democratic, pluralistic rule, and the wonder is audible: "Only under ben Ali. . . ."

Changes, indeed, have been impressive. Besides measures of judicial clemency, extended by mid-1989 to more than three thousand individuals jailed for politically related crimes and bans lifted on numerous long-term political exiles, the ben Ali government has undertaken a number of structural reforms. The presidential term of office has been limited; and so, to some degree, have been presidential powers with the abolition of both the State Security Court and the post of general prosecutor (Laws 87–79 and 87–80). Opposition forces, too, have been allowed new freedoms. Parties, now legalized with relative ease, have proliferated, as has the independent press. And in April 1989 Tunisians—many for the first time—faced a choice in their selection of deputies to Parliament.

I shall argue, however, that the half-filled cup being celebrated with such enthusiasm may also be seen as half-empty; and in the Tunisian case there is much to suggest that even as pluralistic form is introduced, old patterns of personal rule are reestablishing themselves. To put the current period in historical perspective, it is useful to consider two central and enduring dynamics in Tunisian political culture: *rational reform* and *particularism*. Of the two, the particularistic strand is the older; but rational reformism, too, has a long pedigree.

Kheireddine, prime minister from 1873 to 1877, sets the prototype of reformer, but he is followed by a long list of others, including the Jeunes Tunisiens of the early twentieth century, the Vieux Destour, Habib Bourguiba, and groups (like, at various times, the General Union of Tunisian Workers) who called for liberal reform under Bourguiba's thirty-year rule. From the beginning of the 1980s the MDS has been prominent in this role, its leaders persistently and publicly advocating competitive elections. Most recently, the LTDH has been the standard-bearer of reform, through the upheavals of 1987 denouncing arrests and calling for measures to protect the rights of regime opponents (Waltz 1988).

The reformist tradition in Tunisia is the graft of a European tree. Ahmad Bey (1835–1855) prepared the way by introducing ruling elites (of Turkish origin) to European ideals (Brown 1974). French advisors then saw to it that successor Muhammad Bey (1855–1859) promulgated a security covenant, the Ahd al-aman. The covenant protected French interests by assuring civil and religious equality for all Tunisian residents, as well as by assuring access to courts of law. Muhammad Bey's own successor, Muhammad al-Sadiq (1859–1882) was put under further duress by the French and prodded to issue a full-fledged constitution in 1861. This short-lived document was disdained by the reigning prime minister, Mustapha Khaznadar, but it did impress his son-in-law Kheireddine, who in his own brief term of office implemented many of its provisions. Kheireddine had lived in Europe from 1862 to 1869 and in office sought to apply political ideas that had taken shape during his years abroad. Notably, he sought to enhance state legitimacy by installing an administration strong in competence and integrity and by creating a citizenry that would be treated fairly and equally before the law (Krieken 1976).

Consistently, Tunisian rationalists—in and out of power—have emphasized equity in the rule of law, equal access to seats of power, and the predominance of reason in establishing first secular knowledge and then policy. The 1861 Constitution, for example, established equality before the law with respect to taxation and military duty and created a Grand Council whereby the Bey's ability to legislate would be constrained (Anderson 1986, 82–83). One of Kheireddine's lasting contributions was the foundation of the Sadiqi College, priding itself on a secular curriculum emphasizing rational thought (Green 1978, 113–142).

Tunisian reformism—in spirit as in practice—has never reached the extreme of U.S. liberalism, holding the people sovereign and viewing the state as the creation of the governed, there to perform limited and necessary tasks. Tunisians, historically, viewed the emerging state with suspicion and in the post-Independence period learned to mitigate their fears with expectations that unwelcome state intervention in their lives could be offset by state-sponsored benefits in the form of housing, food, medical care, employment, and other welfare goods (Waltz 1982). It is against this admixture of supplication and distancing that reformist efforts must be seen.

Unlike their compatriots in the Tunisian *bled al-siba*, reformists have not actually challenged the right of the state to govern and shape society; but neither have they questioned the state's responsibility to provide welfare in addition to security. They have sought to contain arbitrary application of the state's power rather than limit that power itself. Reformists outside the government, from the Jeunes Tunisiens of the French Protectorate to the contemporary League of Human Rights, have sought fair and equitable application of the law and have denounced personalism as favoritism within government (Anderson 1976, 158–162; Waltz 1988). Reformists in power have more frequently used rational reforms to consolidate their own power bases and simultaneously constrain the power of politically fractious elements. The Constitution of 1861, for example, while extending the rule of law also very deftly cut into the power of local leaders and occasioned a widespread revolt, whose slogan was "No more capitation taxes, no more mamluks, no more Constitution" (Moore 1970, 25).

Particularism, for its part, is traced to times when the Tunisian state was not so strong and effective social groupings—whether tribes, peasant villages, or rare urban settlements—were much smaller. Particularism is a general label for practices by which public policy serves private purposes. It encompasses both patron–client exchange relationships, or *clientelism*, and contemporary forms of what Weber called *patrimonialism*—or government as the ruler's private domain. Weber suggests that coercion is the essential dynamism undergirding patrimonialism, or *personal rule*—though coercion may be tempered by, or supplemented with, patronage (Bendix 1977, 334–360). Exchange, however asymmetric, underlies clientelism (Scott 1977). In nearly all governmental systems, some forms of particularism are tolerated—as, for example, certain pork barrel practices in U.S. politics or "special member bills" allowed by the British parliament—whereas others, viewed as corruption, are not. Tunisia, especially over the past decade, has not been immune to corruption; but the particularism that receives attention here remains within the bounds of law.

The form of particularism most conventionally discussed in the Tunisian context is clientelism, an unequal dyadic relationship wherein some form of fealty is exchanged for some form of protection (Schmidt, et al. 1977; Gellner and Waterbury 1973). Strictly speaking, the dyadic patron–client relationship is a personal one. Such personal relationships of political control persist in contemporary Tunisia, especially in rural areas; but the patron's power base today lies with his connections to the government and its vast store of patronage rather than his own accrued wealth or kinship ties (Anderson 1976, 227, 249). A story circulating widely in Tunisia over the past two years illustrates the practice. In 1956 ben Ali was selected as one of about twenty Tunisians to be trained at the St. Cyr Military Academy in France, an arrangement negotiated at the time of Independence to provide an officer corps for the new Tunisian army. Ben Ali's candidacy, however, was opposed by local leaders in his hometown of Hammam Sousse, who claimed that the ben Ali family had collaborated with the French during the fight for Independence. Hedi Baccouche, at the time a regional leader of the Neo-Destour party, established himself as a patron by defending young ben Ali and seeing his nomination through (Huxley 1989). Years later, as prime minister under ben Ali, Baccouche would assert the privileges of patronage by acting even at cross-purposes to the program of reform designed by ben Ali and followed by the remainder of this cabinet.[1]

Clientelism as a political practice is generally seen as a demand function, that is, as a means by which those relatively deprived of power and political voice make their wants known. In Tunisia such demands are often brokered. A village *omda* cultivates relations with the regional party *délégué* (Tekeri 1981, 41) and at the appropriate moment passes up the request for a new schoolroom or dispensary or bus service. Or, prior to recent reforms, an organization seeking legal authorization used a mutually friendly contact to intercede with the authorities. In the absence of an active associative tradition, such brokered clientelism helps maintain links between people and polity in a way dyadic connections could not on any significant scale.

The argument in the remainder of this chapter is that the most significant expression of particularism in contemporary Tunisia is actually personal rule and that the motor for personal rule appears stationed at the top. But patrons, however attractive, cannot be separated from willing clients; and more must be said about Tunisian *society*. The majority of Tunisians— shopkeepers, chauffeurs, small farmers, factory workers—look to the government to supply jobs, provide health and welfare needs, and keep prices down; they are otherwise grateful for its nonintervention in their daily lives (cf. Zghal 1967, 32–56, 151–170; Rudebeck 1967, 134–138). For thirty years the political role of most Tunisians has been confined to that of listener; the bulk of Tunisians are only marginally engaged in their country's governance.[2] There are times in every Tunisian's life, however, that business must be done with authorities. In those times the rules may work, technically; or it may even happen that they do not work in an equitable fashion. Regardless, from the perspective of the peasant or urban dispossessed lost in bureaucratic routine and perhaps illiterate as well, an intercessor is always useful and often necessary (cf. Tekeri 1981). In 1977, 34 percent of 391 respondents in a survey of twelve Tunisian villages indicated they would find someone else in their village to present their case to authorities in an important matter (Waltz 1982). Basic attitudes of suspicion and feelings of vulnerability are tenacious, and one must conclude that the strategy appears rational for individuals unlikely to argue their cases persuasively before those holding the reins of power. The Tunisian masses thus hold themselves aloof from the rules and remain cautiously available to patrons who indicate a personal interest in their lot.

Behind whatever enthusiastic gestures of support they might offer the state or its leaders on occasion, Tunisians in the current period more commonly express sentiments of passive loyalty, approval of a wait-and-see sort. Remembering failed promises and arbitrary requirements of the past and skeptical about current reforms, they are happy to claim what comes their way now and protect themselves against privations of the morrow (cf. Zghal 1967, 51–56). Their attitude of distance and standoffish loyalty contributes to particularistic tendencies and simultaneously detracts from the impersonal rule of law.

Particularism may characterize the political behavior of society's favored as well as those it has forgotten. In addition to providing an outlet for otherwise inexpressible political demands, particularism may appear as a style of governance, aptly described as personalism or personal rule. Robert H. Jackson and Carl G. Rosberg define it in opposition to institutionalized government. Personal rule is a system of governance where

> persons take precedence over rules, where the officeholder is not effectively bound by his office and is able to change its authority and powers to suit his own personal or political needs. In such a system of personal rule, the rulers and other leaders take precedence over the formal rules of the political game: the rules do not effectively regulate political behavior, and we therefore cannot predict or anticipate conduct from a knowledge of the rules. (1982, 10)

The ease with which rulers—Turkish, French, and Tunisian—have changed the rules to suit their own purposes is testimony to the tradition of personal rule in Tunisia. The colonial power, wanting to encourage settlement and reduce its own domestic unemployment in the aftermath of World War I, simply changed employment requirements to restrict Tunisian access to the bureaucracy (Anderson 1976, 148–149). If not an entirely personalistic measure from the French procedural perspective, it was so perceived by the Tunisian subjects. Bourguiba's own rule bore a heavy personal imprint, from the declaration of lifelong presidency to the whimsical change of ministers during his final year of tenure (Hahn 1972; Vandevalle 1988).[3]

The paradoxical nature of the coexistence and vitality of rational reformism and particularism in Tunisian political culture has led a number of analysts to assume a conflictual and evolutionary dynamic between them. Clement Henry Moore for example, predicted the triumph of rationality in the spread of democratic pluralism and accountability—a paper plan that never translated into reality (1970, 286). More recently, Lisa Anderson's liberal use of "transition" language suggests an evolutionary path over the past century from clientelism to bureaucratic rationalism (1986, 26).

Alternatively, one of these facets may be seen as a mask, or as lacking any substantive importance in the political culture. Michel Camau, for example, notes the same two dimensions of Tunisian political culture and differentiates them as *l'Etat idéal* and *l'Etat réel*. The term *ideal* refers to the language and symbols of political discourse, wherein civic values and rationalism are stressed. In idealist rhetoric, the people are considered "citizens"; but political reality, for Camau, lies elsewhere. In the struggle for power that constitutes political reality, only a narrow group of elites have been allowed access to controls. Elites, rather than addressing the people directly, have sought their support through societal brokers. The people are pacified by idealist rhetoric; but in "real" terms, they are simply clients (Camau 1987).

Neither of these approaches accounts well for Tunisia's political dynamics. In the contemporary period, the rational has not replaced particularism. Likewise, the implication that the ideal is only a rhetorical facade for real politics is unsatisfactory, inasmuch as the ideal, or rational, strand of politics has also had substantive impact on Tunisia's sociopolitical system. Tunisia stands in marked contrast to countries such as Nigeria and Zaire, inextricably mired in personal rule and clientelist politics; and successful bureaucratic containment of clientelism has been responsible for much of Tunisia's success in statebuilding (cf. Anderson 1986). A faithful portrayal of Tunisian political culture over the past century has quite simply to admit both rationalism and particularism, like two dominant threads in a tapestry that periodically rise and recede but never quite disappear.

Accordingly, there is truth to Camau's assertion that there exists a private system in Tunisian state governance that transcends specialization of structures and officially instituted procedures. If reformism has had substantive impact, so, too, has particularism. Ben Ali's rise to power has come on a wave of rational reforms, but that should not be understood as a simultaneous disappearance of particularistic politics. In the current period, as in the historical past, personalism finds expression.

"Private rule" in Tunisia has typically been pursued both positively, in the sense of an active advance of personal interests, and negatively, as impediments to political rivals (cf. Moore 1973). Personalistic interests are pursued negatively when limitations are imposed directly on the rule of law or when personalistic use or interpretations of the law interfere with equitable application. As James Scott notes, the universalistic language of legislation does not easily lend itself to the articulation of particularistic interests. Consequently, such interests are more often expressed at the enforcement level (1972, 19). Political threats to the personal leader may be contained or eliminated through arrests and political imprisonment (as with a variety of

Tunisian socialists in the 1960s, labor activists in the 1970s, and Islamicists in the 1980s); exile, either official or self-imposed (of the sort chosen by former government ministers Ahmed ben Salah and Driss Guiga, who otherwise faced penalties for treason); or more finally, through execution (with which Islamicist leaders were threatened in 1987) or assassination (as appears to have been the fate of Bourguiba's early rival Salah ben Youssef).

Personal interests are pursued more directly when elected officials and bureaucrats extend their roles as executives and administrators to become patrons. Through political brokerage, enticements are extended to sizable constituent groups in exchange for present, and possibly future, loyalty. Two major political strategies of the ben Ali era can be seen from this angle—the National Pact and the proposed common list, discussed in Chapter 1. Because these efforts at coalitionbuilding are rather ordinary political moves—if extraordinary in the contemporary Tunisian setting—particularistic aspects are not so readily apparent. More obvious are other examples from the same period: a dramatic reduction in import duties on taxicabs (whose drivers in the final years of Bourguiba's rule were notorious political critics); a three-day holiday for "tired" *lycéens* (who subsequently proclaimed ben Ali the candidate of the young); and significant real estate discounts for residents of one densely populated and erstwhile low-income area of Tunis (a potential Islamicist voting area). The last incident illustrates the process of contemporary personal governance and so bears elaboration. In the early part of 1989 it became apparent that as a result of rising costs associated with a government upgrading program in the Bab Souika area of Tunis, a substantial number of residents and businesses would be forced out of their locales. The country's president and his cabinet met to discuss the impending crisis, and an executive decision was taken to reduce prices by as much as 75 percent. Newspaper headlines proclaimed "Bab Souika Delivered," and residents were duly quoted: "God Bless ben Ali" (*La Presse*, March 4, 1989). Unlike his predecessor, who depended on informal advisors to the near-exclusion of his cabinet, ben Ali appears to make decisions in consultation with his formally appointed cabinet, who have the merit of technical expertise, in addition to a circle of personally appointed advisors. Yet the process is remarkably the same: governance is largely by fiat; and appreciation, in this extended honeymoon phase, accrues to the personage of the president.

A ruler's personal ambitions, of course, may actually further the cause of reform, depending on personal commitments and political circumstances. Bourguiba, for example, used the 1957 Constitution to consolidate his regime and legitimize his rule (Vandevalle 1988). Through a program of political reform, a ruler may effectively contain forces in competition not only with himself as a leader but with a rational state as well and out of a personal goal of survival build a legacy of rational rule. The relationship between personalism and reform is a tangled one: situations frequently arise where the difference between personal interests and public ones is difficult to discern.

The difficulties for a society torn between patterns of rational reform and particularism appear not when public and private interests converge but when they diverge in serious measure. A leader securing a hold on power through a program of reform may find that power limited by the very reforms that have been sought; but there is likewise a risk that reform engendered by particularist means and serving apparent particularist interests will finally be lost.

■ Human Rights and Personal Rule

Recent attention to the area of human rights reform and performance presents an opportunity to examine these aspects of personal rule as they operate in the current regime. As early as November 1987, key legal measures introduced by ben Ali abolished the State Security Court and limited the practice of pretrial incommunicado detention known as *garde-à-vue*, both of which had been used repeatedly to abridge legal protection for the Bourguiba government's opponents. During 1988 several presidential commissions were put to work studying the penal code and considering changes in laws concerning association, press freedoms, and election procedures. A reformed press code encouraging pluralistic expression by preventing monopoly and reducing penalties for code infractions was adopted in July 1988. Laws of association were similarly revamped in July to facilitate the proliferation of civic and political organizations. Since November 1987, Tunisia has ratified the UN Torture Convention and has also imposed a de facto moratorium on capital punishment. These reforms, the hallmark of the ben Ali presidency, have narrowed the gap between ideal and real political activity. In January 1989 ben Ali was awarded an international human rights prize; and, in conjunction with the United Nations, the Arab Organization for Human Rights named Tunis as the site for a new Arab–African Institute for Human Rights.

For the most part, the ben Ali government actually increased its power, prestige, and legitimacy as it extended civil and political rights through 1988. Under Bourguiba, personal rule had too-long dominated, its excesses readily apparent; and even for those not heavily involved in political activities, 1987 approached a reign of terror. A counterstrategy of restoring the rule of law proved effective in gaining political legitimacy for the new government. In many ways, personal and public interests converged: reform has certainly enhanced ben Ali's hold on power, but personal gestures also paved the way for reform. Personal power embedded in Article 28 of the Tunisian

Constitution allowed ben Ali to initiate legal reforms. In practice, parliamentary deputies may debate proposed laws, as they have done over the past year on a range of issues from press code to amnesty laws; but the legal initiative remains closely linked to the personage of the president. The vast majority of political amnesties over the past year have also resulted from personal decisions, arriving as presidential measures of clemency rather than as judicial acquittals.

In other areas, the convergence of public and private interests is less clear—or, at least, it is not clear where the greater benefit is reaped. If it has been in the interest of the new government's legitimacy to extend civil and political liberties, it has also been an astute political strategy to make allies of erstwhile critics. As minister of interior and the person administratively responsible for security forces engaged in torture and custodial ill-treatment, ben Ali was frequently a target of criticism by Tunisian human rights activists. As president, ben Ali appointed two founding members of the independent and respected League of Human Rights to his new cabinet in July 1988; and a cabinet reshuffle in April 1989 put three LTDH members on the Carthage team. These presidential moves can with legitimacy be interpreted as statements of intent to reform the polity, but they are just as surely attempts to coopt potential opponents and critics and secure power. Several points are relevant. The various portfolios accorded league members and other liberals are largely inconsequential ones politically: Health, Youth and Sports, Culture and Information, Education, and Social Affairs. They involve little or no real power. Through such symbolic gestures, ben Ali's political strength is enhanced on two counts. On the one hand he has quieted potential regime opponents, and on the other he has gained legitimacy by bringing the league and its own credibility into his political fold. It is, undoubtedly, a mutually beneficial arrangement; but it would appear that the largest gains fall to ben Ali.

Similar limitations appear in the area of electoral reform. In its March 1989 Congress, for example, even as Tunisia was receiving positive publicity about its first truly democratic elections, the LTDH expressed concerns about changes in electoral laws that made candidacy more difficult to establish. A new electoral code approved in July 1988 required all candidates to appear on a slate and obtain exclusive support of seventy-five voters within the district of contest. Small parties like the PUP, the Socialist Liberal Party (PSP), and the RSP found it difficult, if not impossible, to compete even at the level of fielding a slate of candidates. Election results of April 1989 demonstrated how effectively opposition qua opposition had been shut out of the political process. An early appeal by ben Ali to form a national unity ticket had been rejected by MDS leader Ahmed Mestiri, who clung religiously to the notion of a pluralistic contest. Difficulties of establishing candidacy and arbitrary application of campaign rules (see

Christian Science Monitor, March 30, 1989) combined with the single-ballot, winner-take-all electoral system, resulted once again in a monopoly of the National Assembly by the RCD. The electoral process, in fact, worked so embarrassingly well for the RCD and ben Ali as its leader that to dilute its influence and maintain credibility in his commitment to pluralism, ben Ali was moved to include, in April 1989, two erstwhile RCD opponents in the Political Bureau of the RCD itself.

There has also been an underside to reforms in the penal code concerning *garde-à-vue*, for decades a focal point of human rights abuses in Tunisia. Tunisian law previously imposed no limit on judicial investigations, allowing political prisoners to be held indefinitely without formal charge. *Garde-à-vue* essentially denies the right of habeas corpus and is widely linked to the practice of torture and ill-treatment (Amnesty International 1984). Ben Ali's government has received many accolades for establishing legal limits to the practice, one of its first reforms; but the terms of the new law (Law 87-70 of November 1987) require scrutiny: Article 85 does impose limits to the period prisoners may now be held without charge but sets them at six months, twice-renewable to a maximum of eighteen months. More than thirty members of a disparate group of Islamicists, customs officers, and military and security personnel were in fact detained nearly the full eighteen months without charge or trial before their release in March 1989. *Garde-à-vue* is now technically restricted, but the state has nonetheless effectively secured for itself powers of preventive detention. Such capabilities enhance the arbitrary powers of a ruler, not the impersonal and institutionalized rule of law.

The rule of law, not least of which is civil rights law, requires fair and equitable application of laws and legal procedures. Personalism in the area of human rights is most rigorously judged in how rules and procedures deemed fair as they exist on paper are actually applied; and it is in this light that any divergence between public and private interest is best detected. In any society there will be contests between public and private interest; and the telling evidence about predominant structures, particularly for newly implemented liberalizing measures, comes not in routine, noncontroversial dealings between state and citizen but in situations where the state must exercise restraint in order to allow the citizen free exercise of rights or where the state may at the least have nothing to gain in extending rights to the citizen.

In the ben Ali era, toleration in widely publicized cases of press and associational freedoms is in some measure offset by less well publicized but no less significant instances where the new freedoms have been abridged. An account of the seizure of two news magazines in successive weeks of December 1988 is instructive. One of the first signs of the new liberties was the restoration, late in 1987, of an independent press. New dailies and weeklies literally mushroomed. Both journalists and their readers were euphoric, and stories ran high in praise of ben Ali. The removal of religious literature—including the rather orthodox official journal of Egypt's al-Azhar Mosque—from Tunisia's literary market has gone largely unnoticed. The test case that was noticed took one year to arrive. When *Mawkaf*, published by the RSP, printed an account of politics in the nonrecognized sector, its copies were seized. Only a few days later, the independent weekly *Réalités* suffered the same fate for an editorial critical of the judiciary. *Réalités's* punishment for the offensive article was extended involuntarily for a second week due to "technical difficulties" at the press used by *Le Phare*, another outspoken weekly (*Le Monde*, December 27, 1988).

Arbitrary restrictions are also apparent in the area of associational freedoms. Changes in the law of association enacted in 1988 did bring recognition for some groups previously considered anathema, such as the left-of-center RSP. A contrary decision, however, was reached for an association calling itself Democratic Women. The group claimed as a central purpose to organize opposition to conservative sentiments regarding women's rights and legislation. Its goals, thus, appear consonant with those of the government; but according to one local commentator, the extraordinary nature of the group—a women's group organized by women—was apparently so great an anomaly as to cause particularistic concerns to take precedence over legal, rational ones. For reasons not explained to the public, the visa that would have allowed it legal operation was denied (*Le Maghreb*, March 3, 1989) until late 1989.

Similar issues arise in the long saga of the Renaissance party's quest for legal recognition as a political party. Through the last years of Bourguiba's rule, this sizable Islamicist group—formerly known as MTI—had made several formal requests for recognition, never honored. Following a revision in the law concerning political parties in May 1988 (Law 88-32), the MTI renamed itself in an effort to comply with new stipulations prohibiting religious affiliation. As the Renaissance party, it subsequently reapplied for legal authorization. Without legal status, the party was compelled to run only Independent slates in the April 1989 parliamentary elections; but it nevertheless garnered 14 percent of the popular vote. In early June 1989, at the end of its four-month wait, the party's appeal for recognition was once again denied, this time because its founders and leaders had served lengthy prison sentences and thus were judged excluded by Article 7 of Law 88-32. Article 7 actually allows interpretation on this issue, excusing party leaders if legal infractions were not "intentional"; but in the case of the Renaissance party, this provision was read conservatively. Ironically, the National Assembly was at the time considering a law proposed by ben Ali on April 9 and introduced by the minister of justice on April 21, restoring civil and political rights to former political prisoners. This measure became law three weeks after the denial of the Renaissance party's appeal. By late December

1989, however, provisions for implementation of the amnesty bill had not been fully articulated, and officials had declined to consider yet another appeal of for authorization of the party. Meanwhile, routine political actions by the party are technically forbidden—tolerated only by governmental grace—and it can hardly be surprising that in late July 1989 dozens of Islamicists across the country were taken into police custody for questioning (*Jeune Afrique*, July 28, 1989). One of the movement's two chief spokespersons, Abdelfatah Mourou, was held by police for several days in October 1989 (FBIS, October 10, 1989); and patterns of arrest and brief detention made life unpredictable for many less notable Islamicists throughout the final months of 1989.

Arbitrary measures have not been applied solely to the Islamicists, widely viewed as the government's principal opponents. In September 1989 the unrecognized Communist Workers party circulated a press release protesting the nighttime arrest of four Gafsa residents charged with belonging to an unrecognized party, defaming the head of state, and distributing tracts. According to the press release, the door of one detainee's home was broken down; she was beaten and forced by police to abandon her infant of four months.

According to other reports, Jelloud Azzouna, professor at the University of Tunis and PUP secretary-general, was arrested in July for having denounced by means of a press communiqué vigilante groups with police connections whom he accused of vandalizing the cars of PUP leaders. Like those detained in Gafsa, Azzouna was charged with defaming the head of state. At his August trial Azzouna's attorney unsuccessfully argued a separation of presidential policy from the personage of the president and was herself arrested for presenting evidence of links between the vandals and security police. Despite several procedural irregularities in the attorney's arrest, she was incarcerated and charged with spreading false news, inciting unrest, and defaming the public security forces. After considerable public pressure and four days in the Women's Prison in Tunis, the attorney was released. Azzouna was sentenced to a year in prison.

Such cases test the relative strength of rationalism and particularism. While the ben Ali government has exercised much greater restraint than did its predecessor, anecdotal evidence gathered over the past two years indicates that temptations to wield personal power continue to run strong in the halls of Tunisian government.

■ **Implications and Conclusions**

A long discourse on the nature and perseverance of personalism in a political culture now apparently in a rational reform phase might seem misplaced, but reminders are necessary for two reasons. First, in popular and journalistic analyses of the current reforms, enduring particularistic interests seem to have been altogether overlooked. In the aftermath of extreme personalism, the new regime has made significant reforms; and personalism in the first year of ben Ali's presidency raised no complaints: those disfavored in the past had been given hopes of recognition. Complaints put personalism in relief; and during the initial honeymoon phase, at least, complaints were minimal. The recession of personalism, however, should not be mistaken for its disappearance.

Secondly, latent particularistic tendencies have important implications for political–economic challenges that lie ahead. Any political system— particularistic or impersonally rational—has advantages and disadvantages; and the relative merits of a given system must be evaluated in light of challenges and circumstances faced by the polity. The international economic environment today presents serious difficulties for the Tunisian polity. Although, psychologically, Tunisians are much more optimistic than only a few years ago, in the overall picture little has changed. The economy's 1988 receipts warrant some cautious optimism, but unaddressed structural difficulties continue to compound. For Tunisia, as for most other Third World countries, the long-term view remains enshadowed. International monetary institutions are now openly recognizing that structural adjustment will not be a single, difficult pill to swallow but should rather be accepted as chronic treatment for chronic difficulties (Riddell 1987, 99).

After eighteen months of silence about economic issues, ben Ali finally broached this topic in a speech following the April 1989 elections. The news was bad: Tunisians were warned that times ahead would require hard work and sacrifice (FBIS, April 10, 1989). High unemployment and deficit spending are among the chronic problems facing the nation, and attempts to redress one of the problems will inevitably exacerbate the other. Significantly, the domestic economic difficulties are situated in an international context of significant debt.

As Stephen Krasner notes, small states like Tunisia operate at a disadvantage in the international system. Under like circumstances, larger industrial states are able to influence the international environment and can also make internal adjustments to soften the effects of adverse international phenomena. Even smaller industrialized states have enough political flexibility to make adjustments in their domestic political economy that can in some measure compensate for an inability to redirect the international environment. Third World states, however, are vulnerable on both fronts. Their small size constrains their international influence, and inflexible domestic structures limit internal adjustments. For such states, shocks and fluctuations of international origin may result in severe domestic political and economic dislocation (Krasner 1985, 11).

In the long run, bad news such as that delivered by ben Ali in April is acceptable only to a people who perceive the hardship as one shared equitably, that is, by impersonal policies impersonally implemented. In such circumstances, the personal ruler is at a disadvantage. It is inherent in the nature of personalism that the ruler who claims personal credit for positive governmental or economic performance will also be held personally responsible for failures, however complex their origins. Under prevailing international conditions, such rulers are highly vulnerable; and even the protective devices of charisma, scapegoating, or political repression may not be sufficient to secure their hold on the reins of power. Robert Wood argues that the demands placed on today's internationally indebted countries may be so extreme that even the most firmly entrenched personal rulers may be forced to share power in order to comply with international requirements without occasioning domestic upheaval:

> The austerity demands imposed on Third World countries have been so devastating in their social consequences that it is unclear whether most governments can continue to implement them without some form of new "social contract" with the rest of society—a contract almost sure to involve the expansion of political rights as a trade-off for economic concessions. (1986, 326)

It is in this context that the dangers of a return to personal rule in Tunisia become most apparent. To meet the challenges ahead, the state will be required to prove and assert its legitimacy. Already that task is a formidable one. Despite the impressive statebuilding that took place over the past century (Anderson 1986), many Tunisians retain what has been called an "exit option"—that is, they claim enough autonomy to thwart intended state policies (Hirshman 1970; Hyden 1983). The failure of the 1960s cooperativist movement attests to this, as does the more recent acknowledgment of failed parastatal enterprises (Pelletreau 1989). University graduates know that a degree alone is not sufficient to secure them desirable employment (Entelis 1974); accordingly, they seek to cultivate whatever personal connections make themselves available.

Tunisia's expansive, well-anchored bureaucracy, which has found its way to the smallest villages, creates an impression of state strength that can be misleading. Authoritarian but weak states are common in the Third World; for explanation of the paradox, Joel S. Migdal points to the existence of nonstate alternatives open to incompletely captured "citizens." Many societies, as opposed to the states claiming to govern them, "have been as resilient as an intricate spider's web; one could snip a corner of the web away and the rest of the web would swing majestically between the branches, just as one could snip center strands and have the web continue to exist" (1988, 37). In Tunisia, tribal loyalties of the past century have virtually disappeared; but during the Bourguiba years, even as the state was expanding and extending influence, a web of alternative structures, generally in the form of informal clans or factions, developed and flourished to advance interests that otherwise seemed neglected. In fundamental ways the state remains unconnected to many of its people. In many villages and urban quarters through the 1970s and into the 1980s, local reality and official descriptions, analyses, and plans shared little in common. It is indicative of the state's relative weakness that it was patently unable to control—let alone destroy—one network, the Islamicist movement, despite a decade of concerted efforts. State policies under Bourguiba—such as restrictions concerning the *hajib*, Islamicist attire for women—were flagrantly violated; and by the end of 1987 it seemed certain that at least some Tunisians had greater allegiance to informal Islamicist structures than to the Tunisian state itself.

In the current period these networks have not disappeared. There remain strong ties of parentage at the highest levels of government, many RCD hacks continue to guard their interests, and cultural strongmen like Islamicists Abdelfatah Mourou and Rachid Ghannouchi have gained sway over important sectors of the population. The existence of structures in competition with the state to control society readily forces leaders into what Migdal calls "politics of survival" (1988, 206–237). In efforts to counteract centrifugal forces that threaten to wrest control from the state, leaders often resort to nonmerit political appointments, political purges, and various forms of political repression.

As James Scott noted a decade and a half ago, a government that depends on law alone operates at nearly fatal disadvantage (1972, 19). Ideological support or the support of key social sectors may in some political situations be sufficient to carry a leader or a program through political challenge and opposition. Such support for ben Ali is weak. Within the RCD, ben Ali has no clearly identifiable social base, despite the fact that in 1988 he handpicked 122 of the 200 members of the RCD Central Committee's members. Beyond the RCD, the small group of Independent Liberals with whom ben Ali has surrounded himself have themselves no sizable power or social base. Tunisia's president, thus, is forced to act by himself to a large degree, seeking support for reforms wherever he can find it.[4]

The particularism toward which such a political reality drives a leader is not necessarily antithetical to reform. Indeed, it may enhance the possibility of successful reform insofar as a leader without a well-defined social or political base is also a leader unfettered by the well-articulated interests of such a base, perhaps comfortable in the existing order. As suggested above in the brief discussion of clientelism, important coalitions and alliances may often be brokered through particularistic acts of patronage. Particularistic gestures may likewise be instrumental in securing political reform that affects not only political players but the rules of the game itself. There is, however, implicit risk in a strategy where means and ends diverge. The ruler for whom the game of survival politics goes well may keep his seat and provide the polity a certain stability, but the temptations to abuse power along the way are many. In providing "stability" through particularism, in fact, the rule may also "deinstitutionalize" society and make it, in the future, ever more dependent on individuals and particularistic rule.

We are thus led to a paradox. The existence, or even the threat, of alternative structures creates a social tension that through competition fosters the practice of personal rule. Citizen loyalty and consolidation of regime support—and by extension, regime legitimacy—is captured by generous application of particularist oil to fix or prevent squeaking wheels. That very particularism, however, soon becomes "survival politics" and undermines the broad social contract that seems one of the few tenable political solutions to chronic economic problems. Symptoms are addressed—sometimes fixed and sometimes only masked—but structural problems remain. The late-twentieth-century challenge to the despot, however benevolent, is to share power; and at this point it seems unlikely that ben Ali and his entourage will truly rise to that challenge.

■ **Notes**

1. After several months of rumor, Hedi Baccouche was dismissed as prime minister on September 27, 1989, apparently for having publicly contradicted ben Ali's program of structural adjustment. See *Jeune Afrique*, October 9, 1989.

2. Moore's (1963) account of politics in what was then the "village" of Hammam-Sousse—which produced both Hedi Baccouche and ben Ali—might give another impression. Moore documents the attachment of local leaders to national politics that has now been characteristic of the Sahelian region for over fifty years and was then characteristic of the epoque (cf. Tessler and Freeman 1981; Tessler and Hawkins 1979). The Sahel region has been an important exception in this regard (Hermassi 1972; Zartman 1975).

3. According to journalists Samir Gharbi and François Soudan, Bourguiba was barely lucid during his final days in office. After reviewing photos and accepting a cabinet slate proposed by then-Prime Minister ben Ali on October 28, he rejected it the next morning, claiming there were too many young people and too many from Sousse. The mention of his planning minister's name, Mohammed Ghannouchi, sent him into a tirade, railing against the bête noir of his later life, Islamicist leader Rachid Ghannouchi (Gharbi and Soudan, "Cette nuit-la . . . ," *Jeune Afrique*, November 18, 1987).

4. For an overview of elite structures in Tunisia, see Zartman 1975, 1982 and Stone 1982. These have not changed in any significant way since ben Ali's accession to power.

3

Tunisian Industrialists and the State

Eva Bellin

During the past decade or so the field of development studies has performed a volte-face regarding the private sector's role in the development process. In an earlier generation of development theory, conventional wisdom put an enlightened state (and expanded state sector) center-stage in development strategy. Over time, however, development theorists grew disenchanted with state-led development given the sluggishness and inefficiency associated with public sector growth; increasingly, they focused attention on the dynamic (and corrective) role private sectors might play in the development process. Policies fostering private sector growth were pressed upon Third World countries; terms like *privatization* and *liberalization* became the watchwords of rhetoric—if not always policy—in much of the developing world. This change in rhetoric spread to parts of the Arab world as well; and, whether as cause or effect, it coincided with the emergence of "an entrepreneurial, production-oriented bourgeoisie" in the region (MERIP 16, no. 5, [September–October 1986]: 2).

The political implications of this development, however, remain to be seen. The question remains, does the rise of a production-oriented bourgeoisie in countries like Egypt, Tunisia, or Morocco signify the appearance of a dominant class, that is, a class able to dictate policy to the state? Or has the Arab bourgeoisie remained essentially parasitic, state-dependent, and hence politically submissive to initiatives from states that are still largely autonomous and self-directing? This question can be answered only after empirical research into the character of the bourgeoisie and its relation to the state in the context of specific Arab countries; this chapter is an attempt to carry out such an investigation in the case of Tunisia. By studying the origin, structure, and organization of the Tunisian industrial bourgeoisie, as well as its relation to the state, this chapter will explore the issue of who is servant and who is sovereign in the context of Tunisian politics (Batatu

1986, 12) and suggest the contours of the relationship between state and bourgeoisie in other Arab countries as well.[1]

■ Tunisian Industrialization

To trace the development of an industrial bourgeoisie in Tunisia we should begin by reviewing the history of Tunisian industrialization. Like other Third World countries, Tunisia was a latecomer to industrialization, though for centuries the country had produced and exported sophisticated consumer goods. Tunisian ceramics, textiles, and leather goods were world-famous in medieval times; items like wool *chechias* (caps) were prized and purchased throughout the Muslim world (Mahjoub 1978, 28). But despite large-scale production and distribution, production processes in Tunisia remained largely artisanal. Nor did the country's opening to European capital in the early nineteenth century alter the system of production. French and British capitalists saw in Tunisia a potentially profitable commercial venture, not a field for industrial development. They sought to procure Tunisian agricultural products (primarily grain, olive oil, dates, and wool) in exchange for European manufactured goods. In fact, Tunisia's first venture into industrialization was delayed until the mid-nineteenth century, when Ahmed Bey began an experiment in "defensive modernization" that involved the creation of mechanized oil presses, flour mills, and cannon and gunpowder factories (Mahjoub 1978, 84). But this first experiment in state-led industrialization was soon abandoned by the bey and, save for the mechanization of the odd flour mill or oil press by a local notable or foreign trader, Tunisia remained largely devoid of industrial structures well up to colonial invasion in 1881.

The imposition of French rule, however, did not necessarily speed the industrialization process in Tunisia. French colons, much like their merchant predecessors, regarded Tunisia as a source of agricultural exports; they invested primarily in olive, vine, and cereal culture. A near-exclusive focus on agriculture was expanded to include mining when mineral deposits (lead, zinc, iron, copper, and, most importantly, phosphates) were discovered in the late nineteenth century. Thus, for the first fifty years of colonial rule industrialization was not a priority; the main areas of economic investment were agriculture and mining. Moreover, the creation of a customs union with France in 1904 (redefined in 1928) opened the Tunisian market to French manufactured goods, a factor that stunted the development of local industry (besides destroying local artisanry). Official statistics from the period make this clear. For the year 1896, Azzam Mahjoub (1978, 234) counts only 103 industrial enterprises in Tunisia (the lion's share of which, 68, were in the agroalimentary sector). Thirty-four years later, in 1928, the number had only risen to 428, with Tunisian industry still heavily weighted toward the agroalimentary sector (358 firms, of which 256 seem to be little more than mechanized olive oil presses).

By the mid-1930s, however, Tunisia's industrial sector began to expand and diversify. But the biggest spurt in industrial growth coincided with World War II and the years immediately following the war (1938–1951). The timing of this spurt had more to do with external factors than internal ones. During the war North Africa was cut off from the supply of European manufactured goods; under these artificial conditions an indigenous industry grew up to answer local demand for manufactured products (Mahjoub 1978, 311–312). This process was expressly encouraged by the colonial state, which perceived the "underindustrialization" of Tunisia as a strategic risk. (France could not guarantee the provision of essential goods to its citizens in Tunisia during wartime [Signoles 1984, 556]). Consequently, the state issued a series of decrees designed to encourage private investment in industry. Between 1942 and 1956 four laws were passed offering tax breaks, customs exemptions, and guaranteed credit to all potential investors. During the course of this period, the French state provided more than six billion francs in credit to new industrial ventures (Gouia 1987, 201–202; see also Signoles 1984, 735 and Romdhane 1981, 180).

Given the protected market and the state's encouragement, local industry flourished. The production capacity of extant industries increased significantly (Mahjoub [1978, 315–317] estimates that the metalworks sector increased its capacity nearly seven-fold); and entirely new industrial ventures sprang up (e.g., food canning, textiles). Unfortunately, a good many of these firms, launched under the artificial conditions of war-imposed autarky, were not competitive enough to survive the resumption of foreign trade with Europe at the war's end. (Mahjoub [1978, 556] counts fifty-two food canning factories in 1947; by 1952 only twenty-two still survived.) Moreover, it should be stressed that although Tunisian industry may trace its roots to the World War II period, a Tunisian industrial bourgeoisie cannot claim such early origins. Throughout this period most industrial sectors were dominated not by Tunisian entrepreneurs but rather by large European trusts (this was certainly the case in mining, transport, and energy); even transformative industries were dominated by foreigners. A 1953 census of large industrial enterprises in Tunisia found that out of 141 establishments employing over fifty workers only 11 (8 percent) were owned by Tunisians (Mahjoub 1978, 338). This meant that Tunisia arrived at Independence in 1956 still lacking an indigenous industrial bourgeoisie of any real consequence.

With the achievement of Independence, Tunisia was finally positioned to steward its own economic destiny. Confronting this task, the Tunisian elite was divided over the development strategy to adopt. One wing advocated a central role for the state in the development process, concentrating capital in the hands of the public sector and orchestrating investment through a careful system of planning. A second wing preferred to make the private sector the engine of growth, arguing that market signals, not planning directives, should guide the development of the economy. After considerable political struggle between these two groups, President Bourguiba ultimately opted for the second, "liberal" strategy. As the success of this strategy ultimately depended on a dynamic, industrializing bourgeoisie, the state proceeded to set in place various legal and institutional structures to foster their development. Colonial decrees offering tax holidays and guaranteed loans to industrial investors were preserved by the state; and more generous laws (such as that of February 1958 guaranteeing stable tax regimes for exceptionally long periods of time to firms with new investments exceeding fifty thousand dinars) were drawn up as well (Romdhane 1981, 179–189). Prohibitive customs tariffs were decreed to protect infant industries in the local market, and wholesale import bans were not uncommon in many sectors. Finally, a number of financial institutions were created between 1956 and 1961 with the express mandate to make credit easily available to potential Tunisian investors. (Among these were the Fond d'Investissement et Developppment (FID), Société Tunisienne de Banque (STB), and Société Nationale d'Investissement (SNI) (Dimassi 1983, 133).

Despite much encouragement, however, the response of the Tunisian bourgeoisie was disappointing. Investment funds made available for industrial projects went begging; Tunisian entrepreneurs apparently preferred to buy up abandoned French businesses rather than risk inaugurating new industrial ventures (Romdhane 1981, 200). Investment levels fell between 1956 and 1961 (a process exacerbated by the capital flight associated with the departure of the French), and many sectors of industry stagnated (pp. 191–192). During the first five years of Independence per capita GNP remained constant, and by 1961 it was at risk of declining. The disappointing performance of private capital and the consequent threat of negative growth disenchanted many political elites with the "liberal" approach to development and made them reconsider a state-led, planned strategy after all.

■ The State Takes the Lead

Reconsideration became official policy in 1962, the year Tunisia published its economic First Plan. The plan's publication marked the ascendance of the *dirigiste* wing of the political elite, an elite committed to setting Tunisia on a "socialist" path to development. But though socialist symbols and rhetoric were much bandied about in the Tunisia of the early- and mid-1960s (the Destour party renamed itself the Socialist Destour party in 1964), the socialist content of the economic program adopted was actually rather thin.

The state's attempt to make agriculture cooperative, monopolize trade networks, and manage the industrialization process represented an attempt more to centralize economic decisionmaking in the hands of state bureaucrats (*étatisation*) than to realize socialism in Tunisia (Signoles 1984, 754). Nonetheless, the Tunisian economy underwent some dramatic changes during the 1960s, and the state played a central role in this process. This is made clear by the investment figures from the period. For the decade 1962–1971, the Tunisian public sector accounted for 72 percent of gross fixed capital investment; in the industrial sector, its role was even more pronounced. State investment dwarfed private participation in nearly every branch of industry, as shown in Table 3.1.

There is no question then that the state took the lead in the industrialization of Tunisia during the 1960s. Under the direction of Super-minister Ahmed ben Salah, state technocrats set up industrial ventures in nearly every industrial sector and geographical region of Tunisia—from sugar refineries in Beja to paper-processing plants in Kasserine. Moreover, this development program was carried out within a particular ideological context, one that prized the public sector as efficient, dynamic, and dedicated to the national interest while denigrating the local bourgeoisie as risk-averse, self-serving followers, not leaders, of the development process. Nonetheless, it is important to realize that even at the height of the etatist experiment, the regime never wholly discredited the private sector, either in rhetoric nor in policy. From the first days of "planned development," political elites from Bourguiba to ben Salah asserted their commitment to the private sector, arguing that the Tunisian economy would be the work of three sectors: state, cooperative, and private. (Even the earliest plan asserted that the state would act largely as "associated partner" to private capital, providing the capital and cadres necessary for private sector promotion and undertaking development projects that surpassed the capabilities of private initiative, such as water, energy, and transport [République Tunisienne, Ministère du Plan 1962–1964, 141].)

In terms of policy, the regime maintained and supplemented earlier decrees designed to encourage the development of the private sector. Throughout the 1960s, tax holidays; protected local markets; guaranteed loans; and subsidized credit, input, and infrastructure were still the rule for private entrepreneurs. These benefits were actually augmented by further decrees in 1962, 1966, 1968, and 1969 (Romdhane and Signoles 1982, 65; see also Dimassi 1983, 515–516). Even in its most aggressive attack on private interests, the state revealed an underlying commitment to private sector development. In the hope of "rationalizing" the commercial sector the state took charge of import and export trade, in addition to reorganizing wholesale and retail networks into a less redundant, state-supervised system. The state's goal was to chase propertied but speculative Tunisians out of the

Table 3.1 Public and Private Participation in Gross Fixed Capital Formation,
           1962–1971 (%)

Industry	Public Enterprise	Private Enterprise
Industrial sector	77.7	22.3
Nonmanufacturing industries	76.8	23.2
Mining	98.5	1.5
Electricity, water	100.0	0.0
Petroleum	54.0	46.0
Manufacturing industries	79.3	20.7
Agroalimentary	70.6	29.4
Metal, glass, construction materials	91.0	9.0
Electromechanics	89.8	10.2
Chemicals	76.2	23.8
Textiles	70.7	29.3
Woodwork	30.4	69.6
Paper	78.4	17.6

Source: Gouia 1987, 280.

commercial sector and into more productive activities like industry. In fact, the process was less successful than had been hoped (even though one-third of former wholesalers in the town of Sfax moved into small-scale industrial activities such as shoe manufacturing and metalworks [Signoles 1984, 759; see also Asselain 1971, 111–139]). Nonetheless, it showed that the state, even at its most intrusive, was still at heart committed to the creation of a private industrial bourgeoisie.

■ Private Sector Encouragement

But if nurturing a private industrial bourgeoisie was only implicit in the policies of the 1960s, it became explicit in the 1970s. Agricultural failure and fiscal crisis precipitated the fall of the *dirigiste* elite in 1969–1970; and the new executive team, led by Prime Minister Hedi Nouira, advocated a very different strategy of development.[2] Henceforth, they argued, the private sector would take the lead in national development; the state would only act as its handmaiden and guardian. Chedli Ayari, then minister of national economy, announced in 1974, "The state seeks to create a generation of industrialists who will be the masters of the country tomorrow" (Signoles 1984, 790–794).

To foster their development, the state spared no effort. A new series of decrees were announced in 1972 and 1974 designed to expand existing fiscal benefits, credit subsidies, infrastructure guarantees, and exchange facilities for private investors in industries. New institutions were created such as the Agence de Promotion Industrielle (API, to help entrepreneurs identify potentially profitable industrial investments and facilitate the realization process), the Agence Fonciere Industrielle (AFI, to make land available to industrial investors, often at subsidized prices) and the Centre de Promotion des Exportations (CEPEX, to help exporters identify market opportunities and improve their marketing techniques, packaging, and transport facilities). Financial measures were taken to make credit easily available to potential investors and one fund, Fonds de Promotion et de Développement Industriel (FOPRODI) was created with the express purpose of creating a new class of private entrepreneurs (providing generous grants of capital to potential entrepreneurs who were rich in know-how but poor in financial resources). A new furlough system was instituted in the public sector to encourage state employees to make the jump from public to private sector work: civil servants were permitted a two-year leave of absence to try their hand in the private sector, during which time their positions and seniority in the public sector would be guaranteed (interview with Fethi Merdassi, July 8, 1988).[3] Thus, many measures were employed to encourage the development of a private industrial bourgeoisie during the 1970s.

The results were not disappointing. The 1970s saw a decade of spectacular industrial growth. Pierre Signoles counts more than eight hundred new industrial enterprises created during that period, projects representing more than a billion dinars in investment (Signoles 1984, 568). Tunisia's industrial park doubled in just twelve years, as Institute National de Statistique (INS) statistics show. The following figures represent the number of firms with more than ten employees in selected years (Romdhane and Signoles 1983, 60–62):

1967	553
1970	640
1975	927
1978	1,205

Moreover, the private sector's share in all this growth was impressive. Private investment in industry surpassed that of the public sector for the first time in 1972, and it remained high throughout the decade (Signoles 1984, 597). Table 3.2 gives precise figures on private and public shares of industrial investment during the 1960s and 1970s.

As Table 3.2 shows, the private sector grew significantly in every branch of industry, save chemicals.[4] It dominated such sectors as agroalimentary, textiles, metalwork, and mechanics and ceded place to the state only in mining, chemicals, construction materials, and utilities. As Mahmoud ben Romdhane and Azzam Mahjoub (n.d., 77) make clear, this pattern of investment reflected a marked division of labor between private and public sector in the industrial field. Whereas the private sector focused on the

Table 3.2   Relative Share of Public and Private Sector Investment in Gross Fixed
Capital Formation in Industry, 1962–1980 (%)

Industry	1962–1969		1970–1976		1977–1980	
	Public	Private	Public	Private	Public	Private
Agroalimentary	72	28	30	70	38	62
Glass, marble, construction materials	93	7	69	31	79	21
Electromechanics, metal	92	8	54	46	46	54
Chemicals	62	38	70	30	91	9
Textiles	83	17	18	82	13	87
Diverse	79	21	23	77	18	82
Total	84	16	47	53	61	39

Source: Signoles 1985, 807.

least capital-intensive, the least technologically sophisticated, and the most immediately profitable branches of industry, the state carried the burden of basic, heavy industries that were beyond the capability and interest of the private sector. (For example, while the private sector focused on simple finished goods like ready-to-wear clothes, canned foods, shoes, and carbonated drinks, the public sector concentrated on cement works, paper-processing plants, fabric weaving, and sugar refining. In fact, the state quite consciously followed this strategy, opening up new sectors of industry for production and then letting future investment opportunities in the sector fall to the private sector as soon as those sectors became profitable (Romdhane 1981, 267–268). But no matter the logic, the 1970s did see the expansion of the private sector in Tunisia; and by 1983 (the latest year for which reliable statistics are available) the INS counted 2,608 private sector industrial enterprises with more than ten employees (Table 3.3).

■ Tunisian Industrialists—Parasitic?

But if I have established that a private sector industrial bourgeoisie indeed exists in Tunisia, the question remains, What is its relation to the state? Is this class largely parasitic? In the context of Third World politics, the term *parasitic bourgeoisie* has rather precise connotations. It implies that the bourgeoisie is unproductive, that it preys upon the state, most often enriching itself by trading on contacts within the state rather than by contributing something valuable to the national economy. A very clear

Table 3.3 Private Sector Industrial Enterprises (More Than Ten Employees)

Industry	Number
Agroalimentary	613
Metal, glass, construction materials	314
Electromechanics	300
Chemicals	110
Textiles, shoes	841
Diverse	430
Total	2,608

Source: Table compiled by M. Sellami of the Institut Arab des Chefs d'Enterprise, based on INS statistics.

example of a parasitic bourgeoisie can be found in the "supply mafia" of Egypt so well described by Robert Springborg (1989, 81–82). These racketeers typically use their personal connections within the Egyptian Ministry of Supply to get access to state-subsidized goods (e.g., flour). The racketeers then sell these goods, at much higher prices, on the black market, pocketing the difference in price. The term *parasitic bourgeoisie* thus connotes private enrichment at public expense; and in some cases it has been extended to include any class of people who have profited from corrupt use of public office.

But does the term *parasitic bourgeoisie* accurately describe the private sector industrial bourgeoisie of Tunisia? No doubt there have been some spectacular cases of corruption in Tunisia. In early 1986, the scandal making the rounds was that of Moncer Bouzgenda. Apparently, Bouzgenda, the head of a construction and engineering firm, made his fortune from public works contracts he had won from the state (thanks to close personal relation to one or two ministers). Bouzgenda routinely failed to deliver the goods contracted or at best delivered bridges and roads way below the quality standard paid for by the state. However, he kept his operations running by bribing inspectors and playing the contacts game within the various ministries. Estimates have it that he bilked the Tunisian government out of millions of dinars.

No doubt the Bouzgenda story is only the most dramatic example of what must be more than a singular case. But is it paradigmatic for the way business fortunes are made in Tunisia? Corruption is notoriously difficult to document, so little irrefutable proof can be offered. However, interviews with over seventy-five Tunisian academics, public officials, and businessmen turned up a near-uniform rejection of this portrayal, at least for the case of the industrial bourgeoisie.[5] Repeatedly, interview subjects pointed out that the largest fortunes in the industrial community had been made in businesses that had no special relations (contractual or otherwise) with the state, whether referring to the case of Abdelwahab ben Ayed of Poulina (Tunisia's poultry king), or Hedi Jelani of Lee Cooper Jeans (an export-oriented textile manufacturer), or Abdessalem Affes of STPA (a major couscous manufacturer). And although most admitted that petty corruption greased the wheel of nearly all business operations (e.g., slipping a sample of free merchandise to a state inspector), interview subjects were unanimous in arguing that by and large Tunisian manufacturers owed their fortunes to shrewd management and hard work rather than to shady relations with the state.

Does this mean that personal contacts with officials in the state bureaucracy are irrelevant to business success? Certainly not. Nearly all the businessmen interviewed emphasized the importance of knowing someone on the inside to getting business affairs done. The businessmen argued, however, that this was important not because it gave preferential access to public goods but rather because the character of the state bureaucracy demanded it. Tunisia is plagued by an overly ambitious and overextended state that seeks to license, monitor, and regulate nearly every aspect of business affairs. A typical project may require signatures from over a hundred offices before it works its way through the bureaucratic approval process. Moreover, the laws and regulations that govern business life are constantly in flux. Consequently, it is extremely easy to get lost in the maze of state bureaucracy; a project may molder under a pile of dusty files for the want of a single piece of paper. Knowing someone on the inside may mean that the businessman's file will get read a little faster or that he will be better informed regarding the best supporting documents to submit with his file.

Personal contacts with state officials are thus important to business success. But in Tunisia one does not need to offer a cut of the action to a public official to get an industrial project approved. Nor is it necessary (as is the case in Syria or Iraq) to get the party's imprimatur to do business in Tunisia. In fact, a good portion of the businessmen interviewed were not members of the Destour party at all. The bureaucratic approval process is a cumbersome one, but it appears equally cumbersome for people of all political stripes. In fact, one might say that (save for businessmen at the extremes of the political spectrum) the bureaucracy is largely politically neutral vis-à-vis businessmen. The clearest evidence of this is the fact that not a few successful businessmen in Tunisia are former political activists who, for one reason or another, fell into disfavor with President Bourguiba. These men fled to the business world as a refuge from politics and, for the most part, were granted "the right to make money" free from politically motivated bureaucratic harassment.[6]

But even if we accept that business–state relations are not essentially ties of corruption and that Tunisian industrialists are much more than just influence peddlers, the question remains, Has the industrial bourgeoisie created enterprises that are truly productive and viable, or is this bourgeoisie parasitic in the sense that it lives off the largesse of the state?

Certainly, state largesse has been crucial to the development of nearly all industrial ventures in Tunisia. All the industrialists interviewed admitted they had benefited in one way or another from state support, whether that meant subsidized credit, protected markets, monopoly prices, or fiscal breaks. In fact, Tunisian industrialists have been so buffered and nurtured by the state that some Tunisian economists refer to them as a "rentier bourgeoisie," arguing that they owe their fortunes not to productive enterprise but rather to the rents that accrue from exclusive production licenses and monopoly conditions created by the state (interview with Abdeljelil Bedaoui, March 14, 1988). Lately, however, these rentier conditions have begun to change. A serious foreign exchange crisis in August 1986 brought in its wake an IMF-sponsored structural adjustment program; this program called for the liberalization of prices and imports (i.e., an end to monopoly conditions and the introduction of competition), reduced public spending (i.e., less subsidized credit to go around), devaluation of the dinar (i.e., accurate world market prices for imported inputs), and a stronger emphasis on export orientation (where prices would be set by the international market, not the Tunisian state). The program essentially demanded that Tunisia's infant industries grow up.

In fact, the state has been reasonably prompt in implementing the IMF reform measures. By January 1988 interest rates had risen significantly, prices had been liberalized for 60 percent of industrial products, and imports had been liberalized for 67 percent of imported goods (*Courrier de l'industrie*, January 1988); the same was done for the rest of imports consisting of finished goods in March 1989. Although it is expected that local producers will continue to be protected by an across-the-board customs tariff (contemplated at 25 percent), the future holds more market competition for Tunisian producers and consequently the prospect of a less cushy rentier situation. No doubt, some producers will be unable to withstand the competition; and numerous bankruptcies may result. But at least according to official rhetoric, save for cases threatening severe political liability (e.g., the closure of a large public sector firm), the state will allow market discipline to prevail and will stand by as firms go under.[7] Foreign exchange crisis, then, has led to a measured retreat of the state from business affairs; and this in turn should lead to the demarcation of a leaner but more independent industrial bourgeoisie.

■ Tunisian Industrialists—Politically Powerful?

As established above, the Tunisian industrial bourgeoisie is by and large not parasitic and that it is now on the road to greater economic independence from the state. But does this class of industrialists constitute a dominant class, namely, one with sufficient political clout to dictate policy to the state? Or does it resemble most other groups in Tunisian society, which are, for the most part, the passive recipients of political and economic initiatives handed down to them by a state largely autonomous of domestic forces.

The political power of any social group is notoriously difficult to measure, especially in political systems where "electoral politics is not central to the design of policy" (Haggard and Kaufman n.d., 20). It certainly cannot be measured by observing policy outcomes, that is, by deducing a group's political strength from the number of policies passed that favor that group's interests. This would be to confuse class partiality with class capture, the inverse of Hassine Dimassi's caution not to confuse state autonomy with neutrality (1983, 65). On the contrary, the state may choose a certain policy thanks to a calculus of its internal interests; this policy may then simply coincide with the agenda of a particular class, without necessarily being the work of that class (Waterbury n.d.).[8]

This has largely been the case in Tunisia with regard to policies favoring the industrial bourgeoisie, at least until the 1980s. The advantageous policies enacted during the 1960s and 1970s were not the result of Tunisian industrialists' clamoring for state favors; nor can they be taken as a measure of pressure brought to bear upon the state by this class. Such a scenario would have been impossible, since, as has been shown, an industrial bourgeoisie hardly existed in Tunisia prior to 1970. On the contrary, the state adopted these policies for its own reasons (largely due to recognition of its own financial and technical limitations),[9] and in the process it *created the constituency* for these policies. Rather than interpret these pro–private sector policies as the measure of bourgeois strength, these policies should be seen as a "gift" bestowed on Tunisian society without struggle. In this they are similar to the liberal personal status laws enacted in the late 1950s, which were not wrested from the state by a powerful women's movement but rather were handed down with paternalistic largesse by President Bourguiba to a still largely inert female constituency.[10] Similarly, the most recent round of liberalization reforms (which serve the interests of at least certain segments of the industrial bourgeoisie) must also not be taken as a measure of that class's clout. Rather, it was a foreign exchange crisis and the IMF's insistence on a structural adjustment program that forced progressive liberalization of prices, imports, and interest rates in Tunisia. No doubt, the fact that a domestic constituency exists for these policies helps prod the state into keeping to the IMF agenda, something that is sorely lacking in Egypt, as Robert Springborg points out (1989, 260–261). Nonetheless, the decisive shove that overcame the state's inertia to liberalizing reform came not from potent domestic constituencies but rather from external forces (like the IMF) and the logic of integration into the world economy.

But if the industrial bourgeoisie has proven less than successful at mustering decisive clout on the domestic political scene, there are a number of factors that help explain it. First, the structure of the industrial bourgeoisie is one source of weakness. A profile of private sector industry shows that the majority of Tunisian firms are small-scale operations. An INS survey carried out in the late 1970s found that 62 percent of all firms in the industrial sector employed fewer than ten workers, while in branches such as textiles, leather, wood, metalworks, and electromechanics, the share jumped to 95 percent (Institut National de Statistique 1979, 41).[11] The small size of the Tunisian firms is confirmed in monetary terms as well; a recent API report found that the average industrial enterprises in Tunisia did not represent more than one-hundred-thousand-dinars' worth of investment, and 94 percent of all industrial projects fell under the five-hundred-thousand-dinar mark (API internal document n.d., 1).[12] Besides being small, most private sector firms are family-run operations with limited resources at their disposal. (Stockholding is still a relatively rare phenomenon in Tunisia [Gouia 1987, 422].) Moreover, most of these small-scale industrial firms are run by entrepreneurs from nonindustrial backgrounds who have little experience in the field and who have chosen to invest in simple, repetitive projects geared to the domestic market, such as brick works, biscuit factories, ready-to-wear textiles, and so on (API internal document n.d., 4).

Small, inexperienced, family-run enterprises lacking in resources, and producing for the local market in relatively crowded sectors are rarely conducive to a spirit of collective solidarity; on the contrary, a feeling of mutual suspicion and competitiveness prevails. (The smaller the firm, the less likely it is to participate regularly in the affairs of UTICA, the official businessmen's association, for example.) Add to this the fact that a good many Tunisian industrialists are guilty of tax evasion, and it is even more apparent why this class is less politically assertive than might be expected. Most industrialists prefer to keep a low profile rather than court the state's attention; their modus vivendi is more likely to be one of seeking favors on an individual basis than demanding rights for the collectivity.[13] Thus, although larger, better-placed industrialists have occasionally demonstrated collective assertiveness, the atomized structure of the industrial class as a whole—not to mention the diversity of this class—certainly works to limit its political clout.

Another factor contributing to its political reticence derives from the structure of state supports and incentives. For years, the state provided a variety of encouragements to private business, whether fiscal breaks, tariff protection, or subsidized credit. These benefits were distributed in discretionary fashion, usually after evaluation of the investment project in terms of stated policy objectives (e.g., the degree of employment creation, energy conservation, or economic integration). In addition, the state sought to regulate many aspects of business affairs. As noted, bureaucratic approval had to be won to launch an enterprise, acquire credit, set prices, or get access to import licenses and foreign currency. This system certainly enlarged the discretionary power of the state over business fortunes, a factor that could not help but hamstring the political assertiveness of businessmen; for although businessmen by and large do not pass a political test to do business in Tunisia, nonetheless, the petitionary quality of their relationship with the state certainly does not encourage an aggressive or confrontational approach vis-à-vis their benefactor.

Finally, organizational weakness comes into play in limiting the clout of the industrial bourgeoisie in Tunisia. Typically, organization (that is, the capacity for collective action) is the power source of labor, not capital; on the contrary, capital finds its classic source of leverage in individually exercised decisions like capital flight or investment strike (Panitch 1981, 27). Nonetheless, organization can be an important source of power for businessmen as well, especially in the Third World, where data is scarce and information is power. Organization (specifically businessmen's organizations equipped with highly skilled research staffs) can wield significant influence by gathering together information on the economy (information often unavailable to overworked and poorly trained civil servants) and using this information to support a particular vision of the economy. An example of such an influential organization is TUSIAD, the Turkish businessmen's association whose widely distributed, well-researched economic studies contribute much to shaping economic opinion throughout Turkish state and society (Arat 1989).

Unfortunately for Tunisian businessmen, an organization of similar character never emerged in Tunisia. In the years prior to Independence the few existing Tunisian industrialists were grouped together with Tunisian merchants and artisans in a coalition called the Tunisian Union of Artisans and Traders (UTAC). The organization ostensibly represented general business interests to the colonial state but in fact acted as an appendage to the Destour party, participating in the Independence struggle and acting as cover for the party when the latter was forced underground (Chekir 1974). During the first fifteen years of its existence the organization went through a variety of structural changes and finally added *Industrialists* to its name in 1963 to become the UTICA; but its character remained essentially the same—a hodgepodge of bourgeois and petty bourgeois interests grouped together in an organization that was organically and financially linked to the party. Although designated the sole corporatist representative of business to the state after Independence, the UTICA remained essentially weak due to its domination by the party and the heterogeneous character of its membership. The organization lacked vision (as well as the research capability to define that vision), and its approach was largely defensive. For the most part it reacted to state initiatives and sought to defend the short-term interests of business (e.g., the price of tomatoes next season, the provision of imported supplies for hairdressers). In the words of the UTICA's long-time director, the organization believed its role was "to rectify rather than to propose" (interview with Abdallah ben M'Barek, June 15, 1988). Consequently, the UTICA did not offer industrialists an effective vehicle for defining and promoting their collective interests; and given the corporatist structure of interest representation imposed by Bourguiba, businessmen did not feel free to organize alternative associations until well into the 1980s.

Despite these organizational and structural impediments, a number of factors have served to augment the political clout of Tunisia's industrial bourgeoisie in the last few years. The most important of these are the result of financial difficulties faced by the state. To start with the most dramatic, Tunisia faced a severe foreign exchange crisis in August 1986, resulting from a long-term decline in petroleum revenues and foreign exchange remittances. As mentioned above, the foreign exchange crisis brought in its wake an IMF-sponsored structural adjustment program that sought to introduce greater efficiency into the Tunisian economy, in part by introducing more market mechanisms and reducing the discretionary power of the state in economic affairs. Among the polices recommended by the program were withdrawal from a license-based system of importation (for example, all firms exporting 15 percent of their production were granted nearly unrestricted rights to import inputs); an end to state administration of prices in favor of their determination by the market (in sectors where monopoly conditions did not prevail); and the replacement of qualitative and quantitative restriction of imports with a standard, across-the-board tariff for the protection of local industry. The decrease in discretionary power for the state introduced by these measures meant that the businessmen would no longer be required to wheedle individual bargains from the state for their prices, protection, and imports. This certainly enlarged the possibility of political autonomy for Tunisian industrialists, since it meant that the state would wield significantly less retaliatory power over potentially "troublesome" members of this class. Moreover, these policy reforms were likely to encourage more collective action on the part of industrialists, since benefits (like tariff protection and access to imports) would no longer be the stuff of individual bargains cut by particular firms with the state but rather would be standardized for distribution on a broader, often sectorwide, basis.

Besides foreign exchange deficits, state fiscal crisis also contributed to a stronger position for the industrial bourgeoisie. From the late 1960s, fiscal constraint forced the state to realize that it did not possess sufficient technical or financial resources to guarantee the growth necessary to provide Tunisians with a rising standard of living. Consequently, the state increasingly shifted economic responsibility to the private sector, calling on the latter to make up for public sector shortfall in investment, job creation, and export earning.

And in fact, the private sector lived up to a large part of the demands placed upon it. For the period 1971–1975 an API report showed that 91 percent of all new jobs in industry were created by the private sector (cited in Gouia 1987, 361). A more recent report by the same agency shows that 72 percent of all industrial workers in Tunisia are employed in the (predominantly private sector) small-scale enterprises (API internal document n.d., 1). In terms of investment, Ministry of Plan reports show that the private sector provided 43 percent of investment during the first four years of the Sixth Plan (1981–1986), and it expected the private sector to play an even larger role in the future (République Tunisienne, Ministère de l'Industrie et du Commerce 1986). In terms of exports, manufactured goods have fast been replacing petroleum and phosphates as a major export earner (the Sixth Plan expected manufactured goods to constitute 57 percent of total exports of good and services by 1986); and the largest share of these manufactured goods come from industrial branches like textiles, shoes, and leather—branches where the private sector predominates (Signoles 1984, 810).

The positive role played by the private sector in the creation of employment, investment, and exports has resulted in a changed image for the industrial bourgeoisie. Whereas in some developing countries the private sector bourgeoisie is still reviled by official rhetoric, in Tunisia the private entrepreneur is increasingly regarded as the new hero of national development. Business leaders are frequently spotlighted in the press; official institutions like API sponsor seminars on "how to become an entrepreneur," and public officials regularly consult businessmen on the direction of the state's economic policy. Recognition of the private sector's contribution to the economy as well as the positive image ascribed to businessmen in the public eye has given this class new confidence; consequently, they have become more outspoken advocates of their interests. The change is especially evident in the associational activities of businessmen. Whereas the UTICA was once the domesticated mouthpiece of the Destour party, the businessmen's organization has taken on new life since Bourguiba's ouster and the subsequent détente in the politics of national associations. A new executive team was permitted to take hold in the UTICA; and led by a highly dynamic, well-educated, export-oriented textile manufacturer, the UTICA has vast plans underway to carry out survey research on the Tunisian economy, draft a businessmen's version of the Five Year Plan (an alternative to the official one), and rally businessmen to more active roles in local and national politics. There is even talk of weaning the UTICA from state-controlled financing in the hope of making the organization more autonomous of the state (Interview with Hedi Jelani, July 22, 1988).

Besides a more dynamic UTICA, an increase in collective assertiveness among businessmen has also been manifested by the creation of another businessman's association, the Institut Arab des Chefs d'Enterprise (IACE).

Founded in 1985 by former minister and current bank president Monceur Moalla, the IACE was designed to serve as a "club" where the elite of the business community would meet with public officials and academics in forums of reflection and debate on the Tunisian economy.[14] Committed to creating an environment "hospitable to the flourishing of enterprise," the institute conducts economic research, organizes conferences, and publishes reports to promote its views. Funded entirely by private subscriptions and contributions, the institute has served as one of the most autonomous channels of business communication to the state and in recent years has emerged as an increasingly influential opinionmaker on the Tunisian political and economic scene.

None of this is to overestimate the role played by businessmen's associations in Tunisian politics. The IACE representatives, for example, were careful to distance their organization from any likening to U.S.-style business lobbies or pressure groups. The IACE, they insisted, served more as an intellectual forum for long-term reflection on the economy rather than as a pressure group promoting the short-term interests of a particular economic constituency. And even leaders from the UTICA, the designated representative of business interests, resisted the term *pressure group* and the antagonistic relationship between state and association that the term implies. They insisted that the relationship between the UTICA and the state was not one of pressuring and weightslinging but rather one of mutual consultation and cooperation (perhaps indicative of their still-limited capacity to "force" their will upon the state).

Moreover, associations are not necessarily the most important venue of communication between business and the state. Tunisia is still a small-enough country that leading businessmen and public officials can often meet face-to-face. This may be at the instigation of either party. Most businessmen pointed out that the largest industrialists rarely relied on collective action or associational networks to solve their problems with the state; rather, they spoke directly to the relevant minister involved. Moreover, as was pointed out by one industrialist, once an enterprise gets to be a certain size, "the ministers come calling on you" (Interview July 14, 1988). Informal consultation by public officials with leading businessmen on economic policy has become routine in Tunisia; and businessmen are regularly called to serve as consultants to commissions at the Central Bank, the Ministry of Plan, and the party. Businessmen thus actively participate in the policymaking process and do so on both an individualistic and collective basis in Tunisia.

To return to the original question—Does Tunisia's industrial bourgeoisie constitute a dominant class?—the answer would have to be *not yet*. First, Tunisian industrialists cannot constitute a dominant class because their role in the economy is still significantly circumscribed. Although the private sector's share of the economy is growing, the state continues to play a large role—even a commanding one—in many branches of the economy. Moreover, the state still provides over half the country's annual investment as well as employment for nearly a quarter of the active population; thus, it cannot help but retain a position of predominance. Second, though programs of structural adjustment and liberalization are gradually weaning the industrial bourgeoisie from dependence on the state (in addition to reducing the discretionary power of the state over business fortunes), still, the state can be expected to play a large role in promoting the private sector for the near future, buffering it (at the very least) from the vagaries of integration into the world economy.[15] Thus, we can expect that a certain degree of dependence between business and state will persist and that the petitionary character of the relationship will never wholly disappear, though it may diminish. Third, Tunisian businessmen cannot expect to play a domineering role in politics so long as they persist in one common illegal practice, that is, tax fraud. Such fraud is standard procedure for Tunisian entrepreneurs (so much so that when Monceur Moalla was minister of plan he appeared on television saying that given Tunisia's quite high tax rates, no businessman could possibly pay all the taxes legally due and still expect to stay in business).[16] Many observers consider this rampant evasion of taxes evidence of state weakness and society's relative strength. In fact, the result shows that the contrary is the case. Tax fraud becomes the sword of Damocles that hangs over the head of nearly every businessman; and, like state-sanctioned corruption elsewhere (Waterbury 1976), it serves as a control mechanism that muzzles the political assertiveness of the offenders. More than one well-placed businessman confessed he had blunted his criticism of the state for fear of retribution from some vengeful bureaucrat armed with a well-documented dossier on his business affairs.

One further issue that can only be touched upon here but has been developed at greater length elsewhere (Bellin 1991) concerns the impact that Tunisia's experiment with democratization will have on the political power of the industrial bourgeoisie. Although it might seem counterintuitive at first, there is reason to believe that the democratization process will serve the interest of this numerically small (and hence vote-poor) segment of Tunisian society. This is because ben Ali's program of democratization has called for the separation of party and state. Specifically, the president promised to wean the government party, the RCD, from financing by the state by January 1989. This left the party scrambling for new sources of funding, and the most likely suppliers turned out to be well-heeled businessmen. The fall and winter of 1988 saw the solicitation and recruitment of many businessmen by the party (in just a few months businessmen had pledged over three million dinars to the RCD); such increased reliance of the party on business financing cannot help but make the party more sympathetic to business interests. And although it is unlikely that the party will make a radical break with its image as party of the entire Tunisian people or abandon its organized rural constituency and metamorphose into an exclusively businessmen's party, still it is not beyond the ken to expect that the party will move rightward, perhaps toward an alliance of business and rural interests, an alliance likely to exclude organized labor and the urban lumpen proletariat.

In short, there are numerous factors at work to enhance the political power of Tunisian industrialists. However, this process is not ineluctable, and the most significant obstacle to political influence may be the industrialists themselves. Thus far, Tunisian industrialists have shown little inclination to test the boundaries of their power, largely because they have not felt the need to do so. The fact that for the last twenty years the Tunisian state has largely anticipated their needs and legislated an extremely favorable context for investment has nurtured a degree of political apathy among Tunisian industrialists. The true measure of their power will come only when the state enacts policies that seriously contradict the interests of this class (or at least a significant portion of it). This opportunity may come sooner than expected, such as when the true impact of liberalized import laws (regarding finished consumer goods) becomes felt in the coming year or two. Only then will we be able to test the political mettle of Tunisian industrialists (their unity, their independence, their capacity to organize) and see whether this class can effectively challenge the state that was its father.

■ Notes

1. I would like to thank John Waterbury, Atul Kohli, Nacy Bermeo, and L. Carl Brown for reading earlier drafts of this paper.

2. The reasons for ben Salah's fall and the abandonment of the *dirigiste* strategy of development are complex and might easily merit an article in itself. Suffice it to say that a variety of factors were involved, including a clash of political personalities, the discontent of the rural bourgeoisie who were threatened by ben Salah's plan to subject their land to cooperative control, the fiscal crisis faced by the state, and the bad luck of consecutive years of drought and poor harvests. For a fuller discussion of these issues see also Dimassi 1983 and Signoles 1984.

3. In fact, a good many of the biggest private entrepreneurs got their start in the public sector. Gouia counts 30 percent out of his sample of 140 large-scale private industrialists as originally hailing from the public sector (1987, 431).

4. As Pierre Signoles points out, the increase in public investment in industry that began in 1975 should not be seen as an abandonment of the state's commitment to private sector growth (1985, 807–808). Rather, the need to overcome certain structural blockages (e.g., the provision of basic goods like cement and the expansion of hydraulic, energy, and transport infrastructure) led to a surge in public spending during the late 1970s. However, the state's goal

remained the creation of conditions most conducive to private sector growth and prosperity.

5. No doubt one would expect some response bias when asking businessmen whether shady connections with the state were essential to business success. Nonetheless, the fact that nearly every businessman interviewed rejected the importance of such relations (even while admitting the prevalence of petty corruption) and the fact that independent academics corroborated this view made a relatively convincing case for the argument that corrupt relations with the state were not the typical way industrial fortunes were made in Tunisia.

6. None of this is to underestimate the important role that *copinage*, or cronyism plays in all aspects of Tunisian life, especially in business. In a small country like Tunisia where everyone knows everyone else, a great deal of business in conducted "among friends." Moreover, in a country where statistical and technical information is scarce, falling back on social networks for data is not necessarily reproachable. In the case of dispensing credit, for example, a bank may lack the technical staff to evaluate properly the merit of a given project. Consequently, bank officials may fall back on personal contacts ("friends in the business") for advice on whether a project is sound or the borrower reliable. So long as such networking provides valuable and true information (rather than mere promotion of meritless friends and projects), it neither introduces economic inefficiency nor can justly be called cronyism (at least not in its most negative sense). Similar processes of networking are no doubt evident in the state bureaucracy's interaction with business. Similarly, the resulting favoritism that accrues to "well-connected" businessmen cannot be accurately called corruption, for there is no misuse (or necessarily inefficient use) of public funds involved. The bottom line in Tunisia is that insider contacts can help a good project get approved faster and may favor the case of a mediocre one; but it will rarely get a thoroughly worthless project approved. Moreover, all the businessmen I spoke to affirmed that a good project could get through even without connections. The process would simply require greater patience and greater persistence on the part of its promoter. (I am indebted to Salah Brik al-Hannachi for his insight into the issue of cronyism.)

7. In the spring of 1988 the state did undertake a program to save approximately 250 firms from the jaws of bankruptcy. Various measures were implemented, such as rescheduling debts and forgiving fiscal arrears. However, when interviewed, the civil servant responsible for the program asserted that the state chose to aid only the firms that were viable (i.e., had a chance of regaining profitability). He claimed the state would not offer a generalized safety net for all failing firms even though there were obvious political incentives for doing so (Interview of July 7, 1988).

8. Ilya Harik also developed this idea in a discussion during the spring of 1988.

9. The hope was that a dynamic industrial bourgeoisie would help fuel the growth process and thus help shoulder the burden of creating employment (among other things), which was a key political goal. Not to be discounted in the state's choice of a pro–private sector strategy is the ideological predisposition of the political elite of the time, especially that of Hedi Nouira.

10. Thanks go to Mondheur Gargouri for this insight.

11. These figures actually exaggerate the size of private sector firms, since the INS calculations average in the public sector firms as well, firms that are generally large and hence skew average firm size in the industrial sector upward. A more recent survey published by the INS for 1983 confirms the tendency of

private sector firms to be small, counting 2,649 industrial firms with ten or more workers but only 358 firms with one hundred workers or more.

12. Again, the figures are biased upward for the private sector, since public sector investments (generally large) are factored into these figures.

13. I owe this insight to Abdelgelil Bedaoui.

14. At one thousand dinars for a first-year membership, the institute certainly screens out any but the largest and most prosperous businessmen.

15. I owe this insight to John Waterbury.

16. Thanks are due to Salah Brik al-Hannachi for this story.

4

Tunisian Banking: Politics of Adjustment and the Adjustment of Politics

Clement Henry Moore

Pays pilote of the 1960s, Tunisia may again be forging a development model. While hardly the first to have embarked on an adjustment program carrying out IMF and World Bank prescriptions, it is pursuing a distinctive strategy that hinges on financial liberalization. Simultaneously, its political arena is undergoing transition from a one-party system toward greater pluralism. The political reform is not directly tied to the adjustment program, but real financial liberalization would support a more pluralistic politics. Even as threatened interests slow down the package of economic reforms, financial changes are taking on a life of their own. By focusing on money and banking, the Tunisian reformers have hit upon a gradualist strategy of political and economic change that is curiously reminiscent of Bourguibism—determined as to the eventual goals, flexible on timing and tactics. Given the nature of the strategy, they cannot yet claim success; but the commercial banks seem gradually to be conforming to an overall design for change. Indeed, Tunisia's official adjustment policies add up to a political, as well as an economic, design; for the banks must be viewed as potential political intermediaries, not just financial ones.[1]

■ Banking as Political Intermediation

Bankers are not only financial intermediators, matching up savers with borrowers. When they allocate credit, they are often performing political as well as economic services. In command economies, lending is inherently political; whereas in market economies bankers enjoy greater discretion and try to appear apolitical. In most Mediterranean countries, as in much of the Third World, the pretense is transparent because political and economic elites are so highly interrelated. It seems odd, in fact, to contrast the hell of

67

atavistic politics, even Lebanon's, with "the benign utopia of finance" (Ajami 1981, 2). The bankers kept the militias shooting.

Of course, bankers usually sit above partisan politics. They only exceptionally identify with particular political parties (or militias) and prefer to balance their risks and to exchange favors with a variety of entrepreneurs; but these borrowers are inevitably tied into political–administrative networks. Bankers are not usually political actors in their own right, but they are important intermediaries: their money solidifies the personal networks that make political organizations possible.

If Cosimo de Medici pioneered machine politics through banking in fifteenth-century Florence (Hale 1977), Tunisia offers more recent illustrations. Mohammed Chenik's Crédit Agricole afforded Habib Bourguiba a financial base for breaking away from the Destour party in 1934. The first congress of the Neo-Destour was held in Ksar Hellal in the home of one of Chenik's clients; and its delegates overrepresented Tunis and the Sahel, the very regions in which the Crédit Agricole was most heavily implanted. In its early days the Neo-Destour "was a party based on extensive patron–client networks. The wealthy, like Chenik, provided the party with funds for leaflets and automobiles, aid to the indigent, and support for the families of jailed militants" (Anderson 1986, 172–174). However big a moral and religious explosion the charismatic leader ignites, he needs selective incentives—patronage grounded in financial obligations—if he is to build an enduring organization. Bourguiba understood financial power, and his lessons of political organization did not escape other Tunisians. In good Bourguiban fashion Habib Achour founded the Banque du Peuple in 1964 with capital subscriptions from the mass membership of the UGTT. The bank was central to his drive for trade union autonomy vis-à-vis the party–state. After suppressing the autonomists, the government had the Banque du Sud buy out the little bank's shareholders in 1968.

Indeed, in his lifelong effort to construct "a monument without cracks," the master statebuilder hastened to gain control over the country's banking system. In 1958 Bourguiba put one of his most trusted political associates, Hedi Nouira, in charge of a new Tunisian Central Bank. When in 1961 he enabled Ahmed ben Salah to begin implementing grandiose designs for a command economy, he was careful to keep Nouira in control of banking. Nouira, who opposed ben Salah's version of state socialism, monitored his economic policies and perhaps limited the commercial banks' contributions to the government's deficit financing.[2] While favoring private enterprise, however, he also shared Bourguiba's vision of the state as a monument without cracks. Even after relinquishing the governorship of the Central Bank to become prime minister, he preserved its Draconian control over credit allocation. As late as 1985, a British financial report described Tunisian banks as "virtually state agencies":

They may not lend sums over a certain amount without Central Bank approval. For most loans the ceiling is TD 600,000 ($720,000) and for medium term farm loans only TD 5,000. Further controls apply to the amounts banks must lend certain sectors—20% of deposits must be lent to the government, 5% to the Caisse Nationale d'Epargne et Logement, a state housing bank, and 18% of funds lent to others must be medium term. The Central Bank fixes maximum and minimum interest rates for each sector, export-oriented enterprises being favored most. (Hughes 1985, 119)

By this time, however, many cracks had already appeared, not just more wrinkles, on Bourguiba's face. Tunisia suffered interrelated crises of legitimacy and overregulation about which much has been written (Camau et al. 1984; Moore 1988a; Mzali 1987; Ware 1984). As its foreign reserves dwindled to $69.6 million[3] (about nine days worth of imports) in 1986, even Bourguiba accepted the need for major reform. The problem was to disengage the state from excessive economic burdens without losing so much legitimacy that the mobs would again take to the streets, as in January of 1984, perhaps this time finishing off Islam's only genuinely civilian republic.

■ **Designing Adjustment: The Financial Priority**

Little more than a year after returning from a second tour of duty in Washington as an officer of the World Bank, Ismail Khelil replaced Mansour Moallah in 1983 as Minister of Plan in the Mzali government and urged some of the bank's policies on the prime minister—in vain (Interview June 6, 1989). "Quant à moi, j'ai pour coutume d'agir énergiquement quand et où il le faut," Mohamed Mzali would subsequently write, "et n'ai pas pour habitude de plier les genoux devant les institutions internationales, fût-ce le F.M.I., pour les entendre me dicter leurs ordres" (1987, 82) In 1986, however, Bourguiba's aspiring close advisors jockeyed for the succession at the same time that diminishing oil revenues, a poor harvest, and a drop in tourism in the wake of Israel's bombing of the PLO headquarters near Tunis and U.S. attacks on Libya precipitated a foreign exchange crisis. With backing from Finance Minister Rachid Sfar, Khelil engineered Tunisia's *plan de redressement.* Circulated by the Planning Ministry as early as May 25, 1986, it challenged the government's complacency six weeks before Bourguiba replaced Mzali with Sfar.[4]

The plan has withstood four changes of prime minister and one change of president and regime in three years. Ismail Khelil became minister of finance as well as planning. Then he was promoted to Hedi Nouira's former post, governor of the Central Bank, before ben Ali took over the presidency. After November 7, 1987, Khelil not only stayed on but became a member of the RCD's Political Bureau—in other words one of the new regime's political heavyweights. As might be expected from his background with the World Bank, financial reform is the cornerstone of the adjustment plan.

Adjustment packages, to be sure, contain a variety of standard short-term, as well as medium-term, objectives—"stabilization," or belt tightening, as well as economic growth and efficiency. Tunisia's was no exception. In return for a badly needed IMF standby agreement, reached November 4, 1986, to release credits of up to $125 million over eighteen months (together with a slightly larger compensatory loan for export fluctuations), a letter of intent spelled out tough government fiscal and monetary targets. Although "there are, nonetheless, some potential trade-offs between stabilization and adjustment" (Nicholas 1988, 4). Tunisia also concluded negotiations with the World Bank for sectoral adjustment loans in agriculture ($150 million, September 18, 1986) and for industrial and trade policy ($150 million, February 24, 1987). In return, Tunisia was committed to deregulating most domestic prices and liberalizing imports within a three-to-four-year time frame. Encouraging competition among banks was only one among many proposed reforms, which included a new tax law, a new code for foreign investment, cutting back on public investments, and privatizing some enterprises, as well as specific trade and agriculture reforms (Safra 1987, 66).

But Tunisia, unlike other countries in similar balance-of-payments crises, immediately embarked upon structural financial reforms even while stabilizing the money supply and cutting the public deficit. One of the Sfar government's first steps was to deregulate most interest rates, effective January 1, 1987. Though the measure had been promised the IMF, it was not in accord with the conventional teaching that "the liberalization of the domestic financial market can only be fully undertaken if the fiscal deficit is tightly under control" (Edwards 1987, 10). Perhaps Tunisia's macroeconomic indicators were already under reasonably tight control—the fiscal deficit was only 6 percent of GDP in 1986, and inflation was estimated at about 8 percent—but the government's attack on interest rates also seems to be part of an essentially Tunisian, rather than IMF, strategy. The IMF was primarily concerned to limit increases in the money supply.

Economists will always disagree as to whether the real economy of production and commerce drives finance or vice versa, but the financial levers will be most readily available to government in a mixed economy enjoying the tradition of a strong central bank, especially if the government is committed to a gradual process of deregulation and privatization of parts of the public sector. Ismail Khelil subsequently tipped his hand at a privatization seminar when he prudently observed that

it is better to speak of "restructuration" than of "privatization." For it is
necessary in a first stage to pass through an intermediary phase, a
necessary relay, banking, for example, to achieve the disengagement of
the state from public enterprises. It is only in a second phase that the
real intervention of the private sector can be envisaged. (*La Presse*,
April 29, 1987, 11)

The banks, in short, could become a useful instrument, helping the state to
disengage from, or "restructure," public enterprises by cutting their credits.
As long as the Central Bank directly allocated credit, cutting back was
politically difficult. It had therefore become necessary to make the banks
responsible for their own credit decisions.

Tunisia had already begun to liberalize its banking system. For instance,
in 1981 the limits for lending without prior Central Bank (Banque Centrale
de Tunisie) approval were increased for most types of loans from TD 150
thousand to TD 600 thousand; and some were further raised to TD 1 million
in 1985. In that year only 561 loans exceeded TD 1 million. Restrictions on
offshore banks were also relaxed. Limited access to domestic bank deposits
was permitted, and the Tunisian dinar was allowed to slide in value against
hard currencies so as to make Tunisian exports more competitive and to
attract remittances from Tunisian workers in Europe. Several months before
signing the letter of intent to the IMF, the Tunisian government had devalued
the dinar by almost 10 percent.

Tunisia was thus economically better prepared than most countries in the
first throes of adjustment to reform its financial structures. The politics, too,
were favorable in a curious way. Already in mid-June 1986, the leaders of the
UGTT, the UTICA, and the Union Nationale des Agriculteurs Tunisiens
(UNAT) were consulted about the adjustment package (Interview with
Mohammed ben Amara, June 5, 1989)—though it was never formally
published, just released in bits and pieces by ministers to the National
Assembly (Safra 1987). In what turned out to be Bourguiba's final year of
power, the government was necessarily weak and vulnerable to palace cabals.
Nobody, in effect, governed; yet structural reforms had to be undertaken.
Perhaps as much by default as by design, the financial system would be the
principal target, and Tunisia's new economic czar would "retire" to the
Central Bank. It is not surprising that well-informed observers considered
his appointment as governor of the Central Bank in October 1987 to
be a demotion (*Middle East Economic Digest* [hereafter *MEED*] October
31 (1987); 56); for Tunisia had become accustomed to its economic
leaders' being (since the time of Ahmed ben Salah) the ministers of
finance and plan. But times and strategies had changed. If the government could no longer run a planned economy effectively, it could refashion
the mechanisms of credit allocation and thereby rule the economy indirectly.
As a French treasury director once described such duties, Ismail Khelil would

be "a symphony conductor who produces no sound but watches over the harmony, rhythm, and volume of music produced by others" (Mamou 1988, 12).

If an emphasis on finance covered a political vacuum under Bourguiba, it also gave his successors a breathing space. Restructuring financial markets is a silent, technical process. If money, in the end, talks, the paths of influence are too obscure to be controversial, at least in the short run. Tunisian adjustment continued to the satisfaction of the international financial community without disturbing President ben Ali's prolonged period of grace; and the politicians could focus upon issues of political organization and electoral reform. In opting for an indirect strategy of market deregulation, Ismail Khelil and his allies in charge of the Ministries of Finance and Agriculture could delay political confrontations and play for time, awaiting an upsurge of business confidence in the form of more foreign and local private investment, while nontraditional exports, tourist revenues, workers' remittances, foreign loans, and foreign currency reserves all increased, some dramatically, almost erasing Tunisia's chronic balance-of-payments deficit in 1987.

Once the grace period ended, in the wake of the general elections of April 2, 1989, discussed in Chapters 1 and 11 it still seemed only prudent to avoid any sharp polarization on economic policies. Already by mid-1988—eighteen months after the agreement with the IMF—Tunisia's adjustment plan was graying at the edges. For instance, the money supply, carefully managed in 1987 to rise no more than the gross domestic product (at current prices), spurted up by 20 percent in 1988 against a 7.9 percent increase in GDP (Banque Centrale de Tunisie, hereafter referred to as BCT, 1989, 13, 71). Official speeches no longer promised liberalizing all imports "except a few luxuries" (République Tunisienne 1987, 6) by 1992. Tariffs were being reduced, as planned, to no more than 25 percent; but some 20 percent (Khelil, 1988b, 3) to 25 percent (Khelil, 1988c, 4) of Tunisia's imports would remain subject to quantitative restrictions "to assure temporary protection of infant industries" (Khelil, 1989a, 5). With the economy stabilized, the Tunisian government could give in to demands from inefficient enterprises for more credit and more protection, but adjustment silently continued. Ismail Khelil persevered with his four pillars of financial reform.

■ The Four Pillars of Reform

The Central Bank governor never tired of repeating that the "dynamization" of Tunisian financial markets occupied a "choice position" in the country's strategy of structural adjustment of the economy and that it rested on "four essential pillars," to wit (Khilil 1988b, 1989b):

1. The improving of the system of monetary regulation by reducing restrictions to the normal functioning of the market;
2. Reinforcement of integration within the financial market by attenuating the segmentation and compartmentalization demarcating the domains of activity of its institutions;
3. Developing the role of the stock exchange as the favored framework for mobilizing savings and financing investments; and
4. Progressive consolidation of the liberalization of foreign exchange and capital controls to facilitate the emergence of Tunis as a regional financial center.

The first of these pillars is really the foundation of the edifice. Removing "restrictions to the normal functioning of the market" has had the greatest impact upon the banking system. It has meant not only removing or altering specific banking regulations but also trying to revive the players— the banks themselves—and inciting them to be more competitive and capable of making their own credit decisions: "The Central Bank must relax its grip on the banking sector in order above all to permit the banks to become responsible" (Khelil, 1988b). To be sure, "one should not think that deregulation means weakening the role belonging to the Institute of Emission. In reality it is only the form of managing liquidity and overseeing banking activity that will be modified" (Khelil, May 23, 1988). But being a symphony conductor requires an orchestra as well as music scores.

The other pillars are really more like superstructure. Integration entails breaking down artificial and legal distinctions between commercial, development, and offshore banks. Ideally, "every financial institution will have three windows, one for commercial activity, a second for development and a third for offshore activities. It may choose voluntarily to specialize in one of these activities just as it can opt for a harmonious evolution of operations in all banking domains" (Khelil, 1989b) In practice, however, deregulation was unlikely to have a major impact upon the principal players, the commercial banks. One commercial banker observed that his (major) bank would be less inclined to increase its loans to enterprises to enable them to pay off their investment bankers if the latter were also commercial competitors. Ironically, though integration is supposed to increase competition, the only illustration to date is in a specific sector, agriculture. The Banque Nationale de la Tunisie (BNT) merged with the Banque Nationale de Développement Agricole (BNDA) to form the Banque Nationale Agricole (BNA), a new bank enjoying a virtual sectoral monopoly.

The third pillar, a more active stock exchange, is also of limited significance because enterprises are generally unwilling to disclose adequate financial information about themselves even if they are willing to raise capital from the general public. In societies like Tunisia, where accounting standards lack credibility for a variety of reasons,[5] stock markets cannot replace banks and governments as the principal sources of capital. Even in financially more open and sophisticated economies, bankers retain their function of financial intermediation to the extent that borrowers insist on confidentiality. In Tunisia, financial reporting conveys little information, despite much talk about *transparence*.

Finally, Khelil's fourth pillar of external liberalization really depends on the first. As a World Bank consultant explains, "The first principle of reform sequencing . . . is that international capital controls should only be lifted after the domestic financial market has been reformed and domestic interest rates have been raised" (Edwards 1987, 10). External liberalization may be urgent because controls cannot prevent capital flight in an economy depending largely on tourism and workers' remittances from Europe (al-Karm 1989); but keeping capital in Tunisia depends on competitive interest rates (as well as a relatively stable dinar propped up by export-led growth).

Perhaps "surprising some by the ambition and rapidity" (Khelil, 1988) of his moves, the governor of the Central Bank implemented the core of his strategy in 1987. After partially deregulating interest rates in January, he lifted all requirements for prior Central Bank approval of loans by the end of the year (just six weeks after ben Ali assumed the presidency). Banks, instead, were ordered to diversify their portfolios, raising the possibility that inefficient enterprises, whether private or public, might be caught in a credit squeeze. Credit allocation was to become more efficient, driven by bankers competing for safer, more diversified, and more profitable loan portfolios. In the world of Khelil, the reforms "incitera les agents économiques et notamment les banques à faire le meilleur choix des opportunités de financement et surtout à s'abstenir de s'engager dans des opérations à risques démesurés" (Khelil 1988, 5). In theory, markets, not administrators, would now allocate and ration most credit to local businesses. Various banking ratios continued to be enforced, such as the requirement that 25 percent of a bank's deposits be invested in government bonds of various sorts; but all regulation became a posteriori after December 23.

Central Bank discounting facilities were discontinued—as had been promised the IMF—except for lending to certain priority sectors (agriculture and export finance); and banks in need of liquidity were dispatched instead (starting January 1, 1988) to a reorganized money market. The Central Bank continued to set the market's interest rate, but the governor announced in May 1989 that variable rates based on supply and demand would soon be introduced: "However, in a first stage, considering the indebted situation of the banks, we will try to satisfy liquidity needs by combining fixed rates with those determined by a Dutch auction" (Khelil, May 11, 1989, 6).

In other words, some of the banks were having difficulty keeping up with the governor's pace of reform. They were first jostled out of an era of comfortable, state-imposed spreads (the difference between interest earned on loans and received on deposits), then told to be responsible for their lending, to weigh their risks carefully and diversify their portfolios, and finally (if they were short or long on cash) to face unpredictable interest rates on the money market. The stakes were high. If they became autonomous allocators of credit, they might push other enterprises toward greater efficiency or toward restructuring. Decentralizing and privatizing credit allocation could also indirectly stimulate a greater diversity of political organizations. How autonomous and competitive, in fact, were the banks becoming?

■ The Liberal Facade of Banking Competition

Structurally, the system was becoming more competitive. For standard commercial banks, a strong deposit base is the key to profitability and growth. Competition among banks will be reflected in struggles over market share for deposits. One way of looking at this competition is to view changes in the concentration of market shares over time. The system displays more competition, the smaller the market shares (i.e., more banks are competing for deposits) and the more evenly distributed they become.[6] Figure 4.1 summarizes the evolution of the market shares of Tunisia's commercial banks' deposits since 1972 and shows that new banks the Crédit Foncier et Commercial de Tunisie (CFCT), the Banque Internationale et Arabe de la Tunisie (BIAT), and the Arab–Tunisian Bank (ATB) were entering the market and gradually increasing their share at the expense of the larger banks.

Holding over 40 percent of the deposits, the STB and the BNT (amalgamated with the BNDA to become the BNA in 1989) still dominated the commercial banking system, however. Together with the Banque du Sud, which had absorbed the UGTT's Banque du Peuple in 1968, and the Union Internationale des Banques (UIB), the public sector controlled 62 percent of the deposits in 1987, compared to 68 percent in 1972. But public sector banks were now, in light of the 1987 reforms, supposed to become as autonomous and competitive as private sector banks. Distinctions between public and private sector banks had never been sharp, for that matter. Ownership of the public sector banks was mixed, so that a minority of shares was held by the general public and quoted on the stock market; moreover, both public and private sector banks had equally shared stringent Central Bank controls, and both had also been subjected to outside political pressures for loans. Public enterprises were not formally obliged to place their deposits in public sector banks; and some of the private sector banks certainly got a share of them, although one of the private banks, the Banque de Tunisie (BT), regretted in a recent annual report that it was unable to attract many public sector deposits.

Figure 4.1 Market Shares of Deposits, 1972–1987

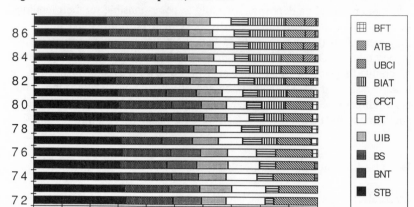

Within the private sector, relics of the old French colonial system endured; but they had been put in Tunisian hands. The BT survived the transition to Independence intact, its ownership gradually altered with increases in capital to reflect a Tunisian majority. The Union Bancaire pour le Commerce et l'Industrie (UBCI) resulted in 1961 from a fusion of French banks but in 1979 became a joint venture half-owned by a leading French bank, half by private Tunisians headed by a businessman from Sfax. These relatively conservative banks should be distinguished from a newer Tunisian private sector, consisting of the BIAT, and ATB. The CFCT, created in 1967, is exclusively owned by a Jerban business group. The BIAT was established in 1976 by a former Tunisian minister who, with some Arab Gulf backing, acquired the local branches of the British Bank of the Middle East and the Société Marseillaise de Crédit (Signoles 1985, 497–498). The ATB is a joint Tunisian venture with the Arab Bank headquartered in Amman.

From virtually nothing in 1976, the BIAT managed by 1987 to capture 13 percent of the commercial banking system's deposits[7] (Banque Internationale et Arabe de la Tunisie 1986). The strategy was risky because the bank became undercapitalized as a result of rapid growth and investment in branches, but it attracted Gulf Arab as well as Tunisian capital. The BT, by contrast, implemented a conservative strategy, generating fair profits with minimal risk from a quality clientele. Although the public sector banks had to dole out credit to ailing public sector enterprises as a matter of practical politics, the influence of the private banks over credit allocation was increasing. In effect, they could serve as monitors, reducing the costs of state supervision. Enterprises refused by BIAT as well as by BT might in future be refused elsewhere, now that Tunisia's stabilization program entailed some rationing of credit.

New private banks, moreover, were entering the field. In 1987 a private Tunisian enjoying Saudi backing briefly achieved control of the Banque Franco–Tunisienne (BFT), an ailing subsidiary of the STB. Offshore banks, spearheaded by the Islamic Beit at-Tamwil al-Tunsi (BEST), gained permission in 1985 to receive up to 1.5 percent of the total domestic deposits and to make loans denominated in dinars. Believing that it could attract up to 10 percent of the deposits, as Islamic banks do in other Arab countries with mixed economies (Moore 1988b), the BEST bank had plans for expansion if banking regulations could be further liberalized. Of the Maghrib countries, Tunisia seemed to be tiptoeing closest to Egyptian-style *infitah*, and Bourguiba's forced retirement opened more doors. Citibank received an official license to do normal onshore commercial banking in 1989, and the Arab Banking Corporation seemed to be next in line. A number of Arab banks were consolidating their presences, hitherto limited to stakes in offshore and investment banks. Qatari investors, "mainly members of the [royal] Al-Thani family," were likely to get permission to establish the Qatar International Bank as an offshore Islamic bank similar to the BEST (*MEED*, June 23, 1989, 22).

The Central Bank policy of integrating the markets served by commercial and development banks would also have at least a modest impact on the distribution of market shares. The Caisse Nationale d'Epargne Logement, about as large in total assets as the UIB, was renamed the Banque de l'Habitat and urged to compete for deposits with the other commercial banks. The other development banks, with assets totaling those of the STB—but no branch networks—were also permitted to collect sight and savings deposits from the general public. Measures of market concentration reflected the growing dispersion illustrated by Figure 4.1 and would no doubt reveal growing competition in the 1990s.[8]

In the aggregate, however, the Tunisian banks did not seem capable of much competition. On average, they were not healthy. Their combined balance sheet of November 30, 1988 reveals them to be undercapitalized. Their equity amounted to only 4.6 percent of their total assets, and all of it (104.6 percent) was tied up in buildings and other illiquid investments. By contrast, the Cooke Commission recommended that banks by 1992 reach an overall capital-to-asset ratio of 8 percent, only half of which could be tied up in illiquid assets (Kapstein 1989, 344). Tunisia's nonperforming loans amounted to almost 20 percent of their collective portfolio, and only 28.5 percent of them were provisioned by reserves. Total deposits of TD 3,203 million only barely covered their loans (TD 3,012.5 million, excluding special state-funded credits), so that some banks obviously faced liquidity as well as solvency problems. Apart from a more accurate reporting of nonperforming loans, the picture had little changed in five years (though in 1984 the equity seemed more liquid).

Averages do not, however, convey the health or sickness of particular banks. Some Tunisian banks were quite healthy even if others were moribund, bringing down the averages. The success of financial reform efforts depended not so much on the degree of concentration of market shares as on whether the healthy banks were really ready to compete—to grow and grab deposits and other business from their sicker sisters—or preferred to live comfortably and dependently off the rents the banking system extracted from other enterprises and the general public to keep the sickest banks in business. Reformers in the Central Bank also faced a dilemma: Could they allow an ailing Tunisian bank to go out of business?

■ Oligopolistic Brakes on Competition

The bank's first collective response to reform was to collude on interest rates to be offered depositors. When the rates were deregulated, as of January 5, 1987, the competition lasted only a couple of weeks before an agreement was reached by the Association Professionnelle des Banques de Tunisie (APBT) to put a halt to competitive bidding. According to some bankers, the STB used its market power (see Figure 4.1) to impose fixed rates. While there may have been some slippage in the monitoring of the cartel's decision, market shares changed only slightly more in 1987—the BIAT and STB being the big winners and losers, respectively, of .8 percent of the deposits—than in 1986.[9] By agreement, all banks stopped paying any interest on sight deposits, so that average rates most banks paid for deposits actually diminished slightly in 1987. Ironically, the STB ended up paying slightly more than the BIAT.[10]

Some banks were chronically short of deposits and in need of various transfusions from the Central Bank and from other domestic banks whose treasuries were in surplus. Figure 4.2 shows their respective surpluses and deficits (defined as the ratio of interbank loans to deposits) cumulatively over the five years ending December 31, 1987.[11] Banks in balance at the end of year had a ratio of one, so that a cumulative score of five or more showed an average positive balance. In contrast to the STB, the BNT, and the very liquid ATB, the Banque du Sud (BS), the CFCT, and especially the UIB were consistently in the red, borrowing more than they loaned out. The UBCI had also been a consistent borrower on interbank markets until 1987, when its treasury showed a slight surplus for the first time since 1981.

By rigging the rates on deposits, the APBT reassured these banks that they could preserve their market shares with a minimum of effort. The banks most hungry for deposits did pay slightly higher rates for their savings and

Figure 4.2 Cumulative Treasury Surpluses/Deficits, 1983–1987

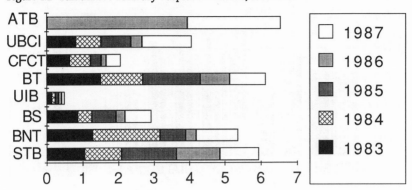

time deposits, but differences were actually less in 1987 than in 1986. The UIB's rates dropped dramatically, from 9.8 percent (two full percentage points above the average) in 1986 to 7.7 percent (just over half a percentage point above the norm) in 1987. The CFCT paid less than one-tenth of a point above the national average in 1987, despite a deposit structure that was relatively low on interest-free sight deposits.

The new era of partial deregulation thus had little impact upon the banks' margins or "spreads" between the interest they earned on loans and paid on deposits. Figure 4.3 depicts these spreads for each bank, as a ratio each year since 1983 of its net interest revenues to its total assets at the end of the year. It can readily be seen that their margins remained intact in 1987 relative to previous performances. Those of the two big public sector banks, the STB and the BNT, diminished very slightly, as did those of the private CFCT; but all of the others', including the troubled UIB's, rose a bit. The available returns for 1988, those of the BT and STB, indicate little further change.

Since spreads are a most important indicator of a bank's basic health and profitability, Figure 4.3 helps to explain why margins will probably remain protected. Not only the UIB but even the state's flagship bank, the STB, appears to be on the defensive. By fixing margins so that the UIB may survive, the other banks, especially the leader, conserved a convenient safety net. Were the margins any lower, the UIB would be out of business. Well-known in the early 1980s for its advanced international department, this bank fell on hard times as a result of too many soft loans handed out to various friends and family members of Wassila Bourguiba. When the senile president turned against his wife, the UIB's chairman was jailed and Bourguiba Junior, chairman of the APBT, was dismissed from the palace for defending the poor banker. In 1987 problem loans constituted 22.1 percent of

Figure 4.3 Spreads by Total Assets, 1983–1988

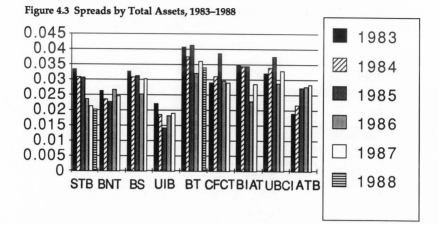

the bank's portfolio; in 1985, the last year the bank's provisions for credit risk were published, these reserves covered only 12.7 percent of the problem loans. The UIB's cash flow remained just barely positive; but it did not offset the annual growth in problematic assets, much less increase coverage of them.

Figure 4.4 sheds further light on the banks' profitability. Cash flow—the sum of net income and allocations to provisions and the depreciation of fixed assets—is a better indication of a bank's basic health than the bottom line alone because banks have a tendency to massage the ultimate indicators of profitability: net income to total assets and to equity (ben Othmane and Souissi 1987, 69). Figure 4.4 measures the cash flow as a proportion of total assets at the end of each year since 1983. With the very marginal exception of the STB, all of the banks increased their cash flow in 1987. Leading the pack, in cash flow as well as in spreads (Figure 4.3), the BT generated almost one-tenth of its average total assets during the 1983–1987 period.[12]

In the past, the public sector banks had generated comfortable cash flows, but Figure 4.4 shows them to be diminishing, just as spreads had also diminished since the early 1980s. The BS appeared to be the most profitable of these banks; but it also carried a disproportionately high share of nonperforming loans—over a quarter of its total portfolio. Had all its cash flow since 1985 (the last year the APBT published provisions for bad debts) been applied to provisions for these problem loans, only one-quarter of them would have been covered by the end of 1987. In this respect, the only bank in worse shape was the UIB, with 6-percent coverage; whereas the STB and the CFCT would have covered more than half of their respective nonperforming assets, and the BNT and BIAT roughly 65 percent. The ATB and the UBCI would have just barely cleaned up their portfolios, while the BT's minuscule

Figure 4.4 Cumulative Cash Flow by Total Assets, 1983–1987

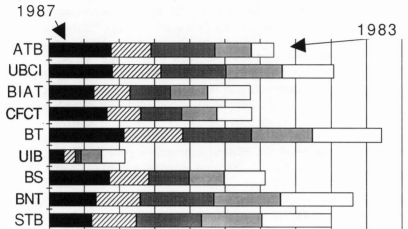

1.3 percent of nonperforming loans was already covered some eight times over. Most banks preferred to maximize their income at the expense of provisions; but the situation became so alarming that the Central Bank prevailed upon the tax administration in 1988 to exempt up to 20 percent of a bank's revenues from corporate tax if they were squirreled away as provisions. Banks were also obliged to be more forthcoming in reporting their problem portfolios (Société Tunisienne de Banque 1987, 9).

The ailing public sector needed generous spreads, as did the BIAT and the CFCT, to cover their questionable credits. A careful look at Figure 4.3 shows, however, that all the public sector banks except the BS were failing by 1987 to keep up with the spreads of the private sector banks; and in 1988 the STB fell further behind. The reason for the lower margins was that the public sector banks (except the BS) earned less on their loans than the private sector banks. Figure 4.5 presents the only publicly available data about the banks' interest charges. They concern only a portion of the respective loans portfolios, namely, overdrafts on current accounts. The private sector banks evidently charged substantially higher rates than the public sector ones. One of the secrets of the BT's profitability, in fact, was to encourage a high proportion of overdrafts among reliable clients and charge them up to 20 percent interest. In 1988 this bank's revenues did not keep pace with its burgeoning loan portfolio (Banque de Tunisie 1988, 9) because the APBT put a cap on the interest rates. Banks "volunteered" to no longer charge more than 2.5 percent over the variable borrowing rate on the money market. In return, in addition to the tax breaks on provisions, the Central Bank relaxed certain reserve requirements. To the benefit of the BT as well as the STB, the

Central Bank also seems to have turned a blind eye to the requirement that 25 percent of a bank's deposits be placed in poorly paying government bonds.

Under the new ben Ali regime there were strong political pressures in 1988 to lower interest rates; and the Central Bank obliged, in part, by lowering the money market rate from some 10 percent to 8.5 percent. One banker took great delight in showing how the Central Bank reformers were manipulating the market. He also poked fun at amateur bank dealers who changed their minds about telephone operations concluded "more than half an hour earlier." He observed that some banks had simply quit the market, resorting instead to "other much simpler mechanisms giving the same results"—presumably direct bilateral relationships between banks (Saidane 1988, 55, 57). Most bankers remained skeptical about the Central Bank's new markets. As for efforts to expand the stock market or in other ways to make debt secure, one leading banker commented that newfangled commissions could never make up for standard spreads. Indeed, some of the banks appeared so financially insecure that the others could be fairly confident that their margins would be protected.

The APBT no longer enjoyed extra political clout once its founder, Habib Bourguiba Junior, retired from banking and politics in 1987. But enmired in their financial prisons, most of the banks had little choice but to follow their leaders. The biggest banks, private as well as public, agreed on most issues. Capital barriers to entry helped to keep out newcomers, yet capital requirements rose flexibly and were applied so as not to disturb members of the club unduly.

Struggles over the ownership and management of the BFT were symptomatic. Restructured as a subsidiary of the STB in the early 1970s, this little bank with a long history (founded in 1879) became a bone of contention between the STB and a Tunisian lawyer–entrepreneur backed by some private Saudi capital. Although the lawyer had bought half the shares of the bank and imported hard currency in 1982 to pay for them, he did not gain a seat on the bank's board of directors until 1985 and finally gained majority control, with other private Tunisian shareholders, in February 1987. When he then discovered in the course of the following year that 40 percent of his bank's portfolio consisted of nonperforming loans left over from the previous administration, an official auditor found sufficient fault with the new manager's rectifications of the ailing bank's balance sheets to enable the STB to contest his management in the interests of the minority shareholders. The Tunisian manager was condemned to eight years in jail and a stiff fine, and some of his Tunisian partners also received sentences; but then the penalties were dropped in return for the bank shares, and a former managing director (who had served the STB owners) was subjected to judicial investigation. As of early 1990, neither the Tunisian nor the international press had unraveled the full dimensions of Tunisia's worst banking scandal.[13]

Figure 4.5 Interest Charged to Overdrafts, 1980–1987

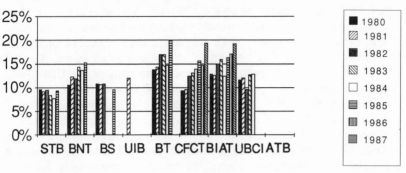

Influential bankers also opposed the granting of an onshore license to Citibank, but the Central Bank overrode their objections because Citibank might invigorate the money market by developing secondary markets for government securities and commercial paper. Earlier, the APBT had tried to prevent the BEST, the Islamic bank, even from functioning offshore. But the BEST was ready to finance the Tunis Lake Project, one of Bourguiba's favorites; consequently, Prime Minister Mzali successfully launched it and subsequently lobbied the Central Bank into allowing offshore banks to collect deposits onshore (in Tunisian dinars). Still at issue—and with potential political implications—was whether the BEST and the new offshore Qatari bank would be encouraged to branch out for more than symbolic shares of dinar deposits.

■ Private Sector Strategies

Though banking remained oligopolistic, the protective barriers largely served the interests of the private sector banks as well as the STB. Relatively stable margins enabled them to pursue distinctive strategies and to keep gaining market share at the expense of the public sector banks. Even the UBCI, whose share of deposits steadily declined in the 1970s and 1980s (see Figure 4.1), showed new signs of life in 1987 (Figures 4.3 and 4.4). After being brought under partial Tunisian ownership in 1979, its capital support—that is, the ratio of equity to total assets—had steadily diminished until 1984, suggesting that it failed to generate sufficient profits to finance both (very modest) growth and good dividends for the shareholders and that the remaining French owner, the Banque Nationale de Paris, was loathe to increase its stake. The UBCI's ratio of capital to total assets improved in 1985 and 1986, however, due to a doubling of paid-up capital that the Central

Bank had obliged the French and Tunisian partners to contribute. Like the UBCI, the BT also preferred to keep equity stakes low, so as to generate high returns on investment to the shareholders. Each of these old colonial banks kept its capital ratio low, at between 4.5 percent and 5 percent of total assets, 65 percent of which was tied up in stocks and fixed assets. The BT consistently paid out 12-percent dividends; and perhaps the UBCI, with similar leverage, was now generating enough cash flow to compete.

The ATB, half Palestinian-owned, was the most strongly capitalized of any Tunisian bank, public or private, its equity constituting 6.68 percent of total assets in 1987. This newcomer had virtually debarked onshore with the PLO in 1982 (see Figure 4.1). It tried to generate attractive dividends, although it was more heavily capitalized than the former colonial banks. In 1986 it managed to distribute 9-percent dividends, half its net income; but it reserved much less of its cash flow to cover problem loans than the UBCI did. It had branched along the coast as far south as Gabes by 1986 and Mednine by 1988; but its growth in deposits seems to have reached a plateau, and future growth perhaps depended on Tunisia's commercial relationships with Arab neighbors.

In terms of domestic politics, the most interesting of the private banks were the BIAT and the CFCT. The BIAT's founder, Mansour Moalla, served as minister of finance from 1980 to 1983, before returning to the bank as honorary president. Habib Bourguiba Junior also served as a founding member of the bank's board of directors. Their excellent political contacts enabled the BIAT to grow rapidly, attracting deposits from the public sector as well as from a core of Sfaxian businesses. While Moalla was minister, his bank surged into third place, surpassing the BS and UIB as well as the UBCI (see Figure 4.1). The BIAT's strategy was one of all-out growth, carefully projected in five-year business plans. Like the BT's general director Abderrazak Rassaa, Moalla injected his years of experience as an economic planner into the bank's strategy. Unlike the BT, however, the BIAT was prepared to sacrifice profits for market share.

The BIAT rarely paid out dividends of more than 6 percent and retained 60 to 75 percent of its annual earnings, whereas the BT usually paid out more in dividends and directors' fees than it retained.[14] The BIAT was nevertheless hard pressed to sustain its growth. It was seriously undercapitalized: its ratio of shareholders' equity to total assets fell to slightly below 3 percent in 1982, and again in 1987 it hovered just slightly above the 3-percent mark. The bank's annual report for 1987 tried to "show undeniably that BIAT behaved [performed] better in 1987 than all banks" (BIAT 1988, 32), for it had to persuade shareholders of yet another capital increase. It could boast of being in the forefront of Tunisia's computer revolution, developing on-line capabilities so that branches could act more autonomously. Its computer planning dovetailed with an organizational strategy that encouraged greater autonomy at the regional and local level. By pioneering decentralized management systems, the BIAT was diffusing more flexible forms of credit allocation that might indirectly affect future political development. Its strategy was risky, for rapid growth prevented the BIAT from being quite as discriminating in its choice of clientele as the BT. Almost 13 percent of the BIAT's loan portfolio (i.e., 6.1 percent of the bank's total assets, against capital, reserves, and provisions of 5.1 percent) was nonperforming in 1987. But as long as much of Tunisia's banking system was less viable than the BIAT, this aggressive newcomer could continue to push. Politically, it was part of the club.

The CFCT is of special interest precisely because it never quite joined the club. The only bank whose shares are not traded on the stock exchange, it is privately held by a family of Jerban entrepreneurs. Its behavior anticipated the Central Bank's efforts to make banks more truly autonomous. An outsider, it occasionally refused to participate in lending packages promoted by the Central Bank before such shows of independence became acceptable.[15] Relatively well capitalized at 5.4 percent of total assets, its reserves, including provisions, easily covered a portfolio of nonperforming loans comparable to the BIAT's. The bank's basic strategy seemed to be to support its owners, the ben Yedder business group, as a ready source of loans. Consequently it competed with the BIAT as well as other banks for deposits. The CFCT was in the vanguard of banks designing new instruments to attract household savings. It had also, like the BIAT, substantially expanded its branch network. The BIAT undoubtedly had its principal competitor in mind when it urged Ismail Khelil, as part of his effort to rationalize Tunisian banks, to make them diversify their portfolios. As of December 18, 1987, no more than 10 percent of a bank's capital was to be loaned to a single client. After a painful transition, however, the CFCT seemed likely to emerge as a leaner, meaner, and more flexible, decentralized competitor to the BIAT.

Competition was indeed at work. As state control became more flexible, the lines between the public and private sector were also becoming further blurred. In 1988 a new chairman of the BS appeared willing to explore possible privatization (though a return to UGTT worker ownership seemed out of the question, and other potential buyers were surely unimpressed with the bank's loan portfolio). Even the STB sought means of escaping public sector controls, especially concerning personnel policies, so as to become more genuinely competitive and adapt to the new Central Bank policies. As the banks strived to be more independent, their credit decisions might gradually cover the state's disengagement from public enterprises. Even before the reforms took effect, private enterprises were gaining at the expense of the public sector: the private sector's share of credit increased from 62.5 percent in 1984 to 64.2 percent in 1985 and 65 percent in 1986 (République

Tunisienne, Banque Centrale 1986, 185). Competition among the banks was also spreading geographically, as branches proliferated.

■ Branching into Civil Society

Setting up a new branch required the approval of the Central Bank, but it also reflected the strategy of the bank in question. From 1971 to 1988 the number of branches quintupled, finally totaling some 496, or one branch for every 16,000 inhabitants. Table 4.1 shows how these branches have been distributed by region since Independence and compares the distribution with that of the general population. The Central Bank provided more detailed breakdowns for recent years. Large urban centers naturally attracted the most branches, even taking into account their greater concentrations of population. Greater Tunis alone supported 119 branches, or one for every 7,000 inhabitants (men, women, and children), in 1988. By contrast, the most neglected governorates (Kasserine, Siliana, and Sidi Bou Zid) averaged a branch for every 36,500 inhabitants. Even so, branches in these poor areas of the country seemed to be a luxury few private sector banks could afford. The UBCI and BT had each implanted a branch, in Sidi Bou Zid and Siliana, respectively, in 1983; but the other twenty-three branches were all public sector. The private sector stayed away completely from Zaghouan and from Kebili and Tataouine in the Far South; and certain of its presences in the Northwest seemed to be relics of the colonial era rather than signs of a competitive strategy.

Figure 4.6 reconstructs changes in the relative number of bank branches fielded by each bank since 1971, when the big expansion got under way. In the early 1970s the BT still had one of the largest branch networks, rivaling those of the younger, more vigorous STB and BNT; but by 1988 the BS, the BIAT, and even the UIB had forged ahead. In the 1980s, however, the private sector banks as a whole had regained the ground lost by the BT to the public sector. They focused their attention on the coastal areas, leaving the poorer, peripheral parts of the country to the public sector. Figure 4.7 maps their penetration of the country, revealing a sharp cleavage between the coastal regions and the interior. Private sector branches were concentrated along the extended Sahel between Bizerte and Jerba; elsewhere their presence was minimal.

From 1981 to 1988 the total number of bank branches increased by 82 percent, and those of the private sector by 23.7 percent—the BIAT and CFCT being the most dynamic, more than tripling their networks. Their main target was Tunis: in 1981 there were only three private sector branches for every five public ones; but the private sector had over half by 1988, as well as a substantial share in neighboring suburban governorates of Ariana and Ben

Table 4.1 Bank Branches by Region, 1956–1988 (%)

Region	Distribution of Bank Branches					Population
	1956	1970	1979	1986	1988	(1988 est)
Greater Tunis	18	20	30	32	32	20
Bizerte, Cap Bon	13	17	14	15	15	12
Northwest	34	18	14	10	10	17
Center	5	6	5	7	7	15
Sahels	19	17	21	23	23	21
South	11	22	16	13	13	15
Totals	100	100	100	100	100	100
Number	(79)	(100)	(257)	(419)	(496)	(7,800,000)

Sources: Signoles 1985, 517; BCT.

Figure 4.6 Shares of Branches by Year, 1971–1988

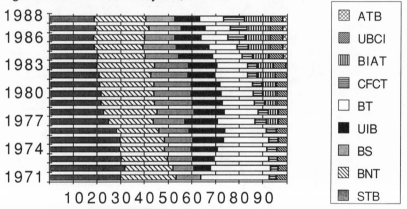

Arous. In Sfax, too, the private sector banks had gained a slight majority, as Table 4.2 indicates. Nabeul, Sousse, and Monastir, homes of much of the political–administrative elite, were more heavily banked than Sfax; but the private banks, having accumulated little over one-third of the total number of branches, did not compete as much as in Sfax. Perhaps the degree of economic activity in these coastal provinces did not justify more forceful presences. In fact, the governorate of Monastir had been home to only one private bank branch in 1981. But the more politically attuned of the private sector banks remedied their relative neglect by 1986. The BIAT opened two branches, and the BT added three to its original presence; while the CFCT and UBCI preferred to stay away from Bourguiba's favored paradise.

In Bizerte the private sector's share actually declined in the 1980s; whereas it held a majority of the branches in Gabes, the center of Tunisian

Figure 4.7 Private Sector Branching by Governorate, 1988

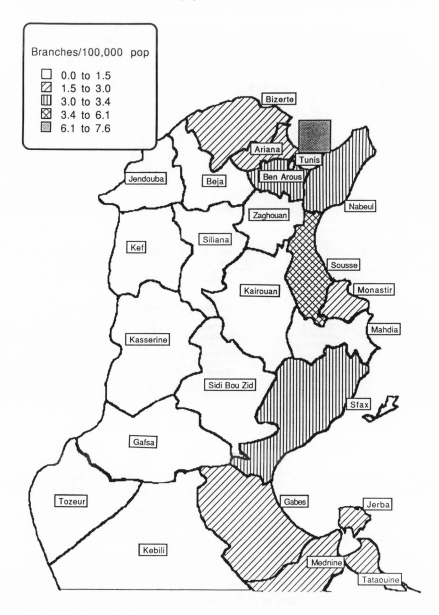

Table 4.2 Bank Branches by Governorate, 1988

Governorate	Banks										Total	Private Sector (%)	Population per branch
	STB	BNT	BS	UIB	BT	CFCT	BIAT	UBCI	ATB	BFT			
Tunis	15	10	10	20	14	20	17	8	3	2	119	54	7,000
Nabeul	9	13	6	4	4	4	4	3	2	—	49	35	10,000
Sfax	7	6	3	3	1	3	11	5	1	—	40	53	17,000
Sousse	7	6	3	5	4	3	4	1	1	—	34	38	11,000
Bizerte	6	6	3	3	3	1	3	1	1	—	27	33	16,000
Monastir	7	5	7	1	4	0	3	0	—	—	27	26	12,000
Ben Arous	5	5	2	2	2	2	2	1	1	1	23	39	13,000
Mednine	5	4	4	2	3	3	1	—	1	—	23	35	15,000
Kairouan	2	5	1	1	2	1	2	1	—	—	15	40	31,000
Ariana	4	4	2	0	2	3	2	1	—	—	18	44	25,000
Jendouba	4	5	0	2	3	0	1	—	—	—	15	27	26,000
Gabes	1	3	1	1	2	2	1	1	1	—	13	54	22,000
Other	20	35	19	7	6	1	3	2	0	—	93	13	27,000
Totals/averages	92	107	61	51	50	43	54	24	11	3	496	37	16,000

Sources: BCT, 1984 Census (projected est. 1988).

petrochemical industries. If Sfax was the major focus of competition outside Tunis, private sector banks varied their emphasis in light of particular strategies. The BT preferred Monastir, for instance, and even built on historic strength in Jendouba, a former colon stronghold in the Northwest of the country—but kept its presence in Sfax nominal. By contrast, the BIAT increased its three branches to eight, overtaking not only the UBCI (whose Tunisian business partner was from Sfax) but also the government's own STB.[16] The CFCT, on the other hand, tied most of its expansion to Tunis and also dominated private sector activity in Mednine, where Jerba was located.

Off the coast, Tunisia's Islamic capital of Kairouan also attracted some private sector attention, though presences remained symbolic. Whether in search of Islamic (interest-free) revivalist deposits or merely a measure of Islamic respectability, three of the four private banks descended upon the city; and CFCT caught up with the herd in 1988.

■ Political Implications

After General ben Ali retired Bourguiba, Tunisia's political system came to life: opposition parties mushroomed, and the ruling party increased its membership by 50 percent. But there were few signs of any relationships between political and economic liberalization. Opposition parties showed little awareness of the need to seek active support directly from business or other interests; nor, of course, did bankers or entrepreneurs project themselves into partisan politics. As in Morocco, where the king subsidized submissive oppositions, the Tunisian parties seemed to expect financial aid from the state. In the longer run, however, the reforms presently being implemented— notably of the banking system—might be creating the material conditions for heartier political competition.

Tunisia's first general elections under the new regime, held on April 2, 1989, mark the conclusion of President ben Ali's political honeymoon. The elections were a disappointment for pluralist reformers because the ruling party won all the parliamentary seats, and they also signified that the only substantial opposition consisted of Islamic revivalists. The RCD's loyal opposition, Ahmed Mestiri's MDS, received little more than 3 percent of the vote; and he complained, "People like us didn't have the means to make our voices heard" (Markham 1989). By contrast, the ruling party had solicited businesses for contributions—some businessmen spoke of "extortion"—so as to lessen the party's dependence on the state budget.[17] Freer competition in the financial sector might help to alleviate some of the imbalances between governing and opposition parties, simply by promoting a stronger, more autonomous private sector capable of making contributions to political parties. More direct relationships between financial and political development also seem possible.

In the Nouira era, the Central Bank had centralized most credit decisions. An entrepreneur in search of a substantial loan needed to key into a centralized patronage network. But as the allocation of credit becomes less centralized, the patronage may be dispersed, becoming potentially available to opposition as well as government elements. Banks will, of course, always avoid identification with particular parties; but their patronage networks may better support a plurality of parties than would a centralized network.

The beneficiaries of credit constituted a tiny but influential minority of Tunisians. As Table 4.3 indicates, only 31,044 Tunisians or firms enjoyed access to any credits classified by the Central Bank in 1986, though these do not include either loans of under TD 3,000 or various other farm or housing credits. Of the beneficiaries, only 1,017 received loans of more than TD 500 thousand. The number of beneficiaries had increased by roughly 50 percent since 1982, but the distribution seemed increasingly skewed, in that the small borrowers received only one-fifth of the total value of the loans in 1986, compared to one-quarter in 1982. Major potential contributors to political organizations—firms and individuals borrowing TD 500 thousand or more—had almost doubled. If, as Mohamed Z. Bechri argues, agricultural beneficiaries enjoyed a symbiotic relationship with UNAT, might the patronage derived from commercial lending not fuel new political organizations? Despite efforts to raise funds from the business community, the RCD seemed to underrepresent businessmen on the Central Committee (almost two-thirds of which was appointed rather than elected at the July 1988 Party Congress).[18] Since the ruling party probably cannot satisfy all segments of the business community, some of them may try to diversify their political support.

While the bank's branching strategies presumably reflected economic rather than political concerns, the provinces they targeted also tended to display the politically most active oppositions while being the least penetrated by the dominant government party. Indeed, if the southern provinces are excluded, private sector banking seems quite closely correlated with opposition voting in the 1989 elections and inversely correlated with the ruling party's ability to mobilize potential electors. Figures 4.8 and 4.9 map by governorate (1) the proportions of voting-age populations voting for the RCD and (2) the votes for opposition lists (including null ballots) as a proportion of those voting, respectively. As Figure 4.9 reveals, Islamically minded Independents were strong throughout the entire southern part of the country; and, of course, they depended more on raw ethical appeal than any selective patronage to attract the voters. Elsewhere, however, the governorates with the greatest per capita number of private bank branches tend to be those with the highest proportions of opposition voters ($r = .73$)

Table 4.3   Credit Allocation, 1982–1986

	1982	1983	1984	1985	1986
Total value (million TDs)	2,281.6	2,708.6	3,283.7	3,773.2	4,165.9
Total borrowers	20,733	23,987	25,689	28,766	31,044
Small borrowers	20,104	23,239	24,815	27,823	30,027
Borrowers > 500,000 TD	629	748	874	943	1,017
Top borrowers					
(50% of total loan value)	110	124	125	132	136
Medium borrowers	519	624	749	811	881

Source: Calculated from BCT memo of May 14, 1987 to author.

and lowest proportions of RCD voters (r = -.72)—with Tunis and Sousse taking the lead.[19]

Sunspot effects for now, banking could well promote competitive politics in the future. The branches are most present in the urban and coastal parts of the country where civil society's organized groupings expressing economic interests are most likely to develop, as in the past. They might then again avail themselves of provincial credit networks just as the Neo-Destour once did. Conversely, the ruling party evidently prefers to keep a monetary, as well as political, monopoly over the agrarian interior.

There is one further point of possible convergence between a competitive banking system and extensions of political infrastructure. "Participatory" Islamic banking has been introduced to Tunisia. Quite independently, the Renaissance party, representing Islamic revival, is on the verge of achieving legal recognition. So also is Qatar International Bank, which is to be run on Islamic principles like the BEST bank. While the BEST bank has less than half a percent of the domestic market for bank deposits, an Islamically oriented economy could grow side by side with a conventional one, as in Egypt—where conventional banks have opened Islamic windows to be more competitive. Although banks tend to restrict themselves to business, not politics, a growing constituency of Islamic credit beneficiaries would probably support the new party and thus help to institutionalize political pluralism. Demystified, Islamic revivalism would be less likely to provoke authoritarian countermobilization by threatened secularists. Conversely, of course, exaggerated perceptions of revivalist threats can keep a broad governing coalition intact so as to postpone hard economic choices and potential conflicts.

■ Conclusion

Banking systems do not determine political change, but they may condition a significant aspect of the environment in which politics occurs. In Tunisia

Figure 4.8 The Democratic Constitutionalist Rally's Share of Population of Voting Age, 1989

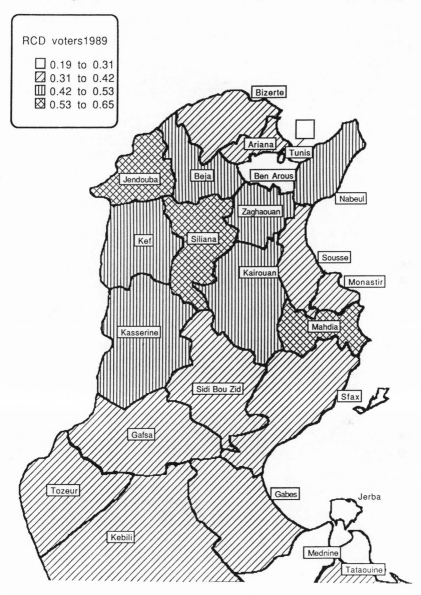

Figure 4.9 Oppositions' Share of Votes, 1989

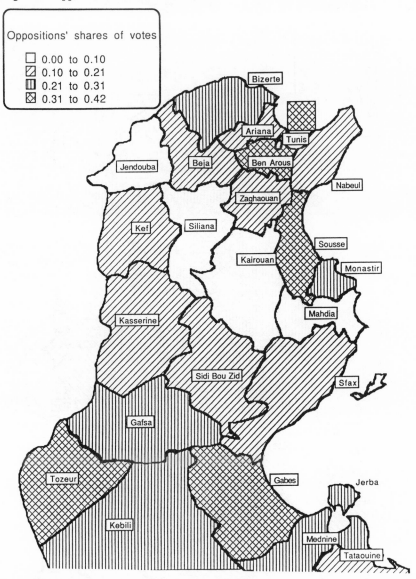

two processes seem to be working in parallel. On the one hand, an adjustment policy is triggering major changes in the banking system, leading to increased competition between banks and more autonomous processes of credit allocation. Hence, valuable potential patronage is being dispersed through a variety of economic agents. On the other hand, a multiparty system has been introduced and allowed to take its first, rather inconclusive steps. Patronage in the form of loans channeled through the banking system may help to cement some of the foundations of these new parties. And possibly, as the young parties learn more about the realities conditioning their financial survival, they will also articulate constructive support and criticism of the adjustment policies that support an economic environment more conducive to competitive politics.

Tunisia's adjustment plan escaped serious challenge during the prolonged period of grace. The salient political issues concerned removing Bourguiba's portraits and statues, constitutional reform, the release of political prisoners, and electoral and party laws—but little about economics. A liberalized system of credit allocation gathered momentum in fits and starts and may become irreversible. "Gentle commerce" (Hirschman 1978) could also soften Tunisia's transition to a multiparty system by strengthening legal opposition parties—patronage and media expenditures are their lifeblood—and by compromising or coopting leaders who would otherwise prefer more ethical but rougher tactics of popular mobilization.

■ Notes

1. I gratefully acknowledge the receipt of grants from the Social Science Research Council, the American Institute of Maghreb Studies, the Centre d'Etudes Maghrébines à Tunis, and the Earhart Foundation for assistance in carrying out fieldwork for five weeks in the course of 1987–1989. I also wish to thank Caroline Attié of the history department at the University of Texas for her research assistance and the University Research Institute for supporting it.

2. The bank's share averaged 14.5 percent of the deficit during the early ben Salah years (1961–1965) but was cut to 3.4 percent during his latter years—hardly a vote of confidence in Destour socialism! From 1970 to 1973, as Tunisia adopted Nouira's more conservative statist orientation, the banks' share of the deficit rose to 14.1 percent. During Nouira's years as prime minister, banking regulations obliged ever greater contributions to the deficit: the banks covered over half of it in 1979 (Bechri 1989 17, 25).

3. World Bank estimate. Ismail Khelil subsequently claimed they had never sunk below $180 million, or twenty days of cover (1989a 5).

4. Mimeographed Tunisian government documents communicated to me bear this date. The Honorable Peter Sebastian, who served as U.S. ambassador to Tunisia at that time, listened to an earlier version of this paper and wished to emphasize the critical and courageous role assumed by Minister Khelil.

5. On a personal note, let me report that my least successful interview—

over a career since 1959 of badgering patient Tunisians with political questions—was with an accountant on February 25, 1987. In response to questions about local accounting conventions concerning the banks, he threw me out of his office.

6. See n. 8 below.

7. The BIAT (1986) did not report deposits for 1976 but estimates that it inherited a market share of about 2.3 percent. The BIAT claims to have captured almost 13 percent of the deposits in 1985, whereas my data for Figure 4.1 show only 11.6 percent. Slight differences are due to different denominators. Mine is the total of the deposits indicated in the banks' annual reports for December 31 of each year. The totals are exaggerated because most banks practice window dressing at the end of the year. They lag payments so as to inflate the totals of slight deposits by a good 15 to 20 percent each year. My data will therefore underestimate market shares of banks that do not practice window dressing. The BTs shares, for instance, are underestimated by a percentage point (interview with Boubaker Mabrouk, president of the board, June 6, 1989). Mabrouk showed me monthly data of his bank, and his point about other banks' window dressing is also substantiated for the banking system as a whole in BCT, *Stats. Fin.*, 8 and earlier issues for prior years.

8. The most intuitively obvious yet academically respectable indicator of market concentration is the Herfindahl–Hirschman Index (HHI). It is simply the sum of the squares of each bank's market share for a given year. The bigger the number, the fewer and/or less equally distributed their shares. From 1972 to 1987 the market concentration of Tunisian bank deposits fell from 19.5 percent to 14.6 percent. Another index of market concentration that is supposed to be "conceptually superior" (Rose 1987, 181) is *entropy*, "which measures the probability that a customer choosing banks at random would choose any particular bank." Its "numbers equivalent" rose from 5.88 to 7.96 during 1972–1987—showing that Tunisian banks were becoming more available, that is, more competitive, less crowded out by a concentrated market structure. But neither of these indices shows much change over 1982–1987. Most of it occurred in the late 1970s, reflecting the irruption of the BIAT into the marketplace. The Market Share Stability Index (MSSI, defined in Rose 1987, 184, as the sum of the annual changes in market share) indicates greatest activity in the years 1973, 1974, 1977–1979, and 1983.

9. The MSSI was .048 in 1987, .032 in 1986. Competitive activity, as measured by this index, had been greater in 1983 and in all the years between 1972 and 1980.

10. On average, the STB paid 3.84 percent for its deposits, the BIAT 3.75 percent; 52% of STB's deposits were time or savings, averaging 7.34-percent interest if no interest had been paid on sight deposits; and 55 percent of the BIAT's deposits were time or savings averaging 6.85-percent interest—according to the annual reports of the banks and of the APBT.

11. The BIAT was excluded because some of its surpluses, measured as the ratio of loaned to borrowed interbank funds, were too large to fit a convenient scale. This ratio measure used in Figure 4.2 exaggerates surpluses and deficits. Even though the BIAT's cumulative surpluses were off-scale, the bank occasionally had to borrow from the Central Bank at punitive rates, as did other competitors, including the wealthy BT. Figure 4.2 measures interbank balances at the end of each year, not flows in the course of each year.

12. If the annual values for total assets had been converted to annual averages, the annual ratios and totals would be a bit longer.

13. The most recent account of the judicial struggles published in *Réalités* is Hedi Mechri, "Majid Bouden: L'intelligence sans artifice," July 16, 1988, 18–19.

14. Before declaring its net income, however, the BT squirreled away more provisions than the BIAT. In the 1980s it ploughed an average of 85 percent of its cash flow back into the bank, compared to the BIAT's 87 percent. Since the BT had the better cash flow (see Figure 4.4), proportionately more funds were available for investment. It chose, however, to build up hidden reserves rather than to invest in more branches for greater market shares.

15. Interview with Ahmed Karm, chief of staff, BCT, June 5, 1989.

16. Like the UBCI, the BIAT has a Sfaxian reputation, because Chairman Mansour Moalla and many of his top cadres come from this city. However, the Tunisian shareholders are a diversified group of some 350 individuals; and there is a significant minority of Kuwaiti and Saudi bank shareholders. Managers claim that the bank's loan portfolio is fully diversified, not particularly skewed toward Sfax businesses.

17. See *Réalités*, November 4, 1988. In 1986 the party is alleged to have received TD 3 million from the presidency's budget; an opposition leader estimated that parliamentary by-elections for five seats in early 1988 had cost the party half a million dinars.

18. *Réalités*, July 29, 1988.

19. If we regress each of the hypothetical variables on private sector bank branch densities, banking "explained" 51 percent of the variance (adjusted r-squared) in opposition voting and 48 percent of the variance in ruling party's capacity to mobilize eligible voters.

_____ PART 2

ECONOMIC
RESTRUCTURING

5

The Social Pressure on Economic Development in Tunisia

Ridha Ferchiou

The social dimension of development is generally expressed through a certain number of objectives, such as employment generation, meeting the basic needs of the population, income redistribution, regional equilibrium, and so on. In the long run, the social dimension of development cannot be dissociated from its economic dimension. However, in the short run, the social objectives of development often enter into competition with the pure economic objectives of growth. In this case, the social dimensions of development act as a constraint to economic growth and exert pressure on it.

Social pressure starts with the first steps of economic growth and becomes more and more important as economic and social and demographic structures of the country become progressively changed. As the per capita income of the population is increasing, the rate of mortality decreasing, education being generalized, the modern industrial and tertiary sectors growing, and the percentage of wage earners in the active population increasing, social pressure on development becomes more and more important. For example, in Tunisia, in spite of the relative growth experienced by the economy during the first thirty years of Independence, unemployment appears to be a more important problem in 1990 than it was in 1960.

The rapid decrease in the mortality rate from 19 percent to 9 percent, which results from economic and social progress, is the main cause of demographic growth. The main objective of this chapter is to analyze the effects of the social pressure on economic development in Tunisia through the study of three social subjects that are considered very important in the 1990s: (1) social pressure generated by the present Tunisian system of basic food subsidies and its consequences on the state budget and on the economy; (2) social pressure exerted through the structural disequilibrium of the labor market; and (3) social pressure through trade unions and relative wage increase on employment generation and on technological choice.

101

■ **The Tunisian System of Basic Food Subsidies**

In 1970 the Tunisian government created a General Compensation Fund
(CGC) as a special fund to subsidize basic consumer goods and protect the
purchasing power of the poor. Ten years later, in 1980, the CGC started to
be the subject of controversy in Tunis. On the one hand, it is accused of
being very expensive for the state budget and the national economy and of
running a deficit: it no longer reaches its social objectives, and it generates
waste on the consumer level and discourages basic food production. On the
other hand, if the CGC is eliminated, poor people would be the first to be
harmed. Under the social pressure of the poor people and of the street, in
general, no government has been able to alter the CGC and substitute a new
income subsidy system for the present price subsidy system. Let us analyze
all these points in detail.

The total amount of the compensation expenses, or subsidies, passed
from 10 million dinars in 1973 to 80 million dinars in 1980 and to 218
million dinars in 1986 (1 dinar was worth $1.06 in 1989). The subsidy
represents 16.5 percent of the total state budget and 3.1 percent of the gross
domestic product. The percentage structure of the subsidies for 1989 is as
follows:

Wheat and derivatives (bread, couscous, etc.)	61.00
Oil	12.00
Sugar	8.75
Milk and other dairy products	8.50
Seeds	4.75
Other basic products (cement, meat, potatoes, paper, etc.)	5.00
Total	100.00

The present system of price subsidies is not efficient and no longer
reaches the social objective for which the CGC was created. All Tunisian
households, whatever their income, take advantage of the price subsidy
system of the CGC. In absolute terms, the subsidy is more profitable for
those who have a higher income than for those who have a lower income. It
is more profitable for those who live in urban areas than for those who live
in rural areas. The rich and the higher-middle-income groups receive greater
benefits from the CGC than the poor and lower-middle-income groups,
because those who spend more get more advantages, since the subsidy is
based on the difference between the official price and the supposed real price
of the product.

In Table 5.1, 15 percent of the total amount of the subsidies goes to the
lowest-income group, which represents 29 percent of the total population. At

Table 5.1 Food Subsidy Concentration (Product Analysis), 1980

Income Levels (TDs)	Population		Total Food Subsidy		Wheat and Other Cereals Subsidy		Oil Subsidy		Sugar Subsidy		Meat Subsidy		Milk Subsidy	
	%	Cumul. %	%	Cumul. %	%	Cumul. %	%	Cumul. %	%	Cumul.%	%	Cumul. %	%	Cumul. %
0-69	10.5	10.5	4.0	4.0	4.7	4.7	6.7	6.7	5.5	5.5	1.4	1.4	.8	.8
70-120	18.8	29.3	11.5	15.5	13.5	18.2	15.5	22.2	14.1	19.6	5.9	7.3	5.6	6.4
121-200	26.6	55.9	23.7	39.2	25.9	44.1	26.2	48.4	24.9	44.5	19.3	26.6	18.7	25.1
201-320	22.3	78.2	26.2	65.4	26.2	70.3	24.1	72.5	25.4	69.9	26.0	52.6	27.5	52.6
321-500	12.9	91.1	18.4	83.8	16.9	87.2	15.5	88.0	16.9	86.8	22.3	74.9	22.7	75.3
501-	8.9	100.0	16.2	100.0	12.8	100.0	12.0	100.0	3.2	100.0	25.1	100.0	24.7	100.0
Total	100.0		100.0		100.0		100.0		100.0		100.0		100.0	
Gini coef.			.22		.16		.11		.15		.39		.41	

Source: This table was prepared by the author in 1980, for the Tunisian Public Accounting Court.

the same time, 16.2 percent of the subsidy goes to the highest-income group, which represents only 8.9 percent of the total population. This inequality in the use of the subsidy varies from one product to another.

The present system of consumer subsidies is not economically efficient for at least two reasons. First, on the production level, the present system of food subsidy has discouraged farmers from producing because the price of the inputs they are using was increasing more rapidly than the price of their outputs, mainly for cereals and olive oil. This was the case mainly in the 1970s. For cereals and olive oil the price indices of outputs were 182 and 141, respectively, in 1980 (basic year, 1971); while the price indices for used inputs were 248 and 232, respectively. Therefore, the present system of subsidies through the CGC has discouraged farmers and has led to stagnation in the production of the main food products. Second, on the consumer level, since the official prices are relatively low and do not reflect the degree of scarcity of the different products, the present system of food subsidies has generated a high level of waste.

Nevertheless, after ten years of discussion and controversy and despite all its defects, the present system of food subsidies through the CGC still exists under the social pressure of the street. It has even become a taboo subject of discussion since the bread riots of January 1984.

In reality, it is not easy to substitute a new income subsidy system to the present price subsidy system for two reasons. First, 70 percent of the poorest Tunisian heads of households are not wage earners and do not have permanent and regular incomes. They include farmers (45 percent), unemployed (14 percent), and independent artisans and traders (11 percent). The bread riots of January 1984 were mainly started and organized by teenage boys from these poor families, not by workers. During the bread riots, the Tunisian trade unions were in discussion with the government and with the UTICA about the amount of wage increase they were supposed to get once the price subsidy was suppressed. Second, Tunisia does not have a system of unemployment benefits, as exists in most developed countries. It is quite impossible to establish such a system now in Tunisia because of the difficulties in defining unemployment and in counting who is employed and who is not.

■ **The Structural Disequilibrium on the Labor Market**

It is very difficult to estimate unemployment in Third World countries because of the coexistence in the same country of traditional, modern, and informal (or unstructured) economies. The informal economy is more and more widespread, although it is not always officially admitted. The official data of the National Institute of Statistics (NIS) show more than four hundred thousand unemployed persons (14 percent of the total active population in 1987); 58 percent of these unemployed persons are young (less than twenty-five years old); 20 percent have been either in the university or in high school; and 25 percent are looking for a first job. This unemployment is more and more urban and therefore more and more open and aggressive. Rural unemployment (mainly disguised unemployment) is decreasing because of the rural–urban migration. This unemployment mainly results from the disequilibrium in the labor market between the additional supply of labor and the number of newly created jobs. It also results from international migration balance. Table 5.2 shows the total deficit in the labor market for the three decades 1962–1971, 1972–1981, and 1982–1991.

Under increasing demographic pressure and mainly because of the decreasing rate of mortality, the average annual additional supply of labor passed from 35,700 during the first decade to 70,000 during the Seventh Plan (1986–1991). The active population is increasing by an average rate of 3 percent per year. The deficit of the labor market is absorbed partly by international migration to Libya and to Europe and partly by the informal sector; and the remainder constitutes the additional unemployed persons.

Why does the labor market deficit constitute a social pressure on economic development? It constitutes a constraint on economic development objectives because for the last fifteen years the formal economy has not been able to generate more than forty thousand new jobs per year, whereas seventy thousand are needed per year in order to satisfy the additional supply of labor.

Since the mid-1970s, employment creation has become the most important economic objective in Tunisia. This priority has been concretized through the economic policy decisions taken during the 1970s and the 1980s. Successive investment laws are favorable to employment generation and to labor-intensive projects. International subcontracting has been developed, mainly to promote employment generation. A large number of jobs—not always economically productive—were created in the public sector in both public administration and public enterprises. As a result, most of these public enterprises are not competitive and show a permanent deficit. Of course, this deficit is supported by the whole community through state subsidies estimated to be about 30 percent of the total state budget.

Since the Sixth Plan—and then mainly with the Seventh Plan— employment generation has not been the only priority: export promotion that is taking on greater importance. The need to promote exports has been imposed by the decreasing oil production and export and by the relative growth of debt servicing. However, it is not at all certain that export promotion and employment generation are two compatible objectives. Export promotion needs a high degree of competition, cost control, and productivity increase. Therefore, the labor market deficit will continue to constitute a social pressure on economic development because the Tunisian

Table 5.2 Labor Supply and Demand in Tunisia, 1962–1991

	First Decade (1962–1971) (I, II and III Plans)	Second Decade (1972–1981) (IV and V Plans)	Third Decade (1982–1991)	
			VI Plan (1982–1986)	VII Plan (1987–1991)[a]
Additional supply of labor				
Total	357,000	469,000	327,000	350,000
Annual average	35,700	46,900	65,400	70,000
Additional demand for labor				
Total	132,000	398,000	200,000	300,000
Annual average	13,200	39,800	40,000	60,000
Total deficit	225,000	71,000	127,000	50,000
Annual average ceficit	22,500	7,100	25,400	10,000

[a]The VII Plan data are previsional.

modern industry is not able to meet the needs of the additional supply of labor.

New dimensions in economic policy should be developed, in agricultural development and informal sector and/or small enterprises development. The informal sector is becoming more and more important in Tunisia. It acts as a sponge and absorbs a large part of the labor market deficit. J. Charmes (1983) estimated the number of employed persons in the informal sector to be 374 thousand, which represents 38 percent of the total nonagricultural employment. The state should also insist on birth control programs and on (urban and rural) female education, which is still particularly low in rural areas.

■ Trade Union Activity and Its Impact on Wage Increase, Technological Choice, and Employment Generation

For a developing country with a relatively high rate of unemployment, Tunisia has adopted an advanced program of legislation and has considerably increased its wages since the mid-1970s. In real terms, the average wage has increased by 4.6 percent per year and the minimum wage has increased by 6 percent per year over the past decade-and-a-half. During the same period, labor productivity has increased by 2.9 percent per year. In the same time, the social charges that are mainly supported by the employer and imposed by a relatively advanced labor and social security legislation have seen a considerable increase. In general, they represent annually about 65 percent of the total wage and 66.8 percent in the construction industry, as shown in Table 5.3.

Table 5.3 Structure of the Social Direct and Indirect Costs Supported by Tunisian Enterprises in the Construction Industry (Percentage of the Total Wage Bill)

Social security paid by employer	20.0
Training tax	2.0
Insurance	9.0
Paid holidays	6.2
Paid official holidays (7 days)	2.3
Working clothes	1.7
Official medical care	1.7
Transportation bonus	6.0
Productivity premium	2.8
Lunch premium	9.4
Other costs	5.7
Total	66.8

Source: UTICA.

Therefore, on one hand, wages are increasing faster than productivity, and neither the wage rate nor the labor legislation reflects the abundance of labor and the existence of unemployment; and on the other hand, the capital factor price has always been relatively low (sometimes negative in real terms) and has not reflected the scarcity of this factor. As a consequence, these factor price distortions have generated a relatively capital-intensive technology, a technology not well adapted to the economic and social conditions of the country. The capital per worker has increased by an average rate of 6 percent per year. For the Sixth Plan, investment objectives were achieved at 106 percent while employment objectives were only achieved at 70 percent. During the Sixth Plan, the amount of investment per worker forecasted at 30,370 dinars was achieved at 44,425 dinars, for an increase of 46 percent.

Therefore, under the social pressure of trade union, the Tunisian economy lives in a situation of factor price distortions and of inadequate technological choice. For example, a large number of Tunisian enterprises use the state subsidies and other fiscal and financial advantages in order to substitute capital for labor. The Tunisian industry is characterized by a high rate of overequipment, estimated at between 40 and 60 percent of the total capacity of production. Finally, one of the reasons that make the informal sector grow and develop fast in Tunisia is the fact that a large number of small businessmen prefer to invest and act in the informal sector in order to have more labor flexibility and avoid the official labor legislation.

■ Conclusions

All the wage increases and all the other advanced decisions in social security and labor legislation aim to protect and improve the economic and the social condition of the Tunisian worker. For the Tunisian labor force and for the trade unions, these wage rates and advanced social legislation are vested interests to be kept and protected. However, for both present and potential nonemployed active population, relative high wages (compared to productivity) and advanced social legislation are obstacles to finding a job and avoiding unemployment. Therefore, in this case, trade union activity and interests could be different from the general social and economic interest, which is employment generation and the reduction of unemployment.

The question under discussion today in Tunis is, Should we limit the vested interests of the workers in order to maximize the number of new employment creations? In order to reduce a certain number of social charges and have more flexibility, employment flexibility and the revision of the social security and labor codes are among the most important demands of the Tunisian businessmen. The trade union and some leftist politicians are opposed to this idea.

I have noticed a certain contradiction and incoherence in the state economic and social policy. On the one hand, its main objective is employment generation, and all its economic decisions are based on this priority; but on the other hand, the economic decisions related to the factor prices favor the choice of capital-intensive technologies and not at all labor-intensive ones, since in real terms the price of capital is relatively low and the wage rate is relatively high compared to the level of labor productivity. Factor price distortions are estimated at 87 percent in Tunisia.

The absence of democracy and the political uncertainty about Bourguiba's succession amplified the social problems in Tunisia, especially after 1978. This politicization of social problems has been a permanent feature of relations between the state and the trade union, which was trying to keep itself autonomous and free from government and from the main political party's influence. The politicization of social problems reached their peak in both situations in the riots of January 26, 1978 and January 3, 1984.

Since November 1987, Tunisia is living a new era of democracy and social respite that are favorable to a direct dialogue between the different social partners. However, this new era is still fragile and weak if a way is not found to decrease unemployment and to solve social problems in general. Therefore, the social pressure is not limited to economic development: it could put in danger the new era of democracy in Tunisia and could favor extremist political tendencies.

6

The Tunisian State Enterprises and Privatization Policy

Abdelsatar Grissa

The Tunisian state enterprise[1] sector started to grow to its present size soon after the declaration of Independence in March 1956. Prior to this date, the only market-oriented state-controlled entities were seaports and the salt, tobacco, and alcohol monopolies. But these monopolies were maintained under the colonial governing authorities mainly in order to facilitate the collection of taxes, not for the purpose of promoting other economic and social objectives. In fact, given that under the colonial administration the role reserved for the Tunisian economy was to export primary products and import French manufactured goods, the relatively limited number of enterprises operating at that time in the country (transport, electricity, finance, construction, mining, agriculture, and the processing of locally produced agricultural and mineral products) were, in addition to being themselves mostly French-owned, by their very nature inaccessible to external competition.

■ Origins and Growth of the State Sector

According to an economic survey conducted in February 1956, one month before the declaration of Independence, there were only 290 enterprises operating in the country employing fifty persons or more. Over 85 percent of these enterprises were owned by European nationals,[2] who also contributed 40 percent of their workforce and occupied virtually all of the technical and managerial posts.[3] But as the European settlers started, in effect, to leave the country on a massive scale even before the advent of Independence, the production capacities under their control started to be neglected before 1956, with the consequence that gross capital formation declined in relation to GNP from 15.1 percent in 1955 to 9.7 percent in 1957. Moreover, despite the precipitous fall in property values during this period, only part of the relatively smaller properties could find local private buyers. The local population lacked both the financial means and the technical and managerial

109

capabilities to supplement the European sellers in the ownership and management of their enterprises. This situation was aggravated by the fact that the financial institutions then operating in the country were generally branches of French banks not accustomed to doing business with the indigenous population. Rare were the Tunisians who had access to bank credit prior to Independence, as Chapter 4 notes.

It was therefore in the midst of the administrative and economic confusion accompanying the transfer of authority from colonial to national hands that the Tunisian government had to intervene by taking control of some of the important foreign-owned enterprises, particularly in the public utilities, such as railways and electricity. However, though the nationalization of these enterprises was justified by the necessity of preserving their productive capacity, so that it might be used as a base for the subsequent promotion of the country's economic development, three other important reasons had also contributed to induce the government to intervene:

1. The assertion of the newly won state authority;
2. The satisfaction of the exigencies of certain interested pressure groups—notably, the relatively well organized labor movement[4]—for greater participation in running the economy and greater control over the distribution of its fruits; and,
3. The apparent lack of Tunisian capital and entrepreneurship to fill the vacuum created by the exodus of Europeans.

These three reasons have subsequently become the main driving force behind the persistent expansion of the state enterprise sector.

The growth of the state sector in the early years of Independence (1956–1961) was therefore the result, on the one hand, of the nationalization of foreign interests and on the other hand, of the creation of new establishments, particularly in banking. In 1958, the Central Bank of Tunisia, two commercial banks, and a development bank were established, accompanied by the issue of a national currency, the dinar, which replaced the franc in 1959. This monetary reform was considered an essential step toward the reinforcement of the government capacity to have an independent economic policy; for soon after the introduction of the dinar as a national currency, two other major monetary policy decisions were taken: (1) withdrawal from the franc zone and (2) the imposition of foreign exchange control.

These two decisions permitted the government to minimize the flight of capital associated with the exodus of European settlers, to increase the mobilization of resources for the acceleration of the country's economic independence, and also to extend the state sector.

However, the most important boost to the growth of the state sector came from the introduction of centralized economic planning in 1961. This resulted not only in the reinforcement of government control over economic decisions and the effective allocation of resources but also to the strengthening of certain tendencies within the ruling party, eager to extend public ownership over the means of production by further nationalizations as well as by the creation of new government-controlled enterprises. In fact, the same people who argued strongly in favor of the introduction of economic planning and the extension of the state sector soon became the masters of the country's economic decisions and of their application.

What happened in fact was much more than the extension of a state enterprise sector; for a wide-ranging collectivization policy was adopted in 1962 under the guise of a "cooperative movement" englobing agriculture and handicrafts, retail and wholesale trade, manufacturing, transport, restaurants, coffee shops, and so on. In short, this movement collectivized every existing economic activity in the country, including shoeshine boys and street peddlers. The consequence was a very rapid decline in production and a growing shortage of supplies, which meant also a marked erosion of government tax receipts and an increasing need for subsidization expenditure. Under the impact of these outcomes, this movement was abandoned in September 1969; but it left nonetheless the state enterprise sector considerably enlarged as a result of

1. The nationalization of most of the enterprises, including farming interests, still owned by foreign nationals;
2. The fusion, during the implementation of the collectivization policy, of privately owned operations with those of the state into entities that were maintained under government control even after the dissolution of the movement;
3. The establishment, with the participation of private—and later foreign—capital, of new enterprises; and
4. The creation of enterprises wholly owned by the state or its agencies.

The number of state enterprises that were the product of the forced incorporation during the cooperative movement was quite large. They constituted, in fact, the most important source of extending the state sector during the period 1962–1969. It should be noted, however, that this method of extending the state sector took place mainly in light industries and road transport. In 1990 there were nineteen state-controlled road transport enterprises whose origins are to be found in this process of incorporation. Moreover, the total number of enterprises included in the state sector rose from less than 25 in 1960 to about 185 in 1970; while their share in the country's gross investment grew at the same time from 1.8 percent to 33.7 percent.

However, the dissolution of the collectivization movement of 1962–

1969 did not put an end to the growth of the state sector. Rather, it merely slowed the process by removing its major source, forced incorporation, under the state umbrella of local private producers. But though the creation of state-controlled enterprises stopped in 1970–1972, their number then resumed growth at a relatively rapid pace. More than 110 new state enterprises were created between 1973 and 1984. The main determining factor of the expansion of the state sector in these years lay in windfalls obtained from the steep increase in petroleum prices between 1973 and 1982 and the availability of international credit at relatively low interest rates. For though the net petroleum exports of Tunisia did not exceed, on the average, 2.5 million tons annually in 1973–1984, the windfalls they produced had a considerable effect on the future expectation and spending behavior of the government. The prospects that oil prices would remain high and the hope of finding new reserves induced the authorities to accelerate the growth of their expenditure not only on the creation and the subsidization of state enterprise but also on the subsidization of consumer's goods. Consequently, total government expenditure relative to GNP rose from 28.7 percent in 1972 to 32.0 percent in 1976 and 40.6 percent in 1984. Government capital transfers to state enterprises also rose in relation to total outlays from 8 percent in 1972 to 17.5 percent in 1984. The enterprises created in 1973–1984 were bigger and more capital-absorbing than those established in the earlier period. Moreover, the availability of these financial transfers had the effect of making the enterprises of the state sector lose the fundamental incentive of relying on their own resources for survival.

■ The Economic and Financial Consequences

The following percentages should indicate the relative importance of the state sector in the Tunisian economy and its evolution between 1970 and 1980:

	1970	1980
Share in gross domestic product	26.0	25.0
Share in gross domestic investment	31.0	34.0
Share in nonagricultured salarial employment	21.0	22.5
Share in total nonagricultural salary payments	20.0	30.0
Ratio of the sector's salary payments to its value added	39.0	47.5
Share in the country's merchandise exports	80.0	75.0
Ratio of government capital transfers and subsidies to the sector's gross investment	10.0	52.4

It is evident from these ratios and their evolution that though the contribution of this sector to GDP and to the creation of nonagricultural employment remained rather stable between 1970 and 1980, its share in nonagricultural salary payments rose by 50 percent. The detrimental effect of this rise on the cost of production and the financial situation of the state sector is clearly reflected in the increase in its salary payments relative to value added and in its growing dependence on government transfers for the financing of its investment. Moreover, the absorption of a proportion of the country's investment resources markedly greater than its contribution to GDP is often attributed to the relative concentration of the sector's enterprises in more capital-intensive activities. This explanation does not, however, justify either the persistent rise of the sector's investment in the face of its stagnating contribution to GDP or the more rapid growth of its labor cost in relation to both its value added and the nonagricultural wage bill.

These ratios indicate, rather, that there has been a steady deterioration in the structural inefficiency of the enterprises included in this sector. This deterioration is also evident from the data presented in Table 6.1. This table shows that while real wages rose faster than the productivity of labor in total as well as in the different branches of manufacturing industries, the contrary has taken place in the private sector. But this absorption of more resources than were being put back into the economy meant that the state enterprises

Table 6.1   Annual Growth Rates of the Value Added, Employment, Productivity, and Real Wages in the Manufacturing Industries, 1966–1982 (%)

Industry	Value Added	Employment	Productivity of Labor	Real Wages
1966–1978 at 1972 Prices				
All industries	8.2	6.8	1.4	1.8
Public	8.1	7.4	.7	3.2
Private	8.5	6.5	1.9	.4
Food processing				
Public	6.9	7.8	-1.0	1.6
Private	4.7	1.6	3.1	1.4
Building materials				
Public	10.5	8.1	2.4	4.4
Private	7.7	5.1	2.7	.6
Textiles				
Public	-.4	4.9	-5.4	.5
Private	13.5	11.6	2.0	1.0
Chemicals				
Public	10.4	12.9	-2.4	2.6
Private	5.6	2.3	3.3	1.1
1980–1982 at 1980 Prices				
All industries	7.5	5.1	2.3	-.7
Public	-5.4	5.5	-10.3	-2.3

Source: Rejeb and Krichene 1983.

had been reducing the flow of funds to the relatively *more* efficient private sector, thus slowing down the pace of economic development and of the growth of per capita incomes in the country.

The negative effect of the state sector on the economic development of the country can be easily deduced from the growth of the capital transfers and subsidies from 10 percent of the sector's investment in 1970 to 52.4 percent in 1980. These transfers and subsidies have been at the expense of private capital formations and government direct investment in the country's infrastructure and at the cost of social services—in particular, education and health. The future of the country was therefore being sacrificed for the sake of maintaining inefficient enterprises and creating unproductive employment. The policy was maintained up to the end of 1985, when growing problems of the external debt and rising balance-of-payment difficulties rendered its abandonment inevitable. From the point of view of this forced return to economic rationality, the fall of petroleum prices and the growth of external debt problems have in effect resulted in more good than harm for the country.

The inefficiency of state enterprises is inherent in the fact that they are not considered by their controlling authorities, their workers, or their local customers as normal enterprises that should make profit in order to survive. The way these units have been conceived, located, and managed, and their objectives determined not only excluded the possibility of their being profitable but rendered the application of the term enterprises to them quite a misnomer. The main objectives of these enterprises have been

- The creation of employment, principally through the production of import substitutes and the transformation of as much as possible of locally producible primary commodities
- The control and development of public utilities
- The distribution of incomes through the manipulation of their prices and wages
- The promotion of regional development
- The laying of bases for the promotion of private initiative
- The development of activities considered beyond the resources of the private sector
- The assertion of state authority
- The rewarding of political loyalties

Practically none of these objectives are compatible with the concept of efficiency and the profit motive. Moreover, given that the decisions concerning their investment, the location of their activities, their prices, their wages, their employment, the primary products they have to use, and the markets to be served are generally made by the central political authorities, the immediate management of these enterprises cannot be held responsible for their results. There is no doubt that the most damaging aspect of these enterprises arises from the difficulty of localizing the effective responsibility for their management. Furthermore, since management has been deprived of the capacity of initiating important decisions, it has also become incapable of mastering the day-to-day execution of those taken for it by the higher authorities. Interested groups—workers, customers, purveyors of funds, suppliers, and so on—knew where the true authority lay in order to exercise their pressure, with the result being a frequently embarrassing loss of face for the management, as it found itself obliged to rescind decisions it had taken, often at the instigation of the intervening authority itself. It has, for example, been quite common for the administrators of these enterprises to be forced to reemploy people they have fired for grave professional faults, renounce contracts, rescind price changes, and increase employment despite an apparent lack of need for it. Under these circumstances, it should be difficult to expect the employees, customers, suppliers, and creditors to take seriously what these administrators say or do. They are shadows, while the effective actors are behind the scene. The problem, however, is that it is difficult to determine who these effective actors are. They do not reveal themselves, mainly in order not to assume the responsibility of the consequences of their decisions.

Being, therefore, responsible neither for the decisions taken nor, sometimes, even for their application, these administrators have become totally ineffective in their control of the various elements affecting both output and costs of their enterprises. The weakness of these administrators is particularly apparent in their control of which workers and how many workers their enterprises should employ and of how much, in what activity, and at what location they should invest. Favoritism, nepotism, and other forms of pressure have resulted in raising the labor employment of these enterprises far in excess of their effective needs.[5] Their excessive employment has been the major source of the growth of their labor cost and of the daily difficulties being faced by their management. As to the decisions concerning their investment and the location of their activities, they are generally determined by the relative weight of regional pressure groups, not on the basis of viable economic considerations.

In this environment of interaction between the exercise of pressures and the granting of favors—and given that the primary objective of the administrators of these enterprises is to conserve their posts—increasing losses become inevitable, and their resulting financial burden has unavoidably to fall on the government. However, though data on the accumulated losses of the state sector as a whole are not available, their importance can be deduced from

- The accounts of some reporting enterprises

- The periodical surveys conducted by research organizations, such as the NIS
- The capital transfers of the government

In Table 6.2 are presented the results of some of these reporting enterprises.[6] They all made losses in 1984 and have debts amounting, in certain cases, to several times their capital and reserves. These result are, however, strongly corroborated by those of Table 6.3, which are the product of a survey covering 216 state enterprises undertaken by the INS. The losses reported in this table are far in excess of profits; and the reported net losses would double if the petroleum sector, including pipelines, was excluded. Moreover, 77 percent of the reported losses are due to five groups of activity: building materials, chemicals, mining, wholesale trade, and transport.

Most of the enterprises engaged in these activities on the one hand are inefficient for structural reasons and on the other hand cannot pass their higher costs to their customers either because of intense competition in their export markets (in the case of chemicals and mining) or because of social and economic repercussions of their price increases (in the case of transport and building materials). As to the wholesale trade, the problem relates to four offices, each of which has a buying, as well as a selling, monopoly in its field: (1) cereals, (2) vegetable oils, (3) wines, and (4) foreign trade. The latter is the sole importer of certain products, notably, coffee, tea, sugar, paper, and spices. These offices are overstretched, overstaffed, and—being trade monopolies of either subsidized or taxed products—lack every rudimentary reason for being efficient.

It has, however, been accepted policy that the clients of the state sector should not be penalized by being forced, even where monopoly power permits, to shoulder the total cost of its inefficient enterprises. The expansion of this sector is supposed to be dictated by national economic, social, and political considerations; and—given the objectives of its enterprises and the way they are treated and managed— it should be both unfair and impracticable to make the local customers support the burden of its development. The decisions concerning the establishment, objectives, and management of state enterprises are taken by government authorities; and it is legitimate that the state budget should be responsible for the financial consequences of this intervention.

Table 6.4 shows how this financial burden evolved in relation to both gross investment by the state sector and total government outlays. The ratio of government transfers to the state enterprises rose in 1977–1981 to over 20 percent of these outlays and to 5.5 percent of GDP. For the period 1972–1987 as a whole, what the government transferred to these enterprises amounted to 45 percent of their gross investment and to 16.4 percent of total government expenditure. These are two important ratios, as they indicate, on

Table 6.2   Results of Some Important State Enterprises for 1984

Enterprise	Capital and Reserves (mil. dinars)	Debts (mil. dinars)	Sales (mil. dinars)	Profit or Loss Capital (%)	Profit or Loss Relative to Capital (%)	Debts Relative to Capital (%)
STIA (cars assembly)	9.7	76.6	81.0	–2.4	–24.7	790.0
CONFORT (household goods)	5.7	15.9	11.7	–1.7	–29.8	279.0
STM (trucking)	7.2	12.0	18.2	–1.0	–13.9	166.7
SIAPE (phosphate fertilizer)	32.2	71.3	64.5	–1.8	–5.6	221.4
STIL (milk processing)	7.4	62.3	99.5	–3.6[a]	–48.6	841.9
STL (forestry products)	1.0	3.6	1.6	–0.2	–22.0	360.0
Phosphate of Gafsa (mining)	67.9	242.6	105.5	–25.8	–38.0	357.3
Tunis Air	54.7	147.5	123.8	–5.9	–10.8	270.0
SNCFT (Railways)	—	—	51.8	–8.1[a]	—	—

Source: Published annual statements.
[a]Excluding current government subsidies.

Table 6.3   Results of State Enterprises by Sector of Activity, 1983 (thousands of dinars)

Sector	Profits	Losses	Net Profits or Losses
Agriculture	377	–5,242	–4,865
Food processing	3,588	–4,322	–734
Building materials	3,076	–16,299	–13,223
Electrical/mechanical industries	1,053	–8,272	–7,219
Chemical industries	3,987	–25,489	–21,502
Textiles	639	–2,470	–1,831
Paper/furniture	622	–3,238	–2,616
Mining	68	–28,700	–28,632
Petroleum	54,728	—	+54,728
Electricity	—	–7,463	–7,463
Water	1,412	—	+1,412
Construction	1,427	–1,558	–131
Wholesale trade	6,441	–15,102	–8,661
Retail trade	4,523	–1,889	+2,634
Transport (includes pipeline)	20,652	–51,131	–30,479
Tourism	1,181	–5,286	–4,105
Others	5,226	–1,539	+3,687
Total	109,000	–178,000	–69,000

Source: INS.

the one hand, the incapacity of this sector to maintain its activity without the government assistance and, on the other, the limits beyond which the government cannot go in providing this assistance without inflicting increasing harm on the rest of the economy. It is evident from Table 6.5 that the government reduced transfers in relation to expenditures to the state sector in 1982–1986, first as a result of a decline of the share of this sector in the country's gross investment and then as a consequence of the decline of this investment in relation to GNP.

As to the contribution of these transfers to the sector's gross capital formation, their ratio rose instead of falling. This increase in the relative dependence on government transfers for financing the sector's investment is undoubtedly the consequence of its growing losses and declining cash flows.

The decline of petroleum revenues forced the government to initiate a deflationary polity in 1983 that led to a progressive decline in the ratio of gross investment to GDP from 34 percent in 1982 to 20.3 percent in 1987 and a fall in the rate of economic growth from 6.2 percent in 1977–1981 to 2.9 percent in 1982–1986. The recovery of the growth rate in 1987 was mainly the consequence of a marked expansion of the exports of goods and services following the devaluation of the dinar in 1986 and the accord of a greater liberty to private initiative. The receipts of tourism rose by 44 percent between 1986 and 1987, while those of merchandise exports increased by 27.6 percent. Thus, for the first time since Independence, Tunisia experienced a genuinely export-led economic growth, alimented essentially by an invigorated private enterprise.

■ The Need for Privatization

It should be evident from the data presented so far that the expansion of the Tunisian state enterprise sector has been associated with

- The aggravation of its inefficiency
- The growth of its financial burden on government budget
- The slowing down of the country's economic growth

However, in addition to depriving private enterprises of resources that they could use more efficiently, budget transfers to the state sector have seriously undermined the capacity of the government to realize other important social and economic objectives, particularly in education and health services. Moreover, the problem of the capital transfers to the state enterprises should also be viewed in relation to the mounting government expenditure on the subsidization of certain consumption goods and services and on the interest of the national debt, as discussed in Chapter 5. The weight in the budget of these two items rose from 25 percent in 1977–1981 to 25.6 percent in 1982–1986. Consequently, the government was forced to curtail its expenditure on, for example, education from 21.7 percent in 1977–1981 to 18 percent in 1982–1986 despite the growth over the same period of

Table 6.4   Government Capital Transfers to State Enterprises, 1972–1987

Year	Transfers (mil. dinars)	Gross Investment of State Enterprises (mil. dinars)	Ratio of Transfers to Gross Investment (%)	Transfers as % of Total Government Expenditure
1972	17.3	74.7	23.2	8.0
1973	31.1	68.5	45.4	12.0
1974	57.7	96.0	60.1	16.6
1975	71.5	172.0	41.6	16.6
1976	98.3	243.0	40.5	19.5
1977	130.6	310.1	42.1	20.5
1978	142.9	343.2	41.6	19.8
1979	161.2	388.2	41.5	20.3
1980	179.4	339.0	52.9	19.5
1981	232.5	461.8	50.3	20.6
1982	232.0	649.5	35.6	13.8
1983	268.3	659.2	40.7	15.7
1984	350.5	741.0	47.3	17.5
1985	377.5	622.0	60.7	18.0
1986	281.5	559.0	50.4	11.9
1987	320.4	614.0	52.2	11.6

Source: Reports of the Central Bank.
[a]Annual average 45.5.

Table 6.5   Government Capital Transfers to State Enterprises, 1972–1987, by Percentage

	1972–1976	1977–1981	1982–1986	1987	1972–1987
Ratio of government transfers to gross investment by state enterprises	41.6	45.1	45.6	52.2	44.6
Ratio of government transfers to total government expenditure	14.5	20.1	15.4	11.6	16.4
Share of state enterprises in country's gross investment	36.8	40.0	36.5	38.0	37.8
Ratio of the country's gross investment to GDP	24.3	30.2	29.0	20.3	27.6
Ratio of government transfers to GDP	3.7	5.5	5.0	4.0	4.7
Total net external borrowing in relation to GDP	2.4	5.2	3.7	1.0	3.8
Rate of growth of GDP	6.9	6.2	2.9	5.5	5.3

Source: Annual Reports of the Central Bank.

primary and secondary school registration by 40 percent and of that of the university by 60 percent.[7]

What is even more damaging is that the government has to finance these transfers mainly by borrowing (see Table 6.6). Moreover, in order to minimize the domestic inflationary impact of the financing of its deficit, it has been obliged to resort to external borrowing for much of its financial needs. In fact, government net foreign borrowing amounted to little less than 50 percent of the increase in the country's external indebtedness for

Table 6.6   Government Transfers to State Enterprises and Borrowing (Annual Averages)

Period	Capital Transfers (mil. dinars)	Borrowing (mil. dinars)		Ratio of Total Borrowing to Transfers (%)	Ratio of External Borrowing to Total Borrowing (%)	External Borrowing by State Enterprises[a]	
		Total	% External			Millions of Dinars	% of Total External Borrowing
1972–1976	55.2	64.6	30.8	117.0	47.7	7.4	19.4
1977–1981	169.3	119.3	58.5	70.5	49.0	85.2	59.4
1982–1986	262.3	159.0	93.1	60.6	58.6	117.0	55.7

Source: Annual Reports of the Central Bank.
[a]Generally, government-guaranteed borrowing by the state enterprises.

1972–1986. The rest was government-guaranteed borrowing by the state enterprises. The result of this external borrowing by the public sector as a whole was an increase in the country's foreign debt, relative to GDP, from 32.6 percent in 1972–1976 to 48.6 percent in 1982–1986 and a rise in the service burden of the debt, in relation to foreign exchange receipts from the export of goods and services, from 11 percent to 20 percent. In fact, the relative weight of this debt rose at the end of this period to 60 percent of GDP; and its service burden rose to 27 percent of the export of goods and services.

In addition to these transfers and external borrowing, state enterprises have absorbed about one-third of the growth of domestic credit. But given their chronic losses, they would have been unable to maintain their access to the domestic as well as foreign sources of this credit without the intervention of the government in their favor.[8] Besides, these enterprises are heavily in arrears with the payment of their taxes and social security contributions, including the deductible part from the monthly pay of their workers. The reports of social security indicate that the state enterprises owe it around three hundred million dinars. How much of these banking and other debts is recoverable is not easy to tell; but their existence undoubtedly constitutes an important handicap for the good functioning of the credit system in the economy.

The state enterprises sector has, therefore, become a *fetter* rather than a *factor* of economic development. Its deficit has been the principal cause of the growth of the country's external debt; and it has, by its insatiable need for funds, forced the government to transfer to it resources for which there is much better use elsewhere.

The most frequently used argument in favor of this sector is employment. This argument is used despite the fact that most of this employment is to a large extent redundant. The fact that the funds being used in maintaining this employment could be used in the creation of more productive jobs and more wealth in other enterprises or activities is never appreciated, especially by the organized labor. The economy as a whole has, then, become a prisoner of this fear of unemployment; and the political authorities were ready to continue paying the price of labor indolence as long as the opportunity cost, in terms of dissatisfaction elsewhere, does not exceed this price. The problem, however, is that this price tends to grow, in relation to its opportunity cost, with the expansion of the state sector and its need for funds (particularly as these funds have to come from taxes paid by a weak private sector) and the weakening potential capacity of the economy to support the growing burden of the external debt.

It is this growth of the opportunity cost of the resources being unproductively absorbed by the state enterprises that finally obliged the Tunisian authorities to adopt the policy of privatization. But these reforms were the consequence of necessity before they became a matter of choice. This fact should have considerable implications for the extent, the speed, and the methods of application of privatization.

There is a world of difference between conviction and necessity. The latter obliges while it lasts, particularly since privatization is being resisted by not only organized labor but also the Left, and above all by an important segment of the bureaucracy. The latter profits enormously from management posts provided by this sector.[9] In effect, it is the resistance of the bureaucracy that poses the main stumbling block to a more rapid application of the privatization policy.[10]

■ Privatization Policy and Its Application

The decision to privatize state enterprises that occupy nonstrategic and monopolistic positions in the economy was adopted early in 1985. The country's external current account deficit reached a record level in 1984, rising to 10 percent of GDP, while the disposable foreign exchange reserves fell to the point of becoming negative by mid-1985. These developments have ruled out the possibility of borrowing further from the international capital markets without being forced to pay excessively high interest rates. The country was therefore forced to resort to the IMF for the first time since 1967–1968. The fund provided a stand-by credit of 180 million dollars in 1986; but this was in order to help the Tunisian government realize its economic readjustment program, which, in addition to the privatization of part of the state enterprises, included the other following main points:

- The devaluation of the dinar

- The raising of real interest rates from negative to sensibly positive levels
- The reduction of the public sector deficit
- The liberalization of prices
- The reduction of import restrictions

All of these measures complement each other, particularly (1) the privatization of state enterprises and the reduction of the public sector deficit, (2) the raising of real interest rates, and (3) the liberalization of prices and imports. However, the privatization policy of Tunisia is more than a simple aspect of its readjustment program: it constitutes, in effect, the determining factor of the longer-run success or failure of the country's future development effort.

Nevertheless, the application of this privatization policy raises three important questions:

- What enterprises should be offered for privatization?
- How should this privatization be implemented?
- Who should participate, and on what terms, in acquiring the privatized enterprises?

The problem raised by the first question is solved on the basis of two criteria: the existence of competition in the fields of activity of these enterprises and the importance of their production for the economy as a whole. The privatization of enterprises having a monopoly in their fields of operation is excluded as long as this monopoly persists. But since one of the main aspects of the readjustment program is the liberalization of private initiative, it is assumed that as soon as other producers enter the market and acquire sufficient competitive power, the question of privatizing the state enterprise in question will be reconsidered. However, there are areas called "strategic" (such as electricity, water, public transport, mining, cement, chemicals, and steel), of which the operating enterprises are to remain under the control of the state, at least for the time being. The problem here is that the application of the term *strategic* is quite arbitrary, as the sections it covers can be extended or reduced as well. In fact, the repeated use of this term is throwing considerable doubt on the real commitments of the government toward its privatization policy.[11] Unlike Tunisia, Morocco has made a clearly pronounced choice, in deciding to privatize all except electricity, water, telecommunication, railways, mining, and the national airline.

As to the question, Who should participate in the acquisition of the privatized enterprises?, the law is quite silent except on the point of encouraging the development of small shareholders, particularly among the workers of the enterprises concerned, by offering them discounts in the form of lower prices or the distribution of free shares and the possibility of paying by monthly installments, deductible from their monthly salaries. However, no enterprises have so far been privatized through the public sale of share, so it is too early to judge the extent of success or failure of this measure.[12]

The question of how to privatize undoubtedly raises the most important problem facing the privatization effort. Here the answer depends much more on the nature of the capital market and the economic environment than it does on the choice and readiness of the government to comply with its policy decisions. In Tunisia, however, these problems are in certain respects relatively easy to solve and in others highly difficult. But before we go any further, let us consider alternative options that the government has to put its privatization policy into effect:

- Changing the statutes defining the state enterprises
- Opening the monopolized activities to private competition
- Contracting to private operators the tasks reserved for state enterprises
- Leasing the assets operated by the state enterprises to private operators
- Selling the factories, farms, hotels, and so on of the state enterprises to the private sector
- Exchanging the shares held by the state against the debts owed by these enterprises to banks and other private creditors
- Selling through the stock exchange the shares held by the state to private shareholders

The Tunisia authorities have used, in the last two years, all of these options (except the last, simply because the stock exchange of Tunis is still at a stage of development that does not permit an important or successively significant flotation of shares).

The most important step taken so far in this privatization effort is that relating to the change of the statutes defining the state enterprises. The law stipulated, up to July 1985, that every enterprise in which the state held directly or indirectly (through another state enterprise) 10 percent or more of the paid-up capital was considered state enterprise, subject to government control and supervision, with the government having the exclusive authority to name the management. This definition had in effect done more harm than any other aspect of the state sector. By depriving the other shareholders, who often held the majority of shares, of the exercise of their rights, it not only encouraged mismanagement but, worse still, undermined the development of the habit of share ownership among the population. The defects of this definition were recognized soon after the dissolution of the collectivization movement in 1969. A commission, presided over by a member of the government, was named in 1972 to study the problems relating to management of the state enterprises. This definition of the state enterprises has been among the points on which they insisted that the law should be changed; and they recommended the acceptance of a definition based on a majority control. But the law remained as it was until it was amended by the law of July 20, 1985, in which a state enterprise was defined as one in which the state held 34 percent or more directly, or 50 percent or more indirectly, of the paid-up capital. This law was amended in its turn by that of February 1, 1989, in which only the enterprises in which the state held directly or indirectly 50 percent or more of the paid-up capital were considered state enterprises.

This change of definition has eliminated from the state sector about one-third of its previously state-controlled enterprises. Some of these have been shut down, and some have found new vigor (as they had thereafter no one else to depend upon but themselves), while some have been taken over wholly or in parts by private operators in their fields and in some cases even by their creditor banks. This sort of debt–equity swap is also being extended—though on a very modest scale—to foreign creditors.

However, as the sale of the important and heavily indebted enterprises as operating entities has proven to be impracticable, it has been decided to proceed with the sale of their assets bit by bit, through public offers. It is in this way, for example, that the biggest hotel-owning enterprise has been liquidated. This enterprise owned fourteen hotels with a capacity of over five thousand beds. Of these, ten have been sold (some of them to foreign operations), and four have been leased for long periods after being transferred to local authorities in lieu of debts.

In total, about twenty state enterprises, according to the definition of the law of 1985, have been privatized. This list is being constantly extended. But the most difficult obstacle to this process of privatization is raised by the important volume of debts owed by these enterprises. Some of these enterprises are listed in Table 6.2—for instance, CONFORT and STIA. However, two main options are here open to the government: (1) to absorb as part of the national debt the debts of the enterprises concerned, since they were incurred under its supervision and authorization and (2) to let these enterprises be liquidated as bankrupt entities. It seems that the moral responsibility of the authorities discouraged them from adopting the second course, while the heavy debts prevented them from resorting to the first. Meanwhile, the clock of interest continues to tick, and the debts to grow.

Another option being strongly pursued is that of encouraging foreign capital to participate actively in this privatization effort. The most noted example of this participation is that of Swift, a subsidiary of the Dominion Textiles of Canada, in the privatization of Sitex, the most important producer of textile products in Tunisia; and the purchase of three important privatized hotels (1,650 beds) by a Swiss group. We should, however, expect this foreign participation in the privatization effort of Tunisia to increase in the coming years. Foreign enterprises are already showing a growing interest in the Tunisian economy, especially after the relatively good performance of the readjustment program and the stabilization of the political environment both at home and with the country's neighbors. In fact, this foreign participation should be vital to the survival of many of the privatizable enterprises, not only because of their need for fresh capital but also because of the technical know-how and the external marketing facilities they could obtain from such an association. The major obstacle that may handicap this development is that posed by the heavy debts of these enterprises—for which the sooner a solution is found, the better.

It should be noted, however, that privatization by liberalization has also been an important aspect of this policy. In fact, it would have been impracticable to have adopted a policy of privatization while maintaining government controls and monopolies. This would have amounted to turning on the tap while blocking the hose. Up to the end of 1988, for example, the Tunisian enterprises and individuals were not permitted to charter airplanes or hire ships, a privilege reserved to the national navigation and airline companies. This privilege has been lifted—like many others considered, until recently, inalienable. In this respect, the most important liberalization measures are those related to imports and investment. The latter is highly significant to the development of private initiative; for as this initiative develops, it becomes less and less justifiable to maintain an inefficient state sector, whose expansion was supported in the first place by an argument based, among other things, on a presumed lack of local entrepreneurship. But it should be stressed that this lack was at first an inevitable outcome of the colonial policy, and it has later been perpetuated by the expansion of the state sector and its monopolization of important sections of the economy. The victim, therefore, has become the cause. It is a farce that has been played in vast areas of the world; and only its growing cost, in relation to what it can really produce, is forcing its rejection.

■ Conclusion

The Tunisian state sector owes its origins to the vacuum created by the exodus of European settlers, who controlled most of the organized economic activity in the country. Its expansion was subsequently accelerated, first during the collectivization period 1962–1969 and later as a result of the windfalls produced by the repeated rise of petroleum prices in 1973–1982. However, the effect of this rapid expansion was accompanied by an equally rapid growth of the sector's financial losses and an increasing dependence on government transfers and bank credit. The consequences of this have been a relative decline in government outlays on other essential services, a fall in the flow of resources to the more productive private sector, a rapid growth in the external debt, and finally an insupportable deterioration in the country's balance of payments.

The resort to privatization is an outcome of these consequences; but though the authorities seemed at first to be advancing in this direction at a reluctant pace, the more they advance, the more they apparently become convinced of the good founding of their choice. Probably the most convincing arguments in favor of privatization are the lowering of the burden imposed on the budget by government transfers and the dissipation of the myth that privatization leads to unemployment. But it must be emphasized that the most important resisting group to privatization remains the higher strata of the bureaucracy. Only their resistance can, in effect, frustrate this effort.

■ Notes

1. The term *state enterprises* is used here to denote only enterprises that have pecuniary objectives and that are wholly or partially owned by the state and its agencies, so that the government has the power to name and control the management. The latter aspect is, in effect, much more important than the ownership of capital itself.

2. The other 15 percent were mostly owned by Jews of Tunisian nationality, who also left the country after its accession to Independence.

3. The number of European residents working in the country fell from eighty-six thousand in February 1956 to twenty thousand in May 1966. Most of this decline took place between 1956 and 1960, particularly as a result of the Tunisification of the administration between 1957 and 1989.

4. The labor movement participated actively in the struggle that led to Independence; and it lost in the process its main founding leader, who was assassinated by French extremists in 1953. Therefore, it considered itself to have a legitimate claim to a privileged share in the distribution of the national cake.

5. Some estimates consider this excess employment to be as high as one-third of the actual number employed.

6. These are forty-six enterprises whose shares are quoted on the "permanent" side of the stock exchange and that are required by law to publish their annual accounts and balance sheets. Of these enterprises eighteen are private, and twenty-eight are state-controlled enterprises, among which are seven banks, two insurance companies, and six trading companies.

7. Those who know Tunisia often voice their surprise at the recent deterioration of roads, public buildings, and the quality of education and health services, due mainly to this transfer of funds to the subsidization of current consumption and of unproductive employment, another form of subsidized consumption.

8. This intervention is facilitated by the fact that more than 90 percent of

the commercial banking done in the country is in the hands of state-controlled banks.

9. The commitment of the governing political authorities to the policy of privatization has undoubtedly been reinforced after the change that took place in the country's leadership in November 7, 1987. This change was not of form but was nevertheless very profound; and it has been frequently emphasized that political liberty cannot be assured without the liberty of private initiative in the economic sphere as well. Moreover, in order to confirm this commitment, the name of the ruling party was changed again to Constitutional Democratic Grouping. The word *socialist* was thus dropped de facto after having lost its significance in form.

10. This point has been developed more extensively in Grissa n.d.

11. It should be noted that the word *privatization* has not been mentioned in any of the official texts of the Tunisian government. The terms used in the French version of these texts are *réadjustment* and *assainissment*. A loose translation of the latter term would give "improvement."

12. In an impartially private enterprise, Société des Industries de Textiles, the workers were offered 10 percent of the outstanding shares at a discount of 20 percent, which has proven to be a very profitable offer.

7

Private Sector Development Through Public Sector Restructuring? The Cases of the Gafsa Phosphate Company and the Chemical Group

Pamela Day Pelletreau

In the waning days of the Bourguiba regime, the economic crisis of mid-1986 impelled Tunisia to liberalization measures in the economy. Internal reforms were supported by the international donor agencies, through both project-related and non-project-related assistance. A searching examination of the problem areas led to a structural adjustment program supported by a $150 million World Bank loan signed in 1988, in which macroeconomic targets were set for the Tunisian economy. These targets reinforced the commitment that was explicit in the Seventh Plan (1987–1991) to decrease the drain of public sector enterprises. The approach was two-pronged: privatization of selected enterprises and restructuring of others. This chapter sets forth the legal and institutional context for reform of the commercial enterprises in the public sector, addresses the social complexity of restructuring the phosphate and related processing industries, and explores the potential for private sector development in the restructuring process.

■ Background

The public enterprise sector plays a large role in the Tunisian economy, as Table 7.1 shows. By the early 1980s it was estimated that public enterprises accounted for approximately 25 percent of GDP value added, 24 percent of non-agricultural employment, 40 percent of investment, 75 percent of exports, and 45 percent of imports (United States Agency for International Development [USAID] 1989).

During the Sixth Plan (1981–1986) public enterprise investment represented 57 percent of total investment in the industrial sector. Over the 1981–1986 time period the total debt of the forty largest public enterprises increased from TD 1.67 billion to TD 3.17 billion. Under the Seventh Plan the government's objective was to shift the balance of investment from 44.8 percent private–55.2 percent public in 1987 to 50.7 percent private–49.3

Table 7.1   Share of Public Enterprises in Salary Payments, Employment, and Value
Added, 1969–1980 (%)

Share of Public Enterprises	1969–1972	1970–1980
In nonagricultural employment	21.0	22.5
In GNP	25.0	25.5
In total wages	20.0	29.5
Ratio of salary payment of public enterprises to value added	39.3	49.5

Source: al-Hannachi and Grissa 1987.

percent public in 1991 (Ministère du Plan, 1986. Tables III-2, III-2-1) and to
reduce the share of investment by public enterprises from 8.2 percent of GDP
in 1986 to 5.7 percent by 1991. As a matter of policy, the government
planned to disengage itself from all public enterprises in competitive
sectors.

■ Legal and Institutional Context

The definition of a public enterprise establishes the parameters for the sector
in the economy. In Tunisia, interlocking shareholdings among public
enterprises and public participation in some private enterprises create a
complex ownership structure. Changing definitions of public enterprises have
progressively reduced their number from approximately 500 (prior to July
1985, when 10-percent state ownership was used as a criterion) to 307 (34-
percent state ownership or more than 50-percent direct and indirect public
ownership) to approximately 190 (50 percent or more state-owned)—as
Chapter 6 discusses. At present, a public enterprise is defined as one at least
50 percent of whose capital is held by either the state (either directly or
through state-owned subsidiaries) or by municipalities or other public
enterprises (Law 89-9 of February 1, 1989; for the full test, see *Journal
officiel*, February 7, 1989).

The 1989 economic budget spelled out guidelines for public enterprise
reform. The guidelines provided for

1. Drawing a distinction between, and separating, business activities
related to production and those related to social service;
2. Establishing, within large-scale enterprises grouping several
activities, autonomous units that could be adapted to privatization;
3. Optimizing the labor force through conversion of surplus personnel
into other activities;
4. Facilitating the state's withdrawal through mobilization of financial
support to erase, partially or totally, debts of the enterprises; and

5. The use of criteria that took into account the specific characteristics of each enterprise and each sector to increase flexibility in the restructuring process.

In addition, the management structures of the enterprises were to be strengthened and vested with increased authority (République Tunisienne, Banque Central 1988b, 36–38).

A law passed in the summer of 1987 (Law 87-47 of August 2, 1987) contained provisions for implementation of the public enterprise–restructuring process honored more in the breach than in the observance. Signed only a few months before President ben Ali replaced President Bourguiba, the 1987 law established a highly stratified administrative review process—in part to assure that withdrawal of the state from the public sector did not cause loss of the public wealth (*broadage*) or create situations of private monopoly.

The three-tiered commission structure envisaged in the August 1987 law was rapidly recognized as unwieldy and never fully put into effect. Instead, a single interministerial commission was established, the National Commission for the Restructuring of Public Enterprises (CAREP). CAREP was chaired by the prime minister or his representative and composed of five members: the director of the Central Bank and the ministers of social affairs, public service, planning, and finance or their representatives. Recommendations to the ministerial commission were made by a technical committee composed of high-ranking civil servants in each of the ministries and chaired by the director of public enterprises in the Prime Ministry.

To strengthen the privatization program, an adviser was recruited and funded through the international donor agencies. He was established within the Prime Ministry to support policy determination and develop implementation procedures. A second adviser was posted to the stock exchange to help in enhancing its capabilities as an instrument in the privatization process. The decisionmaking process for restructuring and divestiture was dependent upon an accurate and complete data base; and provision was made to reinforce the Cour des Comptes and accelerate the completion and publication of its annual reviews. The government planned to withdraw primarily from industrial and commercial activities in competitive sectors.

Less than eighteen months after the August 1987 law, in January 1989, a new public enterprise law was submitted to the Chamber of Deputies to recognize on-going practice and to simplify the legislative framework within which restructuring and divestiture decisions would take place. The new law was discussed in the Council of Ministers by the Economic and Social Council and passed by the Chamber of Deputies. It was signed by the president on February 1, 1989. Public enterprises were defined to be those of a nonadministrative character in which the state held 50 percent or more of the capital (with a few exceptional additions). All nonpublic enterprises were to be governed by the provisions of the commercial code. For the exceptional enterprises, in which the state had more then 34 percent but less than 50 percent, ownership, the state would continue to exercise a supervisory role until 1991 (*La Presse*, January 25, 1989).

The government moved in the direction of structured and systematic supervision of the public enterprises rather than of ongoing involvement in the internal decisionmaking process. The 1989 law provided for representation on the boards of directors of public enterprises proportional to ownership share and established official government representation at general meetings by a single, designated representative of the state who could not be the director-general of the enterprise.

Title III of the law had the greatest implications for the clarification and simplification of the structures of the public enterprises. Article 24 provided for a commission with the power to give advice on the sale or exchange of shares held by the state; the fusion, absorption, or division of enterprises in which the state had a direct participation in the capital; and the sale of any assets able to constitute an autonomous business unit. The commission could consider the award of fiscal and financial advantages. High priority was given to the financial evaluation of the enterprises by specialists from within or without the governments; and, in support of the expansion of the number of small shareholders and the expansion of the stock exchange, specific advantages were envisaged for the employees or former employees of the companies who wished to purchase shares. These advantages included a priority right of purchase with payment delayed up to three months, purchase at a reduced price, and even the possibility of the free distribution of shares. With the approval of the prime minister, a variety of tax exemptions could also be granted to restructuring industries; and provision was made for debt forgiveness by decision of the prime minister on the advice of the CAREP. The commission was expanded to include the minister of the interior and the secretary-general of the government or their representatives. It had the power to convoke the minister of the supervisory ministry (*autorité de tutelle*) of the enterprise under consideration as well as the director-general of the company and any other persons it wished.

The objectives of the law were to clarify the definition of a public enterprise, to spell out the role of the state and other shareholders in its administration, and to provide the statutory base for simplification of the tangled web of cross ownership in which many of the public enterprises had become entwined. Furthermore, it was the intent of the government to favor the employees of the various public enterprises as they moved away from state control.

Decrees 89-376 and 89-378 of March 1989 (*Journal officiel* March 31, 1989) provided that the boards of directors were to meet once every three months and hold discussions on the basis of agenda items sent at least ten days before. A majority of the board had to be present for the meeting to be valid and decisions were to be taken by a majority of those present. A special delegate from the state was to be named by the Ministry of Finance and the supervisory ministry for the enterprise concerned. Detailed procedures established a schedule to ensure the publishing of budgets, the balance sheet, and the minutes of the board meetings within specified periods of time. Approval of the February law was a necessary precondition to the extension of the World Bank's Public Enterprise Restructuring Loan (PERL) signed in Washington in July 1989.

Among the industries contributing heavily to the drain on the government's budget was the related set of industries of the Gafsa Phosphate Company (CPG) and the phosphate-processing industries contained within the Chemical Group. The Chemical Group was among the industries over which the government, although less than a 50-percent shareholder, maintained a supervisory role.

■ The Gafsa Phosphate Company

Phosphates were discovered in Tunisia in 1885. The mining concession was put up for bid three times before a concessionaire was found brave enough to take a chance on a hazardous development in desert territory. A concession was finally granted in 1896, and the Compagnie des Phosphates et du Chemin de Fer de Gafsa (later to become CPG) was established in 1897. Mineworkers were recruited from Algeria, Libya, and Morocco as well as Tunisia; and social services were provided to retain them and their (French) supervisors. In 1899 the Metlaoui–Sfax rail line was completed, and the first exports of raw phosphates took place.

Until 1930 Tunisia remained one of very few producers of phosphates in the world and retained a natural monopoly on sales. During the 1930s, however, the United States developed mines in Florida, and the USSR brought some of its reserves into production. Morocco, too, entered the world market with phosphates of a quality superior to Tunisia's

Production in Tunisia was 3.3 million tons in 1930 (Duwaji 1967, 52–60). In the mid-1950s annual exports averaged 2 million tons, and in 1955 they were equal in value to one-sixth of the total Tunisian exports (Barbour 1962, 332). In 1960 mining provided 3.3 percent of GDP (Duwaji 1967). In 1988 production reached approximately 6.2 million tons out of a total world production (1986) of approximately 141 million tons.

The government established the National Office of Mines in 1962 to search for, and exploit, mineral resources in the country and to represent the state in the joint enterprises engaged in mineral extraction. The extractive industries employed, at that time, roughly thirteen thousand people, or just under half of total industrial employment; and of a total industrial investment of over seventy-one million dollars (1960) the extractive industries received sixty-four million dollars. The bulk of the phosphate was exported in raw form, thus making no sustained contribution to the country's industrial development. In the mid-1960s mineral traffic, carried by the Gafsa railway, which operated over 274 miles of narrow-gauge line from Metlaoui to Sfax on a concession basis, equalled 70 percent of total railroad freight. When the concession expired in 1966, the railway line reverted to the state (Duwaji 1967, 142).

By 1988 Tunisia was producing 6.2 million tons of phosphate, selling 5 million internally and exporting 1.2 million in an unprocessed state, primarily to Romania, Greece, France, Poland and Turkey (Economic Intelligence Unit 1989, 13). The phosphate industry consumed two-thirds of the mining investment budget (TD 21.5 million budgeted for 1989 on a total mining investment budget of TD 30 million.) In addition, the state budgeted TD 19.1 million to cover some financial liabilities of CPG and to help it realize its investment program (République de Tunisie, Banque Centrale 1988b). Sectoral exports (phosphates and chemicals) rose in value (in constant 1986 prices) from TD 343.4 million in 1987 to TD 363.7 million in 1988 to a projected TD 397.5 million in 1989 (République de Tunisie, Banque Centrale 1988b, Table IV-2).

During the period of the 1970s, the world market price for phosphate rock rose from fourteen dollars per ton in February 1973 to forty-two dollars per ton in January 1974 to reach sixty-eight dollars per ton in January 1975 (Reidinger 1981, 27).[1] The CPG was able to sustain its role of provider of social services as well as producer. Moreover, it expanded its involvement in other wholly or partially state-owned enterprises. By 1985, however, the company was operating at an enormous deficit, fifty million Tunisian dinars. Increased production by the United States and other producers brought the price down for the Tunisian low-quality phosphates (Interview, Gafsa, March 1989). The company's current expenditures remained fairly constant and the level of public support required for its operations increased. Direct and indirect infusions of public funds supported the company's activities.

☐ *Reorientation*

Isolated in the barren landscape of southwestern Tunisia, the CPG was the prime employer of the Gafsa Governorate. Its community services extended far beyond the provision of employment, as the early mine management made of Gafsa and the surrounding mining areas a company town. The CPG ran schools and clinic–hospitals. It provided housing and covered utility costs. Retirement and health insurance for the workers, a general store, and a sports facility were company-provided.

In the second half of 1986, a new president-director-general was appointed to make the decisions necessary to reduce the drain of the company on the state budget. The CPG reduced its employment rolls by three thousand, from fourteen thousand in 1986 to under eleven thousand in 1988. The new management reoriented the company toward the production and sale of phosphates and away from the provision of social services and participation in money-losing ventures. Company-supported schools and hospitals had been transferred to the relevant ministries in the late 1960s. The government-sponsored utilities STEG and SONEDE took over provision of electricity and water in 1980 and 1985, respectively. In January 1989 the CPG transferred management of its pension fund to the government, thereby guaranteeing benefits that the company had had difficulty in sustaining during some of its years of loss; and a new private sector purveyor was sought to manage and provide medical insurance coverage. As the premiums required by private companies were very high, the CPG considered the establishment of a separate public insurance company.

The union concurred in these actions, as it did in the purchase of shares in the company through contributions from the worker's salaries, a program undertaken to expand the commitment of the workers to the company and make them appreciate its financial situation, as well as to reduce the company's losses (Interview, Tunis, December 1988).

In the early 1980s the company began to sell its dwellings to the workers who inhabited them, for a nominal fee, simultaneously handing over responsibility for maintenance and utility payments. (Between seven hundred and eight hundred company employees had been detailed to domestic maintenance activities.) Of an original sixty-seven hundred workers' homes, by 1898 only eight hundred remained for sale. Furthermore, some of the services that the company had provided in its own administrative headquarters were privatized through contracts: guard service, custodial service, and the provision of refreshments.

Efforts were made to reduce the exposure of the CPG to deficits incurred through its participation in other companies. A construction company that had been established as a joint venture among the CPG, the governorate, and certain private individuals had, by 1986, incurred ten million dinars of losses. The society was scheduled for liquidation. In accordance with Tunisian law, however, revenue would be applied first to retiring unpaid taxes, second to indemnifying the workers, and, only third to paying back the shareholders. The CPG attempted to have an exception made on its behalf.

The CPG-supported commercial–retail society, also running at a loss, was replaced by a branch of the General Store (Magasin General), another public enterprise but one separate from the CPG. The General Store built new facilities and hired some of the workers from the old store. Although the CPG proposed indemnifying the employees of the company store with capital and assistance in finding a place to open up a new business, their overwhelming preference was for a monetary payment.

The CPG shareholders in a third enterprise, for the production of textiles, were made available to the company's private partners, who bought out the phosphate company while applying to the government for a tax amnesty and for transition funds to adjust the textile enterprise.

The CPG demonstrated the importance of external financing to the reestablishment of public enterprises on a sound financial footing. In 1986 the state defrayed a TD-40-million debt. Of the TD-40-million indebtedness, the government covered slightly over TD 20 million owed to the Social Security Fund and 10 million dinars of bank debt and provided a loan of slightly over 10 million dinars from the treasury. The CPG, which incurred a deficit throughout the 1980s, reduced its deficit from TD 30.5 million in 1987 to TD 12.3 million in 1988, less than one-half the budgetary provision for the latter year; and it hoped to break even in 1989. Debt alleviation enabled it to address other restructuring tasks, among them divestiture.

The CPG has multiple shareholdings in related and unrelated enterprises. After 1987, in accordance with the recommendations of the Interministerial Council and the board of directors of the company, valiant efforts at divestiture were undertaken. Difficulties arose from the lack of buyers at the proposed prices on the Tunis Stock Exchange and from the failure or near disappearance of some of the companies. In the spring of 1989, approximately forty different shareholdings awaited sale or write off (Interview, Tunis, June 1989).

The efforts to divest and refocus the CPG conform to the requirements for decreasing losses and building a potentially profitable company. Although some of the activities trimmed have been transferred to other enterprises in the public sector, some, particularly in the housing area, have entered private hands. The company's production and cost targets are focused on the mining and marketing of phosphates; superfluous related activities have been trimmed away. The CPG is, however, the major employer in an area of the country that experienced external intervention in 1980;[2] and social considerations as well as union pressures constrain restructuring efforts. A workers' conversion fund (fonds de reconversion) is projected, but alternative opportunities for those who find no work in the mines are limited. The world market price for phosphates and phosphate products will also increase or diminish the pressure on company management.

Over 75 percent of the CPG's raw product is sold internally for processing. The principal purchasers are the member industries of the Chemical Group, which produce a variety of phosphate-based fertilizer products and other products, primarily for export. In the summer of 1989, the

CPG took a 49-percent share (four of the nine member companies) in a reorganized Chemical Group, thus creating a vertically integrated company for the production, processing, and export of phosphates and phosphate products.

■ The Chemical Group

Phosphate and chemical exports follow only textiles and tourism in their contribution to Tunisia's foreign exchange earnings (phosphates and chemicals, TD 363.3 million; textiles and leather, TD 489.1 million; and tourism, TD 830.5 million in constant 1986 prices [République de Tunisie, Banque Centrale 1988b, Table IV-2]). The Chemical Group processes Tunisian phosphates into a variety of products and exports them. It also exports technology through licensing agreements. Until recently the Chemical Group without a formal juridical structure (though established in 1972) linked nine companies, four of which (Société Industrielle d'Acide Phosphorique et d'Engrais [SIAPE], Industries Chimiques de Gafsa [ICG], Industries Chimiques Magrébines [ICM], and Société d'Engrais de Gabes [EG]) received Kuwaiti financing and one of which (Société Arabe des Engrais Phosphates et Azotes [SAEPA]) received financing from UAE. The capitalization of the companies varied from one to forty-one million dinars. To clarify and simplify the financial and administrative structure, under the aegis of SIAPE, the four companies with Kuwaiti financing have been reorganized. The CPG, with funds from the Tunisian government has taken over the 49 percent that was the Kuwaiti share.[3]

The fluctuation of international markets has caused considerable variation in the return to Tunisia from its phosphate fertilizer production, but a recent analysis projected absorption of global supply overcapacity by 1995. World supply and demand are estimated in Table 7.2.

Tunisian exports of phosphates and other minerals, fertilizer, and inorganic chemical products showed an increase in the value to processed phosphates over the 1986–1988 period (see Table 7.3). In 1988 the sale of phosphates by the CPG to local purchasers increased by almost 18 percent. The export of raw phosphates, however, fell off.

□ Marketing Issues

Of seventeen products sold, four—triple superphosphate (TSP), diammonium azote and phosphate (DAP), phosphoric acid, and superphosphoric acid— bring 85 percent of export receipts (*Conjoncture*, February 1989, 37). Between 1980 and 1987 the price of TSP (46 percent) free-on-board North Africa fell by more than one-third, from $200–$215 per metric ton (1980) to

Table 7.2 World Supply/Demand for Phosphate Fertilizer, 1970–2000 (Millions of Metric Tons P_2O_5)

Demand	1970	1980	1985	1986	1990	2000	Average Growth Rate, 1986–2000 (%)
Western and Southern Europe	5.0	6.1	5.4	5.3	5.5	5.5	.3
Eastern Europe	4.8	8.6	9.7	10.0	10.0	13.4	2.1
Far East	1.6	4.6	6.4	6.5	9.5	14.8	6.1
Africa	.5	1.0	1.2	1.1	1.7	2.4	5.7
Total demand	19.8	30.8	34.3	33.0	38.3	57.2	3.2
Total production capacity	20.6	33.0	37.1	37.0	40.9	52.6	2.5

Source: World Bank estimates 1989.

Table 7.3 Principal Products Exported

Year	Phosphates and Other Minerals		Fertilizers		Inorganic Chemical Products	
	Quantity (1,000 Tons)	Value (1,000 Dinars)	Quantity	Value	Quantity	Value
1986	1,843	38,029	1,281	160,800	622	92,040
1987	2,308	51,441	1,689	217,400	693	103,292
1988	1,432	32,461	1,624	237,362	999	182,024

Source: INS.

$120–$160 per metric ton (1987). In 1988 the price rose slightly to $150–$170. Simultaneously, the average price for Tunisian-produced TSP (46 percent) per metric ton fluctuated from $203 (1980) to $135 (1987) to rise to $154 (1988). Similar price volatility was shown in the other principle products, among them P_2O_5, phosphoric acid.

Sales of P_2O_5 exemplify the interaction among producers, purchasers, and politics in the international market. Approximately one-third of Tunisia's production of P_2O_5 has been exported to the Indian market as a necessary ingredient in the production of fertilizer. In December 1988 Indian contractors signed for the purchase of Tunisian P_2O_5 at a price considered excellent by the Tunisian producers, $480 per ton. Subsequently, however, the Indian government refused to authorize the transaction on the grounds that the price was too high.

Morocco is an alternative supplier; but, in the context of the Arab Maghreb Union, Morocco agreed not to undersell Tunisia on the Indian market. The Indians were able to obtain manufactured DAP, the fertilizer product that requires the input of P_2O_5, from the United States at a price that, free-on-board U.S. Gulf plus transportation costs, was less than the price of the India-manufactured DAP using North African-supplied P_2O_5 at the \$480-per-ton price. Tunisian export sales contracted sharply, and the Tunisian factories closed for annual maintenance. Reopening was projected at 50-percent capacity. Even if Indian purchasers were renewed, one-quarter of the contract year would have passed before deliveries of the phosphoric acid could be made from Tunisia (Interview, Tunis, March 1989). Simultaneously, a major export market in Turkey closed while the internal Tunisian market was limited by drought.

Eventually, in a situation of great Tunisian oversupply, a new price for phosphoric acid was agreed on with the Indians (\$432 per ton); and by mid-1989 the Chemical Group was considering selling more than its two hundred thousand-ton quota. Maghrib solidarity had broken down, and the Moroccan government brought suit in the Hague for breach of the original contract.

☐ *Restructuring*

Unification and rationalization of the administrative and financial structures of the four companies in which there had been Kuwaiti participation will reduce costs (Interview, Tunis and Sfax, March 1989). The Central Bank allowed for an increase in investment credits of 25.6 percent for consolidation within the Chemical Group. In the sector as a whole, however, investment was reduced from TD 54.8 million in 1987 to TD 18 million in 1988 (République Tunisienne, Banque Centrale 1988a, 170).

Overall, the exporting companies of the group increased their value added and decreased their losses between 1986 and 1987. The four major fertilizer-producing companies in the Chemical Group—the SIAPE, ICG, ICM, and SAEPA—reduced their losses by approximately 20 percent (*Bilans*, September 21, 1988, author's calculation). As the chemical sector exports to sixty countries, with the two largest shares going to Western Europe (43 percent) and Asia (32.5 percent) (*Conjoncture*, February 1989, 38), the potential for flexible marketing of diversified products exists even though the current global surplus in the fertilizer market discourages expansion.

In June 1989 two major loans were signed, one between the Government of Tunisia and the Kuwaiti Fund for Arab Economic Development and one between the Government of Tunisia and the Arab Fund for Economic and Social Development. For thirty-two and fifty-two million dinars, respectively, the loans were to assist the newly restructured SIAPE, which now encompassed three other societies, to reduce its costs of production, renew its material and equipment, achieve its optimal productive capacity, and protect the environment. At the signing of the Arab Fund loan, Muhammed Ghannouchi, the minister of plan and finance, stressed the social importance of the chemical industry as well as its economic role as a major exporter (*La Presse* June 18, 1989; June 19, 1989). These two loans provided more than 50 percent of a global project cost of TD 134.8 million.

The Kuwaiti loan incorporated concern for the environment and addressed the struggle against pollution. The operation of the phosphate-processing plants polluted the waters in an area 20 kilometers square off the shore of Gabes in 1988 and 1989. In addition to disturbing the ecological balance (as certain pollution-consuming plankton increased inordinately rapidly), the high levels of cadmium found in shellfish reduced their marketability and had a consequent negative impact on the economy in the area (Interview, Tunis, June 29, 1989). The Chemical Group commissioned studies; and in mid-1989 its engineers made a breakthrough in development of a purification process that would permit the production of decadmized phosphoric acid while reducing the air pollution currently emanating from the factories (*La Presse* July 9, 1989). As the majority of European companies (with the notable exception of Italy's) had recently adopted legislation limiting the level of cadmium permissible in phosphoric acid, the market implications of the discovery were welcome.

■ Conclusion

Tunisia's adherence to the structural adjustment program on which it entered in the mid-1980s and its commitment to meet certain benchmarks established in negotiation with the World Bank require it to restrain transfers to deficit public enterprises. On the other hand, social costs, internal policy objectives, and Arab world diplomacy inhibit maximum implementation of cost-cutting measures and retard their application. Public enterprise restructuring becomes, therefore, a gradual process, requiring both internal and external negotiations. Divestiture can reduce deficits; service contracts and housing ownership can contribute to private sector development. Even a restructured Chemical Group will encounter, as well as an overbuilt global fertilizer market, environmental clean-up and pollution control costs that add to overhead. The CPG and the reorganized SIAPE are now closely linked financially as being producers and processors of phosphates. Although they will become more efficient public enterprises, the contribution of the restructuring of these two industries, the CPG and the Chemical Group, to private sector development is limited.

■ Notes

1. A massive boom in fertilizer plant investment also took place. Increased demand pushed prices to $340–370 for TSP and over $400 per metric ton for DAP

in September 1974. Farmers refused to purchase and by mid-1975 TSP was down to $125 per metric ton and DAP to $160.

2. In 1980 Gafsa was occupied for three days by forces in opposition to the Tunisian government, and the rebellion had to be put down by force.

3. Kuwaiti participation had been described in a South–South context as "backwards integration by oil-exporting countries into the supply of industrial raw materials from developing countries" (United Nations, Industrial Development Organization 1986). Ammonia necessary to the processing of compound fertilizers had been supplied by Kuwait.

8

Rural Development in Central Tunisia: Constraints and Coping Strategies

Barbara K. Larson

Since gaining Independence in 1956, Tunisia has made major efforts to develop economically and socially, using a strategy of social welfare measures and compulsory state cooperatives in the 1960s, followed by the dismantling of the cooperatives and a gradual liberalization of some aspects of the economy in the 1970s. However, through both of these phases, two things have remained constant. One is that state control of development has remained strong, particularly in the less developed regions. The other is that development efforts have disproportionately benefited the northern and eastern (the Sahel) regions of Tunisia at the expense of the Center and the South.

In the late 1970s and 1980s, the government sought to rectify this situation somewhat by targeting development efforts particularly to the Center and South and permitting a limited degree of decentralization in development planning in order to tailor development more expressly to the needs of particular regions. The motives for doing so were both humanitarian and politically expedient: the government needed to develop these regions in order to stem political discontent and reduce the flow of unemployed labor into urban areas.

At the same time, the government's efforts to implement such plans were both constrained and given added urgency by pressures generated by events in the world and regional political economy of the 1980s: declining revenues from oil, tourism, and remittances and renewed pressures from international lending agencies to restructure the economy along more liberal lines. In addition, the government's effectiveness in implementing these plans was affected by the centralized, politicized, and bureaucratic nature of the government itself.

This chapter will look at the efforts of one regional planning and development agency, the Central Tunisia Development Authority (CTDA) to bring about rural development in the area of Kasserine. Based on the author's experience in 1986–1987 as a consultant on socioeconomic impact analysis, the paper will examine development efforts from two points of view: (1) the aims, goals, and strategies of the development agency and the factors that have enhanced or interfered with its effectiveness and (2) the coping strategies of local farmers and their role in the development process. Both will be analyzed against the backdrop of the political and economic forces just outlined.

■ Kasserine and the Surrounding Area

The governorate of Kasserine and its surrounding area is located in the central steppe area of Tunisia. The region is characterized by craggy, mountainous areas in the North and West sloping to dry and arid plains in the East and South. In the North and West, winter temperatures are cold enough to bring an occasional snow. Rainfall is often scanty (varying from around 200 millimeters in the South to over 450 millimeters in the North) and highly erratic from year to year, which makes dryland cereal cultivation undependable.

As a result, traditional adaptations have been based on patterns of dispersed settlement, transhumance, and opportunistic cereal cultivation, as people combined seminomadic sheep and goat husbandry with cultivation of wheat and barley to wrest a meager existence from the environment. Much of this traditional adaptation is still reflected in the statistics today, which indicate that 70 percent of the population is rural; that percent 60 percent live in dispersed, rather than agglomerated, settlement patterns; and that population density is a meager thirty-five persons per square kilometer. (RONCO 1986, p. 22) in contrast to the eastern coast, where population is ten times as high. In addition, some 50.3 percent of the land is officially classified as collectively owned, though a little more than half of this has recently become—or is in the process of becoming—privatized (CTDA 1986).

The region is one of the poorest and most disadvantageous in all of Tunisia, with the lowest per capita income in the country in 1980—152 dinars, with 14 percent of the population below the World Bank's minimum subsistence level (RONCO 1986, 22; Annex D, 6)—and illiteracy rates (for those under thirty) nearly twice as high as in other parts of the country.[1] Only 10 percent of the rural households are electrified, 40 to 75 percent of the houses consist of only one room (CTDA 1986), and average family size is 5.6 persons per household versus 4.7 in Tunisia as a whole (RONCO 1986, Annex D, 6). Furthermore, the interior regions of the country (which include the governorates of Sidi Bou Zid, Kairouan, and Gafsa as well as Kasserine) received only 3.6 percent of the new factories established during the 1970s; and of the eighty-six thousand jobs created between 1975 and 1978, forty-six thousand went to Tunis and the Northeast, while only four thousand went to the South (Seddon 1986, 214). Unemployment hovers at roughly 20 percent of the economically active population (INS 1984), but most scholars agree that this is a serious underestimate and that unemployment for the young is more likely around 50 percent. One need only observe the number of youths in the streets and cafés of Kasserine to confirm the high rate of youthful unemployment.

The economy of the region is based primarily on agriculture, with 40 to 60 percent of the economically active population employed in agriculture (INS 1984) and 65 percent of the cultivated land devoted to cereals. The remaining 34 percent is devoted to tree crops, and 1 percent to vegetable cultivation (RONCO 1986, 22). While some irrigated agriculture exists (based on either deep or shallow wells), most of the cereal and tree crops are rain-fed.

■ The Central Tunisian Development Authority

Tunisia, as noted, began in the mid-1970s to feel a need for some better way of meeting the development needs of particular regions. Toward this end, the government created several development offices (Offices de Mise en Valeur), which were primarily entrusted with the creation and development of public irrigated perimeters (collections of private agricultural lands for which the government provides and manages the irrigation facilities).

In addition, in 1978 the government created the CTDA in Kasserine, which was entrusted with development of the whole central Tunisian region. For the first time, an organization of regional development was entrusted not only with the task of administering irrigated perimeters but also with coordinating, integrating, and promoting regional activities, as well as planning and monitoring innovative development projects; the last, when proven successful, would be turned over to the line agencies for administration (RONCO 1986, 24). If successful, it was anticipated that this organization could be used as a potential model for development in other parts of Tunisia. Technically under the Ministry of Agriculture, the organization has close ties with other branches of that ministry, with local and regional offices of other ministries sharing responsibility for development, and with the Ministry of Planning. It has had financial support from the Tunisian government, the World Bank, and the USAID and is seen as something of a first effort toward the decentralization of development efforts—even though Tunisia remains a very centralized state, with all real policy decisions still made at the level of the central government.

Up until now, the major activities of the CTDA have consisted in the creation and management of irrigated perimeters, the provision of potable water to outlying areas, the construction and processing of credit applications for the digging and equipping of shallow wells, and the provision of agricultural inputs and extension services to project beneficiaries. In addition, it has coordinated the construction of some hospitals and health centers, funded some experimental projects,[2] and begun (as of 1986) to assume some responsibility for regional planning. The CTDA was given the responsibility for coordinating efforts to develop an integrated plan for the governorate that would be incorporated into Tunisia's Seventh Plan. While the general outlines of major policy directions are determined primarily at the national level, the CTDA was given the task, in cooperation with other agencies, of identifying the specific projects within the region that were deserving of consideration in the Seventh Plan. However, this chapter focuses primarily on the organization's efforts at agricultural development in the region.

The major thrust of development policy for the area has been to develop agriculture in order to increase agricultural production, promote agricultural self-sufficiency, generate more employment, and provide a standard of living in rural areas reasonable enough to stem the rural exodus to the already-overburdened cities of the coast (*La Press*, September 26, 1986; *L'Action*, September 14, 1986). Toward this end, government efforts at agricultural development (backed by international and binational development agencies such as the World Bank and the USAID) have been directed toward the development of new water resources on the one hand and a commitment to research and the provision of backup services to the farmer on the other. The development of new water resources is essential for a number of reasons: water is *the* limiting factor to agriculture in Tunisia. What limited rain falls, particularly in the dry interior and the South, is often erratic and torrential, either coming at the wrong time for the crops or coming with such force that it destroys crops and contributes more to erosion than to crop growth. In good years it will support a meager grain crop; in bad years the farmers are lucky to get enough to use for fodder. While some improvements can be made in dryland agriculture through improved varieties of grain and fodder crops or even improved natural pasture land, they are necessarily limited. Substantial increases in productivity can be brought about, however, with a shift to irrigated agriculture; and Tunisia, despite its marginal rainfall, does have underground water resources still capable of being exploited.

As a result, the government in recent years has made a heavy commitment to the promotion of irrigated agriculture. Toward this end, it has been involved in building dams, creating public irrigated perimeters (fed by deep wells constructed at government expense), and offering loans to farmers to construct private shallow wells, generally capable of irrigating 2 to 10 hectares depending on the uses to which the water is put. At the same time, it has made major efforts through the agricultural extension services to teach farmers the art of irrigated agriculture and to encourage farmers to use their water wisely and well, both from the point of view of water conservation and of growing the crops best suited to existing soils and water availability. Hence, in central Tunisia, the government has tried to promote fruit trees, fodder crops, and winter vegetables at the expense of summer vegetables, which require much more water.

Since government agencies—including those like the CTDA—have up until now been the chief developers of these resources and providers of these services, I might at this point ask just how effective government policies and programs have been in achieving government goals. As usual, the balance sheet is somewhat mixed. There is no question that water is the key to agricultural development in the region and that the government has made major strides in developing and conserving the country's water resources. In general, the government's record in providing new projects is good. The CTDA has, since beginning effective operation in 1979, irrigated some 1,000 hectares of land through the creation or operation of small public perimeters and has facilitated the creation and financing of some two thousand shallow wells (RONCO 1986, 1). In addition, the government has brought about some shift in cropping by promoting arboriculture and winter crops, and it continues to supply agricultural inputs and extension services that are sorely needed and much appreciated by the farmers.

However, the goals of attaining increased production, higher revenues, and improved standards of living are much more elusive for a number of reasons. Improvements in these areas are hard to measure because good indicators and statistics in these areas are often lacking; and in most cases adequate baseline data was not collected. It is too soon for many of these efforts to bear fruit, since trees require several years to come into production and many of the irrigated perimeters are quite new. It takes time to transform seminomadic pastoralists and cereal farmers into irrigation fruit and vegetable farmers; and there are many risks to agriculture from forces beyond the farmers' or the CTDA's control (such as hail, locusts [see Chapter 9], erratic weather, and so on). But in addition, there are a number of obstacles on the level of planning and implementation that hamstring development efforts and prevent them from being as effective as they might otherwise be. Chief among these are conflicts in goals, attitudes, and orientations and the existence of political and institutional constraints.

The differences in orientation and the lack of clear-cut success in these areas lead to frustrations on the part of both the farmers and the CTDA personnel, even though both feel that CTDA has done some good. This leads the CTDA cadre to complain about the ignorance, laziness, and noncooperation of farmers, as well as to decry the farmers "gimme" attitude. And it leads farmers to complain about the CTDA's failure to deliver on promises and the politicization of the development process.

■ Conflicting Goals, Strategies, and Orientations

What, then, are the differences in goals and orientations that complicate and undermine the effectiveness of development efforts? To begin with the national level, there is first of all the question of equity versus growth. Should the primary emphasis in development be on more equitable distribution of resources and access to services? Or should it focus on increased production and macrolevel economic growth? Obviously, the Tunisian government is interested in both. Increased equity and improving standards of living are seen as important, partly for humanitarian reasons but also to stem the rural exodus and stave off political discontent. The disadvantaged South and Center has produced more than its share of uprisings and discontent in recent years in the form of the bread riots of 1984, which originated in Kabili and Douz; the "Libyan-inspired" coup attempt in Gafsa in 1980; and labor strikes in Kasserine in the 1980s. But growth is seen as even more essential to the nation's well-being. And the growth of agricultural production is considered particularly important in order to feed cities, increase food security, lessen imports, and increase GNP.

However, in some sense, there is a conflict or contradiction between the strategies for growth and equity, because what is needed to keep people content and down on the farm is not necessarily the same as what is needed to increase agricultural efficiency and maximize production and profits. This is because the goals of, and constraints on, farmers (especially poorer farmers) are not necessarily the same as those of the state, even if both kinds of actors are *for* development.

A number of theorists (e.g., Chayanov 1966; Scott 1976) have argued that peasants (i.e., traditional farmers) have as their major goal not maximum production and profit but rather security and minimization of risk. Though they want increased production and profit also, they are not willing to assume excessive risk to get it. Therefore, they may have problems with agricultural plans and techniques that have high capital costs and uncertain returns. Instead, their security lies, or has traditionally lain, in subsistence agriculture and diversified production. Producing the bulk of their own subsistence needs protects them from fluctuations in market and supply, while crop (and income) diversification may protect them from the vagaries of weather, delayed inputs, irrigation delays, and market fluctuations in price.

Furthermore, pursuit of these goals may make different demands on capital or labor that make it impossible or undesirable to follow the agricultural technician's advice. For example, should the farmer's limited capital go into agricultural inputs or schooling for their children? Since most families see diversification of family income as the best strategy for survival, the latter may seem a better investment. And indeed, this is currently the case on the majority of small family farms, where fathers and elder daughters perform most of the agricultural work while sons seek schooling or off-farm employment.

Similarly, while technicians deplore the intercropping of trees with traditional summer vegetables (tomatoes and peppers), farmers continue to plant them because they know that there is a market, that diversification is a hedge against bad weather, and that they need to have reliable alternative sources of income until their tree crops come into full production. Farmers further irk technicians by neglecting to weed their crops. But in an economy where livestock (sheep and goats) are considered a more valuable asset and a more reliable source of income, saving the weeds for fodder is not (from the farmer's perspective) an irrational point of view. Hence, there is often a discrepancy between the goals of farmers and the government concerning optimal strategies for farm management and income generation.

■ Other Biases and Constraints

This discrepancy is further exacerbated by other biases on the part of the government and donor organizations. The government's emphasis on growth generally assumes a bias in favor of big operations over small (in order to achieve economies of scale); high-capital, high-technology agriculture over more labor-intensive forms; and a drive for privatization and economic liberalization, which is thought to promote competition and efficiency. This approach, however, is often at odds with the resources and needs of smaller farmers and ignores the hidden costs and difficulties of maintaining that kind of agriculture under local conditions. In particular, the foreign exchange costs of importing machinery and the difficulty of getting replacement parts means that even large, mechanized operations often encounter shutdowns or delays that leave them operating at less-than-optimal efficiency.

Another reason why the Tunisian government and international donors favor big projects over small and construction and infrastructure over education and technical training is that they are easier and cheaper to administer, have high visibility, and are easier to evaluate and assess. Consider, for example, the difference between trying to evaluate whether a hundred wells were built versus those of determining whether a hundred small farmers profited from agricultural extension. As such, the big, technical projects make a bigger splash vis-à-vis the many political constituencies that need to be placated or impressed (whether we are talking about Tunisian public opinion or U.S. officials).

High-tech biases are also reflected in the organization, training, and recruitment of a cadre for the CTDA. This cadre consists mainly of specialized technicians. Some have little direct practical experience in agriculture; and some may have little vocation for agriculture, since grades, rather than dedication, determine the specialty one goes into and many are willing to settle for any government job to take advantage of the security that it provides. In addition, training is often based on techniques and norms that may not have been tested under local and real farm conditions (e.g., some yield estimates are based on European or laboratory norms); and the agricultural staff is, by virtue of their training, biased in the direction of their specialties rather than a whole-farm approach.[3] This emphasis on technical specialties, plus the lack of field experience, means that technicians often lack an adequate understanding of the real constraints under which farmers operate. Hence, they become frustrated when farmers, under pressure to balance off their limited capital and labor resources against the needs of family and different crops, fail to conform to the optimal technical specifications for any one crop. These biases are further exacerbated by a preference for top-down, authoritative, centralized planning rather than a planning capability that is more pragmatic, flexible, and responsive to field-oriented strategies and bottom-up types of concerns.

Finally, there is the problem of political and bureaucratic constraints that impede the flow of information upward, since the organization produces statistics that are desirable but not empirically grounded in order to safeguard their careers, get promotions, and curry favor with the powers that be. This leads to an avoidance of risk and responsibility at the lower levels, and feeds into the already-existing bias in favor of centralized, top-down planning. In addition, the politicization of the development process has repercussions at the farmer level as well. Because the distribution of benefits to farmers (in the form of credit, demonstration plots, subsidized inputs to agriculture, etc.) is a highly politicized process (local party officials often draw up the lists of potential beneficiaries), some farmers are encouraged to think of benefits as "free" and to play the game of courting political connections rather than buckling down to work or assuming full responsibility for their agricultural operations—hence the "gimme" attitude so often attributed to the farmers by the CTDA cadre.

The factors cited above, in turn, lead to planning and implementation of projects that are not finely enough tuned to local conditions. While technicians think in terms of the vocation of the land (e.g., this land should be devoted to trees) and get annoyed when farmers intercrop tree crops with water-intensive vegetables, farmers need to live year-round, live until the trees produce, and survive bad years when the climate is unfavorable or market prices low. Therefore, planning to be effective must take this into account. In other words, planning and implementation would be better if planners and technicians were more empirically and pragmatically oriented, paid more attention to local conditions and constraints, and were better able to cast off the need to tailor information to what they think their superiors want to hear.

■ Conclusions

Free market and statist economies have different strengths and weaknesses. Capitalist economies are generally good at stimulating macrolevel production and growth, but they are not so good at seeing that the benefits are distributed equitably. Socialist or statist regimes and economies, on the other hand, are better at resolving issues of equity but are not so good at production and growth. The question, then, is how to arrive at a satisfactory resolution of this dilemma.

This is not a definitive answer, but it seems that an ideal system would want to incorporate elements of both; that is, it would need to allow sufficient incentives for initiative and competition but at the same time provide opportunities (credit, training, skills, and so on) and safety nets to those who do not have equal access to the opportunities available under the free market system. Particularly for Tunisia, it may be cheaper for the government to provide these resources in the countryside rather than to bear the political, economic, and social costs of having large numbers of unemployed migrants in the city.

For this reason, the current efforts and zeal, under pressure from the IMF and USAID, to restructure and liberalize the Tunisian economy as a solution to all Tunisia's ills need to be looked at with a cautious eye. Though one can find much fault with Tunisia's bureaucratic and statist system, it is nevertheless true that government organizations have provided much-needed services. And despite the many problems in development planning and implementation outlined, rural beneficiaries of government services and projects in areas such as Central Tunisia are better off than they were before (Larson 1986, 1987).

While it undoubtedly will benefit Tunisia's economy to be freed from some of the bureaucratic bloat and unduly restrictive controls, one should remember that not all segments of society will benefit equally from such measures; and the political and economic cost of throwing out the baby with the bathwater may be high. Increased GNP is not synonymous with development, and trickle-down theories have rarely worked.[4] Hence, one would hope that Tunisia would not proceed so far down the path of privatization that the needs of the less advantaged in society are forgotten.

■ Notes

1. For men between the ages of ten and thirty the illiteracy rates are 19 to 31 percent in Kasserine Governorate versus 9 to 17 percent nationally; for women the comparable figures are 49 to 70 percent versus 25 to 40 percent (INS statistics). Overall, illiteracy rates are 45.6 percent for men and 75.7 percent for

women in Kasserine versus 34.6 percent and 58.1 percent in the country as a whole (RONCO 1986, Appendix D, 6).

2. These are intended to generate and test new ideas that if successful, might later be picked up and duplicated by other government agencies. Examples of such projects are establishing mother-and-child centers, creating small-scale mat factories using local products, using oil press residues to stabilize dirt roads, and using windmills to run irrigation pumps.

3. This, however, was beginning to change as of 1987, when a new whole-farm approach was just in the first stages of being formulated.

4. Even in the contemporary United States, statistics indicate a rising gap between rich and poor and no growth in real average family income over the last fifteen years despite the fact that there has been overall growth in the economy (*Christian Science Monitor* September 2, 1988; *New York Times* May 1, 1989), while elsewhere in the developing world, in countries such as Egypt and China, efforts to liberalize the economy have also led to growing inequality.

9

The Desert Locust: Agricultural and Environmental Impacts

Christopher S. Potter
Allan T. Showler

Locusts have been an adversary of the African farmer since cultivation began. Historical plagues were reportedly capable of migrating hundreds of miles a day and devouring 100,000 metric tons of vegetation at each resting place (Pedgley 1981, 65; Steedman 1988, 4). The desert locust (*Schistocerca gregaria* Forskål) has returned to North Africa many times over the centuries. Each time locust populations have increased to plague proportions with swarms up to 20 miles long, entire cash crop harvests in Morocco, Algeria, and Tunisia are suddenly placed at risk of destruction.

North Africa is a major food-producing region on the continent (Steiner et al. 1988, 90). National governments are compelled to protect valuable cash and food crops from the menace of locust swarms, since millions of dollars in agricultural revenue are at stake. From a modern crop protection perspective, Tunisia's wheat and barley crops are particularly susceptible to desert locust invasions during the early summer harvest when locusts can attack plant stems and cause total grain loss in affected areas (Steedman 1988, 6). Fruit trees are also vulnerable to attack by immature desert locust swarms, which can completely defoliate citrus trees and subsequently affect fruit yields for years afterward. Similarly, large tracts of rangeland can be lost within days.

In early 1988, for the first time in almost thirty years, desert locust swarms entered Tunisia and threatened to cause significant agricultural losses. In response to desert locust invasions, the government of Tunisia, with assistance from donors, launched a large-scale emergency locust control campaign to save agricultural and livestock production. The decision to use pesticides against desert locusts in Tunisia was made primarily on the basis of immediate regional political necessity, rather than long-term, environmentally sound crop protection strategies. Internal pressure from Tunisian agriculturalists and lack of alternatives to chemical controls made pesticide use the only viable option for rapidly combatting desert locust swarms. To date, little attention has been focused on the long-term environmental impacts of pesticides on the natural resource base that supports agricultural production in Tunisia.

The objective of this chapter is to examine the potential adverse human health and environmental impacts of antilocust pesticide application practices in Tunisia. A description of desert locust population dynamics in Africa is reviewed and basic desert locust biology is outlined. Current accounting of the potential agronomic costs and benefits of the 1988 Tunisian Locust Control Campaign (TLCC) are examined. Finally, implications of chemical desert locust control are suggested, in light of trade-offs between environmental and crop protection tactics.[1]

■ Recent Desert Locust History

Early in the summer of 1987, desert locust swarms invaded Niger following migrations from the Sudan and Chad. Extensive breeding also occurred in northern Mali and Mauritania. In October, desert locust swarms moved northwest across the Sahara into Morocco and Algeria (Showler and Maynard 1988, 10). Swarms moving into western Tunisia were first sighted in February 1988, and relatively successful crop protection measures were conducted by Tunisian farmers and Crop Protection Service (CPS) personnel (Khoury et al. 1989, 12).

Climatic conditions are thought to be the major factors that govern desert locust outbreaks in Africa (Pedgley 1981, 32; Steedman 1988, 34). During the summer of 1988, rainfall in the Sahel provided unusually favorable breeding conditions (moist soils coupled with warm temperatures) for desert locust populations, which permitted reproduction and survival of two overlapping generations and a significant increase in the overall desert locust population size. On prevailing fall winds, desert locust populations moved from the Sahel to North Africa to commence winter breeding.

Predominant easterly winds in November 1988 forced most desert locust swarms into Mali, Mauritania, Senegal, and the Gambia from the eastern and central Sudan. Dry conditions at the end of the rainy season, combined with southerly winds, instigated swarm movement northward to Morocco and Algeria. Effective control efforts, consisting of large-scale terrestrial and aerial pesticide applications in Morocco, Senegal, Mauritania, Algeria, and Tunisia halted further eastward migration of desert locust swarms. In addition, cool, dry North African weather that dominated the region in the second half of November 1988 through January 1989 mitigated desert locust activity. Before the decline in desert locust activity in early 1989, S. gregaria had spread, at one time or another, to the leeward Caribbean Islands, Cape Verde, the Sahara, North Africa, the Sudan, Ethiopia, Somalia, the Arabian Peninsula, Jordan, Iraq, Iran, and Afghanistan.

■ Desert Locust Biology

The life cycle of the desert locust involves eight stages: egg, five nymphal instars, fledgling, and adult. Ovipositing by sexually mature adults occurs in damp soil. The eggs, deposited in frothy pods, absorb soil moisture and develop to the larval stage over a period of ten to thirty days, depending on the soil temperature. The nymphs, also known as hoppers, emerge from the soil and go through a series of five molts. Hoppers are incapable of flight, and may begin to move about on the ground or roost on vertical surfaces in progressively larger groups called hopper bands (Pedgley 1981, 8; Lecoq 1988, 80). When environmental conditions lead to an increase in the number of locusts crowded together in bands, these insects have the remarkable ability to alter their color, behavior, shape, and physiology (Steedman 1988, 21). Locusts can therefore exist in different *phases*, either solitary or gregarious (swarming). Solitary desert locusts inhabit most of the Sahel and Northern Africa and normally pose little threat to agricultural production (Lecoq 1988, 78; Steedman 1988, 21). Gregarious desert locusts, on the other hand, migrate in swarms and can consume enormous amounts of vegetation.

When hoppers complete their final molt, they become sexually immature adults capable of flight. Immature adults are pink in color and have relatively soft body parts. Locusts become sexually mature in a few weeks to several months, depending on environmental conditions. Mature adults, on the other hand, are yellow in color. As locusts of mixed ages fly together in large groups, mature adults will break away from the swarm and begin egglaying in suitably moist soil (20 millimeters of rainfall is sufficient) while immature members of the swarm fly on to continue feeding. The success of adult desert locust survival relies upon the existence of green vegetation scattered throughout the Sahel and North Africa (Pedgley 1981, 17). The life span of an adult desert locust in the field varies from two to five months (Steedman 1988, 21). Information on the mechanisms of phase transformation (gregarization), swarm dynamics, and pheromonal communication, however, is scant. Research continues on control-related efforts including surveillance, biorational insecticides, more effective and environmentally sound alternative insecticides and application techniques, forecasting, and crop loss assessment (Appleby, Settle, and Showler 1989, Annex IV, 1–21; Showler 1989a, 1–5).

■ Desert Locust Control Strategies in Tunisia

Under plague conditions, desert locust invasions into Tunisia are expected to come either from the Southwest via Algeria or from the Southeast via Libya. The Tunisian Plant Protection Operational Plan for 1988–1989 described only the southwestern invasion scenario and lacked recognition of the possibility of a southeastern desert locust arrival. A southeastern invasion is, in fact, likely if gregarious swarms developed in the Sudan and northern Chad and adult desert locusts moved in a northwesterly direction with prevailing winds.

In 1988 Tunisia was invaded by desert locust swarms along two principal corridors that began at the Algerian border (near Tebessa) in the West and continued along topographic boundaries, one centered on the central Tunisian city of Kasserine, and the other just south of Gafsa. These areas may be categorized as arid-to-semiarid steppe with annual vegetation occurring for approximately six weeks during and soon after the winter rains. Livestock grazing (principally sheep, goats, and camels) occurs wherever forage is available. Central Tunisia is a favorable feeding habitat for migratory desert locust swarms. In the spring of 1988 swarms continued to move northeast, diagonally across Tunisia to Kairouan and Tunis. From Kairouan, some swarms moved north to Cap Bon (a major agricultural area) and even reached the shores of southern Italy. The desert locusts that had escaped control along the Gafsa corridor traveled as far as Sfax on the southeastern Mediterranean shore. There were two major infestation periods: all governorates except Gabes and Soussi received insecticide treatments from late March to April 10; Gafsa, Kasserine, and Kairouan were also treated from April 17 to April 25.

The 1988–1989 desert locust control strategy developed by the Tunisian CPS described two main lines of defense against swarm invasion. The "lines" are actually loosely linked regional zones organized around major urban centers that serve as points of dispersal for ground crew and aircraft pesticide treatment teams. The first line, extending from Le Kef to Kasserine, Gafsa, Tozeur, Kebili, and Tatahouine was designed to protect the country from desert locust invasions coming either from the South or the West. The second line of defense was located along the Beja—Siliana—Sidi Bouzid—Gabes—Medenine axis and was established to protect crops from desert locust swarms that escaped control from the first line (Khoury et al. 1989, 9).

The Tunisian government had several response options to desert locust invasions, including (1) no action, (2) nonchemical control/mechanical destruction, (3) biological control, (4) chemical control, and (5) integrated pest management (IPM) (TAMS/CICP 1989, D21). However, each of these options, except chemical control, offered little promise for crop protection. Taking no action in the face of desert locust invasions allows infestations to run their natural course. The country would have to depend on cold and/or dry weather to halt the insects. Some desert locust breeding would be inevitable, although North African environments are not ideal for long-term desert locust reproduction, due to periodic low temperatures (Khoury et al. 1989, 12; Showler and Maynard 1988, 13). A decision not to act is considered by many to be morally irresponsible due to the ever-present threat of malnutrition and famine in Africa and is politically unpopular in a chiefly agrarian nation where crop production is considered vital.

Nonchemical control consists of crushing or burning adult desert locusts after they have landed on vegetation—or, in the event that hoppers emerge, directing hopper bands into trenches for mass burial. These measures are labor-intensive and considered by many crop protection experts to be inadequate during desert locust plagues, when billions of adults must be destroyed within a few hours. Although local farmers often attempt to discourage desert locust swarms with smoke, such efforts are generally ineffective.

Effective methods of biological control for desert locust have not been adequately researched. One major limitation to the study of natural desert locust predators and parasites is that locusts are only present in sufficient numbers for scientific study purposes (particularly with reference to the gregarious phase) as highly mobile swarms. When swarms arrive, the primary concern of farmers, crop protection specialists, and decisionmakers is control, not research. Further, when desert locusts exist in relatively small population numbers indicative of their solitary phase, biocontrol research is often impractical due to the tendency of solitary desert locusts to live in remote and often inaccessible areas of Mauritania, northern Chad, Niger, Mali, and the Sudan, which are known as traditional desert locust recession areas between major population resurgences. In addition to peculiarities of the terrain, the growing environmental concern of some African nations regarding toxic wastes has, ironically, hindered field-testing of biorational pesticides (i.e., *Nosema locustae*; Appleby, Settle, and Showler 1989, Annex IV, 8). Efforts to conduct research on the development of biopesticides, nevertheless, are now underway in some countries and the Government of Tunisia has expressed interest in conducting field trials using *Nosema locustae*.

Despite the potential of biological control, chemical pesticides remain the politically popular choice in Tunisia for desert locust control. The government has used the following insecticides in its 1988 desert locust control program: malathion ultralow volume (ULV), fenitrothion ULV, deltamethrin (trade name Decis), and benzene hexachloride (BHC). The contemporary TLCC includes a mixture of modern treatment techniques, such as handpump sprayers, gasoline-powered backpack sprayers, vehicle-mounted mist blowers and exhaust nozzle systems, and ULV aerial application from rotary- and fixed-wing platforms. The method applied in each particular instance depends on an array of site-specific factors, including the time of day that locusts arrive, desert locust life stage, swarm size, air temperature, wind speed, topography, and logistical constraints.

The final option, IPM, consists of employing a coordinated combination of control techniques, including chemical, biological, and cultural methods in an economically and ecologically sound program that makes maximum use of surveillance in order to prevent or control pest outbreaks at the earliest possible stage. In the case of desert locust control, IPM would consist of a combination of available biological and chemical control technologies, provided that the former methods had been adequately developed. Greenness maps, produced by satellite remote sensors, can be useful in future IPM programs for indicating vegetated areas where desert locust swarms may settle, roost, and breed. This technique streamlines survey efforts considerably (Appleby, Settle, and Showler 1989, Annex IV, 11). However, until an organism such as *Nosema* is proven effective against the desert locust, chemical pesticides will be the mainstay of the Tunisian anti–desert locust arsenal.

■ Crop Loss Assessment

There is a great deal of guesswork involved in estimating the potential damage that locusts might inflict upon the agricultural sector (Appleby, Settle, and Showler 1989, Annex IV, 17–20). The last major desert locust infestation in North Africa before 1987–1989 occurred thirty years ago. Actions taken in the late 1950s in response to locusts centered on chemical control to prevent crop damage, rather than research to estimate locust-related crop losses. The same plant protection priorities existed in 1988, with relatively little investment for assessing overall costs and benefits of pesticide applications in the context of potential impacts on agriculture in North Africa. For the time being, generally accepted figures are available only on the amounts of vegetation locusts can consume in a given time period, so that it is possible to construct a worst-case scenario for annual desert locust injury to annual crop production.

Locusts consume a wide range of plant parts, including leaves, fruits, seeds, and bark. Many crops are subject to desert locust attack, such as cereals, citrus, fruits, vegetables, and even pines (Potter 1988, 9; Steedman 1988, 6). In Tunisia, therefore, nearly all crop items are at risk during large infestations. Each individual desert locust is capable of eating its own weight (ca. 2 grams) in food every day. To put this consumption rate into perspective, it is estimated that a relatively small desert locust swarm (made up of approximately half a million insects) can consume as much food in one day as an average village of twenty-five hundred people (Steedman 1988, 4).

Historical estimates of crop damage caused by desert locust swarms provide a framework for evaluating potential annual agricultural losses in Tunisia during the 1980s and beyond. Examples from Africa include Ethiopia, which lost 167,000 metric tons of grain during the 1958 locust invasion, an amount sufficient to feed one million people for one year (Steedman 1988, 3). This represents an annual crop loss of approximately thirty-eight million dollars of wheat or barley, based on recent commodity prices in Tunisia (INS 1987). In another instance, the value of all crops lost in Morocco in 1954–1955 due to locust invasions has been put at approximately seventy million dollars (Steedman 1988, 3).

To construct the scenario for potential crop losses in the absence of chemical control efforts in Tunisia, a hypothetical situation must be constructed. Official figures for potential desert locust crop damage in 1988 have yet to be made available. In fact, such figures may be impossible to calculate, due to the lack of documentation on desert locust movements and crop damage assessments. Furthermore, a major drought in 1987–1988 reduced grain yields dramatically (*Le Temps-Hebdo* [Tunis], November 21, 1988, 4). The amount of vegetation available to desert locust swarms was therefore below that of production years with average rainfall.

Nevertheless, a reasonable estimate of desert locust impacts on the Tunisian grain harvest during a hypothetical year can be constructed. If one assumes that the heaviest desert locust infestations come in the central and southern portions of the country around the cities of Kasserine and Gafsa, as they did in spring 1988 (Khoury et al. 1989, 9), a total of about 552,000 hectares devoted to grain production would be at risk to locust damage. This surface area is less than the maximum amount of land that the CPS was prepared to treat in 1988 (approximately 1,000,000 hectares—Khoury et al. 1989, 9). Converting area cultivated to crop production, the net worth of grain that could be easily lost to desert locust consumption during such an invasion equals about twenty-nine million dollars (INS 1987).

To put these potential losses into perspective, the amount of arable land devoted to grain cultivation in Tunisia was approximately 1,363,000 hectares in 1986 (INS 1987). This harvest normally represents seventy-two million dollars of net annual cereal production. Under the scenario presented above, Tunisia could lose 40 percent of its yearly wheat and barley production if desert locust swarms were not controlled and they completely consumed grain crops in the principal infestation zones of the central and southern regions.

Looking at potential crop losses due to desert locust impacts in another context, Tunisia received between 59,000 and 210,000 metric tons of food aid annually from 1972 to 1984 (Food and Agriculture Organization 1985). These figures represent from fourteen to forty-eight million dollars per year of grain donated by the international community. It is therefore reasonable to conclude that desert locust swarms are capable of consuming a cereal harvest equivalent in value to the current annual food aid received by Tunisia.

■ Costs of the Tunisian Locust Control Campaign

The costs of modern crop protection include expenses for surveillance (vehicles, scouts), pesticides (purchase, transport, storage, and handling), aerial treatment (aircraft, fuel, pilots, ground crew, and spotters, posttreatment survey teams, and protective equipment), ground treatment (vehicles, crew, sprayers, protective equipment), the salaries of local and national coordinators, and special technical inputs (meteorological and satellite data). The costs of conducting effective desert locust control is between fifteen and thirty dollars per hectare treated, a range that includes local inputs and varies with equipment and labor costs in a given country (FEWS 1987; TAMS/CICP 1989, D83). The Tunisian government reported that approximately 360,000 hectares were treated for desert locust swarms in 1988 (Khoury et al. 1989, p. 9). The scenario presented in the previous section therefore reflects the level of effort needed for desert locust control under heavy plague conditions. If the Government of Tunisia effectively treated to protect the 552,000 hectares of grain mentioned above (effective treatment means killing at least 90 percent of target locusts), the annual control costs would range from about eight to seventeen million dollars. Compared to the potential savings in grain harvests (ca. twenty-nine million dollars), chemical control of locusts would result in a net yearly saving of between twelve and twenty-one million dollars in cereal production alone.

It should be stressed, however, that the net benefits of desert locust control shown here are only rough monetary estimates and do not include potentially adverse environmental effects of chemical insecticides on humans, livestock, and wildlife. Such impacts are extremely difficult to quantify in economic terms. The following sections review potential negative environmental consequences of the 1988 TLCC.

■ Impacts on the Human Population

The two insecticides that were most commonly used against desert locust swarms in Tunisia, malathion and fenitrothion, are only moderately toxic to humans if applied properly (TAMS/CICP 1989, E75); and, fortunately, control operations for the most part have been conducted in uninhabited areas or rangeland, where public exposure was minimal (Potter 1988, 16). Both chemicals are degraded relatively quickly in the environment; residues cannot be detected in soil or water after about one week following application

(Dynamac Corporation 1988, v.). If such pesticides are applied prudently so that population centers are avoided, humans heed warnings not to eat treated locusts, and pesticide handlers adopt precautionary measures, human health impacts following desert locust control operations can be reduced.

Accurate information on the adverse effects of pesticides on human populations is scarce in developing countries. For instance, the highly toxic and persistent organochlorine compound BHC was applied as a dust formulation in the Gafsa area in 1988 (Potter 1988, 22). Although human toxification has not yet been reported by the Tunisian government, the potential seriousness of this situation merits further attention. Benzene hexachloride is not approved for use in the United States and is known to accumulate in the human liver and fat cells much like DDT (p. 22). Benzene hexachloride dust was used in Tunisia after stocks of malathion and other relatively nonpersistent pesticides were exhausted. Unfortunately, there are no medical testing programs in place to monitor pesticide exposure to the human population; nor are there any emergency mobile units available to treat toxification in a timely manner (p. 26).

Proper safety guidelines have yet to be fully developed at many local pesticide storage and handling facilities in Tunisia. The authors have personally observed that pesticide handlers do not always wear protective clothing (plastic gloves, boots, coveralls, respirators, goggles, and hats) during transport and application operations. In addition, pesticide storage practices often do not meet the requirements for proper shading and upright storage, which may lead to pesticide stock degradation, drum overheating, and leakage. Contingency plans for pesticide spills should also be considered a priority concern. Pesticide storage facilities do not always have running water within easy access, making emergency washing in the event of an accident difficult. Training of handlers and improvement of physical plants are needed in most rural areas, where adequate knowledge of precautions for safe pesticide use is rare.

Disposal of spent pesticide containers is another issue that must be addressed by the Government of Tunisia and other locust-affected nations. At the minimum, these drums should be punctured and crushed, a practice that requires only an ax and a truck. There were, nevertheless, over four hundred empty, intact pesticide drums reported by USAID officials as of December 1988. This situation poses a human health hazard if empty drums are used by local people to hold food or water. The authors have observed empty pesticide drums often left unattended at airstrips, inviting public theft and misuse. To complicate matters, the government has proposed the implementation of a farmer-run, collective desert locust control campaign, in which rural inhabitants would treat swarms with small spray devices. This plan is highly impractical from logistic and safety perspectives because the collective campaign has not planned for proper farmer training in pesticide handling and could increase the risk of pesticide misuse. For example, regular washing of pesticide residues from clothing presents a practically insurmountable problem in many rural areas, where water sources are often tens of kilometers distant from farms and bathing is a relatively low-priority use for scarce water supplies.

Finally, it appears that the efficiency of pesticide treatments against desert locusts during the spring 1988 locust control campaign was often lower (60-to-70-percent mortality) than could be reasonably expected (at least 90-percent mortality) if the pesticides were applied properly. The low desert locust mortality rate commonly resulted in insecticide dose increases and/or repeated applications in certain areas to achieve effective control (Potter 1988, 17). There is justifiable concern among international donors that overspraying could occur again, particularly in the event of unexpected reinvasions.

■ Impacts on the Natural Environment

Pesticide applications in Tunisia occur against a backdrop of widespread natural ecosystem degradation. The country covers an area of approximately 16,000,000 hectares. Climatic conditions vary greatly throughout the country, with annual rainfall ranging from a few millimeters in the South to over 1,500 millimeters in the northern mountains. Consequently, Tunisia is an amalgam of ecosystems, including Mediterranean coastal zones, wetlands, islands, mountains, steppes, deserts, and oases. Major environmental concerns in Tunisia are water and air pollution in coastal zones, wetlands drainage for irrigation, deforestation, overgrazing of rangelands, desertification, erosion, and destruction of critical habitats for endangered species (Posner 1988, iv).

Tunisia has an essentially arid or semiarid climate, with moderate winters and hot, dry summers. Most of the precipitation occurs between October and April, with very little rainfall between June and September (Arid Land Information Center 1980). About 35 percent of Tunisia's labor force is involved in agriculture, a critical sector in the Tunisian economy (Posner 1988, 2). Nearly 25 percent of Tunisia's land is cultivated, with grazing on most uncultivated or undeveloped land. Major activities include cultivation of wheat, barley, olives, and citrus fruit (covering 70 percent of all arable land) or raising sheep, goats, cattle, and camels.

Forests cover about 680,000 hectares, less than 270,000 hectares of which are in their natural (relatively undegraded) condition (Posner 1988, 194). The remainder of the forested areas are occupied by plantations and *marquis* (woody shrub associations). Major forest types include *thuya* (*Callitris articulata*, 30,000 hectares), cork oak (*Quercus suber*, 80,000 hectares), and aleppo pine (*Pinus halipensis*, 200,000 hectares). In the past decade, Tunisia suffered a loss of over 13,000 hectares of forested land per year. At the current rate of deforestation, Tunisian woodlands could disappear altogether in less than a century (p. 198).

Tunisia is a country dedicated to environmental protection and conservation of great biological diversity, as evidenced by its role as a signatory nation to the World Heritage Convention (1975), the Ramsar Convention (1976), and the Barcelona Convention (1977), all of which endorsed international conservation efforts. Tunisia has five established national parks, two proposed parks, and nine protected reserves (Posner 1988, v). One of the goals of the national park program is to set aside an area representing each of Tunisia's major ecosystems. Nongovernmental sources have recommended the establishment of nineteen additional protected areas. The Ministry of Agriculture is responsible for administration and management of protected areas.

Definitive information on the current status of the flora and fauna of Tunisia, however, is not readily available; and little is known about the distribution of endangered species. Nevertheless, habitat loss from overgrazing, depletion of forests, and other nonsustainable resource uses have led to severe ecosystem degradation and are thought to result in serious detrimental impacts on indigenous species (Posner 1988, iv). In addition, Tunisia's coastal wetlands, particularly along the Mediterranean Sea, are fragile and provide important habitats for migrating and wintering waterfowl from Europe, as well as several indigenous species.

With the arrival of desert locust swarms, pesticide application has been superimposed on Tunisia's environmental degradation problem. Aerial application of pesticides can cover hundreds of square kilometers per treatment. If spraying occurs during moderate-to-high-wind-speed conditions, insecticide can drift well beyond the intended treatment zone into protected and fragile ecosystems already under human-imposed environmental stress.

Animals, including humans, can be exposed to pesticides either directly through dermal contact or indirectly by ingestion of contaminated vegetation or animal prey. It appears that several nontarget organisms were affected by chemical applications during the spring 1988 TLCC (Potter 1988, 18). No major environmental perturbations were observed, but several incidents of accidental animal poisoning have been reported. Tunisian CPS officials reported that the most dramatic case of animal mortality occurred near Tozeur; thirty sheep died after having grazed in pesticide-contaminated rangeland. The pesticide involved in the poisoning is not known. Several reports of gazelle mortality were noted in November 1988 but were not confirmed by CPS representatives. It is difficult to conduct accurate gazelle population counts, due to the inaccessible terrain and the presence of scavengers (hyenas and vultures) that rapidly remove carcasses.

Several pesticide treatments were carried out in or near fragile wetlands and oases during the spring 1988 desert locust invasions. Deltamethrin, a pyrethroid pesticide, was used to control locusts in the Al-Faouar oasis near Kebili. There were also treatments on the edge of Ibn Chabat oasis near Tozeur. Effects of these treatments on nontarget organisms are unknown. Tunisia's oasis ecosystems are, however, intensively cultivated and extremely fragile due to a dependence on scarce water sources at the edge of the Sahara. All pesticides used in desert locust control in Tunisia are considered toxic to aquatic life, and contamination of irrigation systems could seriously affect the oasis ecosystem productivity. The Tunisian government has, in a prudent policy decision, prohibited future anti–desert locust pesticide applications in oases.

In addition to oasis protection, the Government of Tunisia has expressed particular concern that substantial damage to apiculture efforts occurred during anti–desert locust pesticide applications. The pesticides most frequently used by the CPS are known to cause 75 to 100 percent mortality of honeybee colonies if applied in proximity to foraging worker bees (Potter 1988, 19). If allowed to continue, the impacts of pesticides on insect pollinated crops could be substantial. Apiculture is an important economic activity in northern and central Tunisia, providing supplemental income for many small farmers. Modern beekeeping is practiced in the Cap Bon and Beja areas, while a mixture of modern and traditional apiculture is common over much of the mountainous and steppe zones. Flowers of citrus, eucalyptus, and rosemary are primary nectar and pollen sources for honeybees. It appears, however, that during the 1988 anti–desert locust campaign beekeepers were not always warned in advance of pesticide applications, especially in the northwest and central zones of the country; nor was technical information on protective measures for colonies disseminated. Unless a large-scale educational campaign to protect beekeeping is organized before the next desert locust invasion, the Tunisian apiculture industry at the small-farm level, already weakened by drought and disease, could be debilitated for years to come.

It is conceivable that all endangered animal species will be at risk from exposure to pesticides during the next TLCC, due to the absence of an official policy to avoid pesticide treatments in most fragile and protected areas. Tunisia's emphasis on desert locust control regardless of environmental consequences is not consistent with the country's stated commitments to environmental protection as per its several international conservation agreements. Aerial and ground application of insecticides will continue to have unavoidable, possibly significant, deleterious effects on some nontarget organisms, including desert locust predators and parasites; pollinators and other agriculturally beneficial insects; birds; and possibly even fish, amphibians, and mammals. It is likely that insecticides will continue to be applied near some or all of Tunisia's protected and/or sensitive ecological areas. In cases where treatment does occur, judicious and carefully executed application is vital. Biological monitoring of impacts on nontarget organisms is an important component of future control efforts (Showler 1989b, 1), and the results of these studies should feed back into overall management of the desert locust control program.

■ Future Prospects

Cool weather in December 1988 and January 1989 reduced desert locust activity and minimized further invasions into Tunisia from Algeria. The hurricane in fall 1988 swept a tremendous desert locust population from West Africa into the Atlantic but resulted in no major impacts on Central American island nations where locusts were deposited. In early 1989, conditions for reproduction and survival became less favorable across the Sudan. A relatively cold North African winter, combined with zealous human intervention in Morocco and Algeria, contributed to the recent demise of desert locust activity in North Africa. It should be emphasized, however, that should Sahelian conditions change to support concentrated desert locust populations, the plague could begin anew.

The concept of "strategic control" (Appleby, Settle, and Showler 1989, Annex II, 9) has been embraced by the Maghrib countries as the best approach to controlling locusts in Africa and certainly represents the most promising means of long-term protection of both crop lands and natural ecosystems. This effort would necessarily involve an internationally coordinated approach to killing locusts before they become gregarious. Most of the major desert locust breeding areas, however, are located in remote and often inaccessible regions of Sahelian nations (i.e., the Adrar des Iforas of Mali, the Air Mountains of Niger, northern Mauritania, and the Red Sea Hills of the Sudan). Many of the Sahelian governments have indicated that because the breeding areas do not immediately threaten their own agricultural production (primarily located in the southern portions of each respective country), strategic control is not their sole responsibility. The fact that desert locust populations can move from the breeding areas to neighboring nations provides a rational for this stance. Most of the Sahelian nations that harbor breeding grounds, ironically, will not permit cross-boarder control operations by adjacent countries. Unmanaged desert locust populations in such breeding areas can produce gregarious swarms that are capable of affecting the entire northern African region, given favorable climatic conditions. Thus, regional control is mandatory, and aid should be provided to Sahelian countries with breeding areas to preposition equipment, pesticides, and personnel more effectively for timely anti–desert locust action (Appleby, Settle, and Showler 1989, Annex II, 16).

Although this approach holds promise, there are still many political obstacles to enacting strategic control. These include (1) close international cooperation among all donors and host country governments of the Sahel and North Africa; (2) willingness among the Maghrib nations to divert pesticides and aircraft from domestic crop protection to hopper control in Sahelian nations; and (3) resolution of military and political conflicts in areas where locusts are likely to breed in order to reduce the danger to pilots and ground control specialists operating in politically sensitive areas. The prospects of alleviating these problems, however, appear scant in the foreseeable future.

In conclusion, the decision to use chemical control in Tunisia to combat desert locust invasions should be continually reevaluated in light of estimated crop protection benefits and potentially adverse environmental impacts. The effects of pesticides on the environment can be serious in any nation, especially in a country such as Tunisia, where natural resources are rapidly deteriorating due to growing population pressures. During prior desert locust plagues in Africa, decisions to use pesticides have been made in the absence of the knowledge of realistic crop loss assessments. This need not be the case in Tunisia in the 1990s and beyond. The Tunisian government is well informed; and adequate information, albeit approximate, now exists upon which to base environmentally sound policy decisions concerning the net benefits of pesticide use. Policymakers worldwide have the responsibility of educating themselves and the public on the environmental and health impacts of pesticides. Only then can all the costs and benefits of locust control be assessed in the context of sustainable development for Tunisia.

■ Notes

1. The authors wish to acknowledge the contribution of the members of the 1988 AID locust control technical assistance teams to Tunisia: H. Corn, C. Heming, H. Khoury, A. Messer, H. Moore, R. Stiliha, R. Thibeault, and J. Walker. Thanks also to L. Mammel for critical review of an earlier version of the manuscript. The Government of Tunisia kindly provided much of the information upon which this paper is based. The views expressed herein are those of the authors, and do not necessarily represent the position of AAAS, AID, or the U.S. Government.

PART 3
SOCIAL RESISTANCE

10

Islamic Reform in Contemporary Tunisia: Unity and Diversity

Douglas K. Magnuson

This chapter will highlight the results of three years of anthropological research in Tunisia, focusing on three groups—the Group of the Call and Communication (jama't al-da'wa wa al-tabligh, or the Da'wa), the Movement of the Islamic Way (harakat al-ittajah al-islami), and the Progressive Islamicists (al-islamiyun al-taqaddumiyun)—actively undertaking to reform Islam there.[1]

There are two central concerns. One is the issue of unity and diversity within a religious tradition, which will be approached by showing how three Islamic groups that began within the same broad movement (to return to Islamic roots) in a single Muslim society have over a period of time diversified, carving out for themselves unique identities as Islamic reformers by variously drawing upon the symbols which constitute formal, scriptural Islam. Their different understandings of what is wrong with Islam in Tunisia and what needs to be done to rectify the situation, their central reform concepts and activities, and other group distinctions will be presented.

The other main concern is the issue of comparing and classifying groups within the broad category of Islamic reform, in terms that are as true as possible to the groups themselves. A framework for comparing these three groups that is more data-sensitive than those prevalent in recent writings on Islamic reformism, will be used.

■ **The History of Islamic Reform in Contemporary Tunisia**

The beginning of the 1970s in Tunisia witnessed a stirring of Islamic forces that had been quiescent for some time. The Neo-Destour party of Habib Bourguiba, from its beginnings in the early 1930s, was committed to a Western–secular path of modernization. In the years after Independence (1956)

Bourguiba embarked on a series of bold initiatives of religious reform affecting law, family life, education, and personal religious practice.

His disassembling of the infrastructure of institutional Islam in Tunisia was so complete that social observers in the 1960s questioned whether Tunisia might have entered a post-Islamic or de-Islamicized age (Brown 1966, 98, 106). There was little or no indication that an Islamic reform movement might arise and captivate the attention of large sections of the Tunisian public.

This, however, is what did happen. During the late 1960s and early 1970s—a time of societal upheaval that included the failure of various development plans of the Neo-Destour party—several individuals came together in a broad Islamic movement, driven and held together by the idea of renewing the teaching of Islam in Tunisia. Their goal was to give voice and direction to the deep-rooted Muslim sentiment of the masses, which had been obscured and suppressed—but not destroyed—through the course of Bourguiba's many anti-Islamic "reforms."

At least two separate sources contributed to the development of this movement. In the late 1960s the Pakistan-based Da'wa gained a foothold in the country.[2] At the same time, Rachid Ghannouchi returned from studies in Syria "overflowing with the idea of religious reform" (Ghannouchi 1979, 3–4; see also Ghannouchi 1988). Upon returning to Tunisia, he met 'Abd al-Fattah Muru, who at the time was studying under Shaykh ben Milad at the Zaytuna Mosque. Together with others who were concerned about the state of Islam in Tunisia, they began a group aimed at religious reform.

In the beginning, this broad Islamic movement bore most heavily the stamp of the Da'wa, known at the time as the Group of the Communication (Jama'at al-Tabligh). From 1970 to 1973, members of the movement traveled in groups to the various villages of the country, "calling people from the streets, cafés, and shops, to listen to lessons on Islamic consciousness" and to remind them of their religious obligations (Ghannouchi 1979, 5–6).

A number of the members of this early group, however, soon split from the Da'wa, for at least three reasons.[3] The first was that the practice of moving about the country in groups and "calling" others to faith caused problems with the government, who opposed this activity, reportedly thinking it political. A second reason was that many members of the group came to feel that the traditions of the Da'wa, issuing from the Islamic life of Pakistan and India, were out of touch with Tunisian society. Finally, some members became dissatisfied with what they considered the Da'wa's limited focus, especially the principle of "not paying attention to that which does not concern us" (referring especially to political activity). The discontented members, believing that there was nothing that does not concern the true Muslim, gradually split off and formed their own group, emphasizing the idea of the *comprehensiveness* of Islam.[4]

Those who split off from the Da'wa (in 1974) became known as the Islamic Group (al-Jama'at al-Islamiyya) and developed their own means of working and of diffusing information. They founded a magazine, *al-Ma'rifa* (*Knowledge*), for the dissemination of Islamic ideas and began mosque circles in various locations. Through these channels, which were until the late 1970s their main means of spreading ideas, the Islamic Group began by emphasizing Islamic conviction and character and issues of thought, culture, and society.

As time went on, some of the members of the Islamic Group, which came to be known as the Islamic movement, began to question the direction of the movement. They particularly questioned the commitment of the movement to the path of the Egyptian Muslim Brotherhood, wondering whether this approach would be able to solve the problems that had begun to occupy the Islamicists in Tunisia, especially in light of the fact that the brotherhood had failed to realize its goals in spite of nearly fifty years of struggle.

In 1977 and 1978, Ahmida al-Nayfar wrote a series of five articles that were published in *al-Ma'rifa* under the title "Where Do We Begin?" (1977a–c, 1978a–b). These articles represented a preliminary attempt to articulate some of the issues that were of concern to several members of the Islamic movement. According to Salah al-Din al-Jurshi, the "questioners" intended to be an ideational reform tendency within the movement rather than a separate group. The Islamic movement, however, was unable to handle the tensions brought about by the radical questioning being done by these progressive thinkers, due to a reported "lack of possession of democratic traditions for dialogue" within the group. Al-Nayfar, al-Jurshi, and several others consequently separated from the movement, forming in 1978–1979 an independent association of Islamicist thinkers that they named the Progressive Islamicists.

In 1982 al-Nayfar founded a magazine dedicated to the case of developing a modern, progressive Islamic thought. It was named *15*21*, calling for a new dialogue between Arabic–Islamic civilization and Western civilization, which are entering the fifteenth and twenty-first centuries by their respective calenders. *15*21* is the focal point of the activity of the Progressive Islamists, the essence of which is the search for a modern Islamic thought able to lead Muslims in the work of building a civilization that will be both fully Islamic and fully in touch with the modern age.

While the Da'wa held to its original course, the Islamic movement, encountering harsh opposition from the Tunisian government and faced with difficult challenges in the form of severe social problems, became politicized. This culminated in 1981 with its self-designation as the Movement of the Islamic Way, an official declaration of organization, and an application for permission to exist as a licensed political group. It later led, in 1989, to the

changing of the group's name to the Renaissance party (Hisb al-Nahda), in a
further attempt to meet the rules of the political game in Tunisia, as already
discussed in Chapter 1.

■ Reform in Tunisia: Unity and Diversity

The Da'wa, movement of the Islamic Way, and Progressive Islamicists
have all attempted to address the credibility gap that opened up in Tunisian
society through the 1960s and early 1970s between political discourse and
social realities (Salem 1984, 165, 190). While agreeing that there is a
problem, however, the three groups have differed substantially in their
understanding of that problem and of what to do in response to it. They
have all agreed that "Muslims, if they interpreted their religion correctly and
then lived by it, could rebuild strong, effective societies" (Brown 1964, 58);
but they have differed in their understanding of correct interpretation and
living.

This chapter will now consider each of these groups in detail, presenting
their perspectives on reform, how they have confronted the desacralized reality
of modern Tunisia, and how they have attempted to speak to the Tunisian
masses in the name of Islam. The goal is to shed light on the issue of unity
in diversity. The question is not simply where the diversity lies but how it is
constituted by actual groups within a broader unity and how three groups
who are undertaking the same task (reforming Islam) can at the same time be
significantly different, as they variously draw upon and interpret the symbols
available within scriptural Islam to constitute viable, unique identities as true
Muslims in the modern world.

□ The Da'wa

The Da'wa, as a group focusing on rightly living the Islamic life—which in
their understanding encompasses the minutest details of an individual's daily
existence—stands in especially stark contrast to the surrounding
socioreligious reality.[5] To use Geertz's terms, Islam in Tunisia seems both
weak in *force* (i.e., "the thoroughness with which [Islam] is internalized in
the personalities of the individuals who adopt it, its centrality or marginality
in their lives") and narrow in *scope* (i.e., "the range of social contexts within
which religious considerations are regarded as having more or less direct
relevance") (1968, 111–112). Islam has been limited in scope to the realm of
personal practice; and there seem to be few Tunisians for whom "religious
commitments are the axis of [their] whole existence," who are *god-
intoxicated*. The Da'wa, in contrast, *are* god-intoxicated and *do* have religious
commitments as the axis of their whole existence. They present an

understanding of Islam—and a way of living out that vision—that is unique in the Tunisian setting.

All contemporary Islamic groups, as Wilfred Cantwell Smith (1977, 41) has pointed out, believe that there is a problem, that something has gone wrong with Islamic history. Where groups tend to differ is in their understanding of exactly what is wrong and what to do about it. Those in the Da'wa understand the basic problem to be that Muslims, as individuals, have gone astray from Islam. The underlying assumption on which Da'wa members operate is that Tunisians are in a state of heedlessness or negligence, knowing the truths of Islam but not wanting to think about them, being busy with the world and not having time for the demands of religion. The solution, then, is to call individuals back to practicing Islam— to remind them of what they know and encourage them to practice that to which they give their assent.

The long-range goal of the Da'wa is to build an Islamic society—which in their terms means a society of upright individuals, those who truly live Islam. A basic assumption of the Da'wa, however, is that true reform must be from the bottom up. The individual, they are convinced, is the building block of the society. If individuals return to true Islam, an Islamic society will develop naturally. If, on the other hand, Islamic principles are instituted in the economic, political, cultural, and social realms, in a society in which the majority of people are not truly Muslim, that is, not committed to following Islam and to living in an Islamic society, the society will not succeed and will certainly not be rightly Islamic. The individuals must be reformed, before the society can be. "We believe in changing things from the roots," one individual told me, continuing to explain that "the first 'revolution' is how to follow Islam in your own life." Thus, their immediate goal is the formation (*takwin*) of Islamic individuals.[6]

The reform emphasis of the Da'wa is twofold. Group members are concerned, first of all, with reforming themselves—with rightly living the true Islamic life. They exist as a group partly for this purpose: to exhort and help each other to live this life. But the Da'wa also exists, as its name (the Call and the Communication) signifies, as a group committed to calling others (both Muslims and non-Muslims) to the true Islamic life.

The key reform concept of the Da'wa is *taslih* (restore, fix, make right or righteous). Their goal as a group is to create *salih* (righteous, virtuous, godly) individuals, as a means of arriving at a true Muslim society. Such a society, by the definition of the Da'wa, is one "in which all people are virtuous." "By [creating] virtuous individuals," one Da'wa member told me, "you arrive at a virtuous world"; and vice versa: if individuals are *fasid* (corrupt, immoral —the opposite of *salih*), the world will be fasid.

The virtuous individual, according to Da'wa members, is one who lives by sunna (the sayings and doings of the Prophet Muhammad). The Da'wa consider themselves part of the People of Sunna. They alone, in modern Tunisia, hold strictly to a traditional Islamic understanding of following sunna, that a Muslim is to pattern his life after Muhammad in every area.[7]

The Da'wa divide Tunisians into the following categories, on an ascending scale:

- incomplete believers (sometimes called incomplete Muslims)
- true Muslims
- true believers
- complete believers

Incomplete believers are those who say the *shahadah* (the Muslim creed) with true intention, but who do not practice the Islamic obligations of prayer, fast, alms, and pilgrimage. Da'wa members often condemn these (seemingly a majority of Tunisians) as not Muslim at all, since they do not practice the basics of the religion. True Muslims are those who fulfill these requirements. A true believer is a Muslim who fully believes (e.g., in God, the angels, the books, prophets, the Last Day) and who lives by that faith. The final category, complete believers, is defined by an increasing patterning of life by sunna in all areas.

Many of the specific details of this patterning of life after the example of Muhammad distinguish the Da'wa from other Tunisians. Da'wa members are easily noticeable in Tunisia for the way their men dress. In general, men's dress in Tunisia includes Western and traditional styles. Da'wa men, by contrast, dress in a way that is modeled after Pakistanis and other Eastern Muslims' dress.[8] In fact, Tunisians often mistake Da'wa men for foreigners.

Men and women are strictly separated in Da'wa homes (even from visual and voice contact) except among closest family members, a practice that is highly unusual in the Tunisian context.[9] Da'wa women avoid public places, staying in the homes except when they have errands (e.g., shopping, visiting, meeting together with other Da'wa women) to attend to. When it is necessary to venture into public domains, they will interact with men only to the extent of accomplishing their business. Other than these situations, the women are rarely in the public realm.

Other examples of how Da'wa members attempt to follow sunna, also unique in Tunisia, are in accordance with traditional understandings: sleeping on the floor (by design, not simply out of habit or poverty); eating while sitting on the floor (again, out of principle) and by hand rather than with utensils; doing all activities (such as putting on clothing and passing and accepting objects) beginning with the right side.

One aspect of the significance of the particulars of the life of faith by the Da'wa has to do with the way that they set the group apart from the Islamic Way and the Progressive Islamicists, as reform groups. All three groups utilize available Islamic symbols to construct unique and viable identities as true Muslims and as reformers, but they do so in different ways.

Reform is a relative concept. *Reformers* are those who are dissatisfied with the existing situation, offering both criticism and an alternative. The Da'wa, in a less desacralized Islamic society, would perhaps be a traditionalist group, supporting a status quo in which their dress, behavior, and other group distinctives would not differ significantly from those of the majority of Muslims. In Tunisia, however, their group distinctives set them apart. Their insistence, furthermore, that these patterns of individual and group life should characterize all Muslims make them a reform group, condemning the status quo and offering a clear alternative.

The Da'wa has many significant group activities that are unique to themselves in the Tunisian setting: *weekly study times* centering around their group text *Hayat al-sahaba* (*The Life of the Companions*, written by their second leader, al-Kandahlawi), which gives examples from the lives of the Companions of the Prophet of how to live out the life of the "call," and aiming not at theoretical knowledge but at the practical knowledge of how rightly to live the Islamic life; *i'tikaf*, times of seclusion in the mosque for study and prayer; *mashwara*, a consultation session in which various Da'wa members come together to discuss and make decisions regarding personal and group concerns; and *jawla* and *khuruj*, organized outings for practicing the Islamic life and calling others to that life.

These activities perform various functions. A key purpose of all of them is to create true Muslim individuals. Their outings to call others to the life of faith, for example, serve both of the major purposes of their existence as a group: to put themselves right and to put others right. For both of these, they use the reform concept *taslih*.[10]

Da'wa group activities also create a standardized experience of life as Muslims and a paradigm for viewing life. They are the means for creating the Islamic life of the Da'wa, shaping worldview and practice together into a self-confirming unity, and socializing new members into the life of the Group of the Call. In doing this, group activities act as symbolic expressions of the true Islamic life, giving a distinct sense of identity as the people of the call, those truly following Islam in a pagan society.

Perhaps the best way, then, to appreciate the Da'wa's practice of sunna (as well as other aspects of their group and individual lives) is in terms of their attempt to create a unique and viable Muslim identity in modern Tunisia. Living according to sunna, as well as carrying out their various group activities, are, for the Da'wa, symbolic expressions of the true Islamic life. They have a particular conceptualization of that true life; and the separation of men and women, the clothing they wear, the way they eat and sleep, and group activities are all concrete ways of expressing their understanding. They are all the more conspicuous in Tunisia because other groups do not employ these same symbols, and others do not customarily dress and act in these ways. Thus, through these various symbols Da'wa members are able to make a clear and powerful statement of what it means to be true Muslims and, in so doing, to carve out for themselves a unique identity within the realm of Tunisians working to reform Islam.

☐ The Movement of the Islamic Way

The Movement of the Islamic Way, like the Da'wa and the Progressive Islamicists, is concerned with reforming Muslims and Islamic society in Tunisia. Its approach to the question of reform, however, is significantly different from that of either of the other two groups. From the definition of the problem and the solution to the symbols its advocates use to create a unique identity as reformers and their relationship to Tunisian society they focus not on personal uprightness or Islamic thought but on social action.

Those who formed the Movement of the Islamic Way split off from the Da'wa because they came to see the problem of Islam in Tunisia—and the solution—differently from Da'wa members. The problem, from their perspective, is the decadence of Islamic state and society, the waning influence (or noninfluence) of Islam in legal, political, cultural, economic, and educational domains. The issue they have chosen to address is the official conceptualization of Islam and the pervasive secularism (and secularization) of Tunisian society. The Islamic Way decries the fact that Islam is no longer practiced as an all-encompassing religion but has been relegated to the realm of individual piety, while the social realm has been modeled after Western society. All of the current crises (e.g., moral, economic, political, familial) in Tunisia, in their view, can be traced to the neglect of Islam and the implementation of Western ideas at the societal level. The solution, therefore, is to bring about social change, to recreate a Muslim society and an Islamic state, and to revive Islamic civilization in Tunisia by actively participating in various societal realms, criticizing existing structures and attempting to articulate Islamic alternatives.

The key reform concept of the Movement of the Islamic Way is renewal (*tajdid*) and is integrally connected with the focus of the movement on the society. In discussing the saying, "God sends to this umma every one hundred years those who renew its religion," Ghannouchi asks the question said to have occupied the Islamic world since the beginning of this century, "Why have Muslims gone backward, and others advanced?" (1979, 87, 89; 1981, 12). His answer is that Muslims have abandoned Islam in its "true form" and have thus suffered decline. The solution to this decline, he says, is a movement of renewal (*haraka tajdid*), which entails "wiping from Islam the dust of the decline, retrieving its vitality and its ability to lead in the establishing of Islamic societies which are not only advanced, but which represent the highest form of advancement."

Ghannouchi defines *tajdid* as the broadest category of "reform," including various possible approaches. As long as the Islamic state existed, according to his view, the work of renewal took the form of *islah* (restoration, reform). The total fall of Islam from dominion and authority, however, means that renewal now must take the form of a rebuilding from the foundation (*ta'sis*) (Ghannouchi 1979, 90).[11]

The important point is that the reform idea of the Movement of the Islamic Way is one that focuses not on personal uprightness (as for the Da'wa) but on Islamic society. It is Islamic society and civilization that is to be renewed, either reformed (if still existing) or rebuilt (if absent).

The Islamic Way is a social movement, highly visible, present in the public arena, known by the Tunisian people, and closely watched by the government. It is struggling to activate the Islamic consciousness of the masses and to turn them *en force* against the reigning non-Islamic system in order to accomplish the renewal of Islamic civilization in Tunisia.

What is striking about the Movement of the Islamic Way, in contrast with the Da'wa, is that the movement pays attention to Tunisian society and is actively engaged with it. What it does is done with an eye to others. Various symbols of identity and protest and the writing of articles and the issuing of statements on particular topics all are done with a consciousness that they as Islamicists are struggling in the social arena and exist in distinction from others in the society.

The focal point of the Islamic movement is Islamic ideology as it relates to the social realm. They are not, as a group, concerned with many matters which occupy the Da'wa, such as the particulars of living by sunna or with matters that are the focus of the Progressive Islamicists, such as reformulating Islamic thought. These may concern group members as individuals but are not the focus of the movement as a group.

As a group undertaking the renewal of Islamic society, the movement has utilized different symbols from the Da'wa or the Progressive Islamicists, and has presented to the general population a significantly different symbolic formulation of what it means to be a true Muslim. Their primary symbol is that of the true, socially active Muslim, which they refer to as an Islamicist. They categorize Tunisian Muslims as

- practicing traditional Muslims
- nonpracticing traditional Muslims
- Islamicists

Most Tunisians are traditional Muslims, having an Islam of inheritance and allegiance. At worst, these traditional Muslims do not practice Islam. At best, they observe the fundamental requirements of Islam but are still lacking, having only an Islam of personal practice.

Islamicists, on the other hand, are those who have become dissatisfied with traditional Islam in its various forms and who are striving to rediscover whole Islam. They desire to be complete Muslims, who not only practice Islam in their personal lives but who also understand the social side of Islam, seeing the religion as "a weapon in the [social] struggle," as a political, economic, and cultural movement. "There is no separation of religion and state, of piety and politics, in Islam" is the rallying cry of the Islamicists (al-Sadrin 1983, pt. 1, 58; Ghannouchi 1979a, 78; Ghannouchi 1979b, 91; Ghannouchi 1979f, 1–2).

The struggle of the Islamic movement, rather than being against paganism in the individual (as for the Da'wa), is against paganism in the society. Their most visible opponent has been the Tunisian (Bourguiban) regime, as the force held responsible for the de-Islamicization of Tunisian society.[12] The Islam of the Tunisian government is referred to as official Islam (al-islam al-rasmi), as opposed to the struggling Islam (al-islam al-munadil) of the Islamic movement. The former, which is taught in the schools and communicated through newspaper, radio, and television, applies only to the individual's religious life—it concerns, for example, prayer, fasting, ritual washing, family relationships, and laws of inheritance. Struggling Islam, on the other hand, is based on the concept of comprehensiveness (al-shumuliyya)—a rejection of the separation of religion and politics in Islam and an insistence that Islam presents a program for all areas of a society's life. Its adherents believe Islam to be relevant to societal problems, such as poverty, injustice, and the exploitation of workers and women. Struggling Islam, therefore, is in direct conflict with the regime, which is represented as the cause of various societal problems through its neglect of true Islam.

Many of the slogans of the Iranian revolution became part of the rhetoric of the struggling Islam of Islamic Way Islamicists and part of the symbolic repertoire that they have used in constructing their identity as socially active Muslims. These slogans broadcast the concept of com-prehensiveness; the call to revolutionary Islam; the alignment of the Islamic movement with the oppressed in their battle against the tyrants of the world; and a rejection of dependence on East or West in favor of a third, independent, Islamic alternative (Ghannouchi 1979a–f, 1980a–c, 1981; Muru 1979; Islamic Tendency Movement 1981; Sadrin 1983, pt. 1). The hijab (cowl) for women, beards for men, and fasting and feasting by the moon (rather than by the officially set time) all become, for Islamicists, more than matters simply of personal practice. They are, rather, aspects of consciously constructed Islamicist identity, as well as being overt symbolic statements of commitment to comprehensive, struggling Islam, and, as part of this, of resistance against the inadequate official Islam of the Tunisian regime.

The Movement of the Islamic Way is fully participating in the society—not simply going its own way, following God's path with no concern for the rest of society, but doing and saying what they believe to be particularly appropriate to the circumstances and the setting. The movement's use of Islamic symbols, in constructing a unique identity as true Muslims, and in presenting an image to other Tunisians, reflects that participation. All of the many changes that the Islamic Way has undergone—moving from a harsh, condemnatory stance toward the Tunisian government to an emphasis on commitment to democratic freedoms; distancing themselves from the Iranian revolution; coming to speak of themselves as one Islamic group rather than *the* Islamic group; coming to support worker's rights and union activity; liberalizing their positions on women's roles, polygamy, and social intercourse between men and women; and changing their name to Renaissance so as not to include an Islamic reference—should be seen in this light. All of these changes have involved in some way a manipulating of the symbols that they have available to them, as part of the process of constructing a viable identity as Muslim reformers and of seeking to present to the Tunisian public an image that will be received positively.

The Islamic Way has attempted to tailor its message to the realities of the Tunisian situation. It has created an Islamic identity from symbols that are believed to be readily understandable to the Tunisian masses. It speaks of social injustice, corruption, exploitation, and other evils of a pagan society and presents the Islamicist as the one who combats these problems in the name of true Islam. The movement's message, conveyed through simple, easily understood slogans that resonate with underlying Islamic values, aims at the felt economic, social, and political needs of the average Tunisian and the feeling that the masses have both of being disillusioned with the system and of being victims of the decisions and actions of others.

The Movement of the Islamic Way's slogans, reform concepts and activities, interactions with the realities of the Tunisian social situation, and other group distinctions, all reflect the focus of the movement on social action and the attempt of its members to create a unique and viable Muslim identity in modern Tunisia (particularly as reformers) of a different sort than the identities created and presented by the Da'wa and the Progressive Islamicists.

□ *The Progressive Islamicists*

The Progressive Islamicists represent a third tendency within the broader category of Islamic reform groups in contemporary Tunisia. They are similar to the Da'wa and the Islamic Way, in that they exist as a group for the purpose of reforming Muslims and Islamic society in Tunisia. They are also, however, significantly different, approaching reform through a focus on Islamic thought.

As previously discussed, some of those who split off from the Da'wa as part of the Islamic Group came to question the fundamental concepts of the group and the ability of those concepts to lead to the accomplishment of the Islamicists' goals in Tunisia. Those who became the Progressive Islamicists, while agreeing with the Movement of the Islamic Way on the need to call into question societal, as well as individual, life, gradually became convinced that the central problem did not lie in Islamic state and society but in the decadence of Islamic thought. They attribute the decay of Islam in Tunisia to the stagnation of Islamic thought and its inability to develop in response to the demands of the modern age. Their reform effort, consequently, has centered on restructuring Islamic thought through a rethinking of the fundamentals of Islam. They have relied more on thinking than on living (the Da'wa) or taking action (the Islamic Way).

One of the leaders of this group is Ahmida al-Nayfar, who wrote the series of articles entitled, "Where Do We Begin?" (al-Nayfar 1977a–c, 1978a–b). In these articles are found, in embryonic form, the essential elements of the reform position of the Progressive Islamicists. The focus of the articles is Islamic thought, as the main source of the problems in which Muslims find themselves and as the key for effectively solving these problems. Current Islamic thought is seen as impotent, due to its reactionary, isolationist mentality. It is said to have withdrawn from modern life, refusing to interact with "pagan" society. This thought, according to al-Nayfar, must be replaced with a modern, progressive Islamicist thought fully engaged with the issues of modern man and with "pagan" society, given to thorough analysis of the problems that face them, and able to change current situations until they gradually become more Islamic. Such thought must be diverse, nonpartisan, and tolerant.

Ghannouchi of the Islamic Way has answered the question "Why have Muslims gone backwards, and others advanced?" by saying that the problem lies in Muslims, who have left true Islam and are in need of a movement of renewal. The other answer, he said, is that the problem is in Islam itself, which must be transformed until it is in harmony with the modern age (Ghannouchi 1981, 15–16). The Progressive Islamicists, in their answer, fall between these two extremes. They believe that Islam is able to face the modern age but that Islamic thought needs to be transformed. The major problem, according to the Progressive Islamicists, is the frozenness and lethargy of Islamic thought, resulting in its inability to be in touch with the new and unique problems of the modern age.

Their basis for this distinction between Islam (which is good) and

Islamic thought (which is in need of transformation) is indicated by a fundamental question posed by the Progressive Islamicists. Al-Jurshi criticized the Islamicist slogan "The Islamic alternative," asking, "What do we mean by 'Islam'? If the answer is 'the Qur'an and sunna,' i.e., the texts, then why, in spite of the existence of these texts, have we not progressed—not at the economic, or the political, or social, or cultural, or even the moral or religious levels?"[13] The Progressive Islamicists' conclusion is that the solution is not simply a matter of Islam in the sense of texts traditionally understood but rather has to do with the concepts Muslims derive from those texts, concepts that need to be brought under review.

The reform tendency of the Progressive Islamicists, then, is characterized by thinking, that has led them to some concepts and positions that differ radically from those of other Islamicists. The basic reform concept of the Progressive Islamicists is correction or rectification (*tashih*). They have called themselves a correctional tendency (*tayyar tashihi*) within the broader Islamic movement in Tunisia (al-Jurshi 1984, 38). The focal point of the needed correction is Islamic thought. "The important thing," al-Jurshi has said in explaining the existence of the Progressive Islamicists, "is the necessity of the rectification of modern Islamic thought" (p. 37).

The Progressive Islamicists also speak of renewal (*tajdid*), again focusing on thought. One member has said that Islamic thought has suffered backwardness and decline, and is in need of renewal—even a revolution—to rid it of its rigidity and "mumification" (Krishan 1982, 9). Da'wa members, we have seen, speak of the backwardness of Muslims—meaning backward in the righteousness of their lives as Muslim individuals. Those in the Islamic Way also speak of backwardness and decline but locate them—and the needed renewal—in Islamic society and civilization. The Progressive Islamicists use these same words but refer to the thought of Muslims, as individuals and as a group.[14] It is Islamic thought that needs to be corrected.

As their thinking has clarified, the Progressive Islamicists have developed a set of symbols and slogans that differ significantly from those employed by the Movement of the Islamic Way or the Da'wa, by which they have sought to construct a unique and viable identity as authentic modern Muslims and Islamic reformers. Desiring to reform Islamic thought within the context of the broader Islamic movement, the group has taken a stance against other Islamicists, focusing their criticism and their slogans on Islamicists and Islamic thought and tendencies. Their symbols have tended to be conceptual and verbal ones, employed to contrast themselves, as Muslims with the right understanding of Islam, from others.

One of their fundamental concepts is that Islamic thought, and the Muslims who have developed and hold to that thought, are divided as follows:

- progressive (*taqaddumi*), leftist (*yasari*), futurist (*mustaqbali*)
- reactionary (*raj'i*), rightest (*yamini*), "pastist" (*madawi*)

The label *leftist*, according to al-Jurshi, comes from Western political analysis. Referring to the French Revolution, he wrote that the Left was the group that stood in opposition, the term coming to mean "radicalism, radical analysis, an orientation to comprehensive change and to criticism." Some Islamicists, he said, have called for forming an Islamic Left, which was to be "a search for change, for radicalism, and criticism of traditional thought and of traditional religious thought," as well as "a call to the use of reason" (al-Jurshi 1983, 15).

The terms *futurism (al-mustaqbaliyya)* and *progressivism (al-taqaddumiyya)* have related connotations. To be futurist or progressive is to believe that each society and stage of history has its own special characteristics, which can be understood and learned from, but not recreated in, another time and place. Futurists believe that society is progressing with time, according to social laws, and that it is therefore possible to create an Islamic situation that is better than all previous situations. They favor "putting the experiments of the past [the inheritance] to work for the demands of reality, rather than [oppressing] reality . . . according to the molds of the forebears." To be futurist, in other words, is to look for the creation of a new Islamic society that will be in tune with the current historical situation of its people. The Progressive Islamicist's slogan, rather than "Return to Islam," is "Progress toward Islam" (al-Jurshi 1983, 14–15).

The Progressive Islamicists, in other words, in focusing on Islamic thought, conceptualize mindset and intellectual orientation as the crucial factors that distinguish Muslims from each other. They have attempted to represent their orientation toward criticism of existing structures and ideas, openness to change, flexibility, and struggle on behalf of the masses symbolically in words such as *progressive, leftist,* and *futurist.*

The Progressive Islamicists have attempted to give these symbols (and their program of *tashih*) concrete manifestation by endeavoring to develop progressive perspectives on various issues within Islam that they take to be crucial domains for the application of right thinking. These areas include one's perspective on the nature of Islam, diversity within Islam, and some of the fundamental aspects of Islam such as the relationships of purpose to form, the use of reason, and one's view of the Islamic inheritance.

The Progressive Islamicists are firmly committed to diversity within Islam, believing that there is no original Islam that can be recovered but only various interpretations and understandings. They are committed to finding the broad purposes of Islam, rather than focusing on particular judgments. They take a historical–critical approach to Hadith (narrative relating the deeds and utterances of the Prophet Muhammad), accepting or rejecting Hadith based on their congruence with Qur'anic teaching. They are firmly committed to *ijtihad* (systematic original thinking) and the use of reason (*'aql*), relying on reason when it clashes with revelation (*naql*). They also call for a desacralization of the Islamic inheritance, freeing Islamic thought to begin to develop in light of historical realities. All of these commitments are integral to their progressive approach to Islam.

Socially, the Progressive Islamicists apply their convictions by taking a firm stand in favor of democratic freedoms, rejecting the idea of divine sovereignty (*al-hakimiya*) in the realm of human society. Their belief is that individuals should be free in matters of worship, the government having no right to interfere in this area. They also are not afraid to adopt values from other civilizations (e.g., from Marxism) and to seek to integrate them into an Islamic framework.

Regarding issues of women and the family, the Progressive Islamicists believe that true Islamic character, rather than the separation of men and women, is the answer to problems of immorality in society. They stand firmly against polygamy, on the basis that historical analysis shows it to have done more harm than good. Many of the Progressive Islamicists are convinced that the *hijab* is prescribed Islamically for women, but female members are not compelled to dress this way.

The group does not rely on particulars of dress or life-style for several reasons. They do not want to create barriers between themselves and others that would prevent them from influencing these others. They do not want to have distinctions, moreover, that are merely formal, with no significant meaning, purpose, or content. Their focus, rather, is on what they see as the underlying issues. The search of the Progressive Islamicists is for distinctions that will bring about significant and lasting change. Al-Jurshi made the comment that many Islamists dress in a certain way and think that they have changed the world when in reality "they have not changed anything." Even the basic obligations of Islam are not stressed by the Progressive Islamicists, he states, because "we don't believe that preoccupation with carrying out the religious obligations, changes our reality as a group, or the reality of Muslims."

Thus, this lack of distinctions of dress and lifestyle is in itself a distinction, a positive, symbolic statement of the underlying commitments of the Progressive Islamicists, of their fundamental convictions regarding the nature of Islam and of true and lasting reform. It is an attempt to apply their beliefs (e.g., that not separation but true Islamic character purifies the relationship of men and women) in practice, to express their convictions symbolically. Thus, the social lives of the Progressive Islamicists reflect their thinking and are a domain of application of their attempt to work out an Islamic commitment that is appropriate in the modern age.

As with the other two groups, then, the Progressive Islamicists have chosen a particular focus for their reform activity. They have sought, through slogans, positions on different issues, and the way they approach matters of living as Muslims to create an identity as Muslims and as Islamic reformers that is viable and that sets them apart from other reformers in the Tunisian setting.

■ Classification and Comparison

One of my concerns is to explore the nature of comparative study. Comparative study is essentially concerned with typologizing and with the issue of diversity within unity. The comparative enterprise has as its most crucial question the definition of the unity within which diversity is to be explored. The central task is to discover the proper light (i.e., the appropriate framework of comparison) by which to look at diverse phenomena, so as to see how "their very differences connect them" (Geertz 1968, 55).

The Da'wa, Movement of the Islamic Way, and Progressive Islamicists are groups that are obviously similar and yet significantly different. In what terms should they be compared? One viable option would be to employ the system of categorization of scholars who have studied the modern Islamic resurgence or revitalization in terms of "stances toward the Islamic inheritance and the modern world" (e.g., traditionalist, fundamentalist, modernist, secularist). Several authors have presented a system of ideal types and have then categorized various Islamic phenomena according to those types. Since a number of the groups, individuals, and tendencies studies appear to have much in common with the three Tunisian groups of this study, one approach would be to present the Da'wa, Movement of the Islamic Way, and Progressive Islamicists as examples of types that other authors have discussed.

Table 10.1 compares various systems that have been employed for categorizing and comparing Islamic groups, individuals, and tendencies. The categories are numbered for the sake of comparison. As nearly as can be determined, similarly numbered categories refer to essentially the same phenomenon.

Fazlur Rahman (1981) sets out to trace the roots of neofundamentalism as a particular manifestation of modern Islam. He labels four different groups within modern Islam, which cover a wide range of individuals and groups, tendencies of thought and action, stances toward Islamic tradition, and issues (e.g., politics and religion). John L. Espositio writes of revival and reform in the context of a broader discussion of Islamic politics (Islam, that is, is the primary frame of reference). His categories represent four "positions or attitudes toward modernization and Islamic socio-political change" among Muslims today (1984, 216–218).

Table 10.1 Comparative Categories of Islamic Groups, Individuals, and Tendencies

Source	(1)	(2)	(3)	(4)
Rahman 1981	traditionalist/ conservative	secularist	modernist	neofundamentalist
Esposito 1984	conservative	secularist	contemporary Islamic reformer	neotraditionist
Pipes 1983	traditionalist	secularist	reformist	fundamentalist
Sharabi 1970	traditionalism	modernism	reformism	—
Badawi 1976	conservative	Westernizing	Muslim secularist	revivalist, Islamic reform
Aly & Wenner 1982	traditionalist	—	modernizer	conservative reformer
Voll 1982a	conservative	adaptationist	—	fundamentalist

Daniel Pipes discusses Islamic revival in terms of political power, from the standpoint of the role of Islam in *politics* (1983, 114). He organizes his discussion around Shari'a, presenting four different "new attitudes toward the Sacred Law" found among Muslims who are "compelled to choose between Islamicate and Western civilizations." Unlike Rahman and Esposito, Pipes does not distinguish between premodern and modern reform movements and activity but develops four broad categories that cover the whole range of Muslim thought and activity since the Western colonial onslaught of the eighteenth and nineteenth centuries.

Hisham Sharabi's (1970) concern is the intellectual history of the interaction between the Arabs and the West at the turn of the century. His is a study of individuals (Arab intellectuals) and the three broad outlooks they comprise.[15] The basis of his categorization is significantly different than that of Rahman, Esposito, and Pipes in that he is concerned with Christian as well as Muslim Arabs and focuses not on Islamic politicoreligious resurgence but on the intellectual response of Arabs to the challenge of the West in the domain of thought. M. A. Zaki Badawi (1976) writes about three specific Muslim reformers (al-Afghani, 'Abduh, and Ridha), in the context of the development of modern Muslim thought, again in response to the impact of the West. In his scheme, reformism was only one of several reactions that emanated from the Umma in response to the challenge of European civilization.[16]

Abd al-Monein Said Aly and Manfred W. Wenner (1982) have studied the Egyptian Muslim Brotherhood as an example of modern Islamic reform movements. They discuss brotherhood reform in the context of Islamic political thought that existed at the time of Banna. Their discussion of the brotherhood is not limited to Islamic thought, however, but also considers dimensions such as political action, relationship to the government and to other groups, and changes in ideology. The final system of classification

represented in the table is that of John Voll (1982a), who is concerned with
the current Islamic resurgence in light of the modern history of Islam. He
discusses the interaction of what he calls four styles of, or orientations
for, action and the way each of them meets the challenges of the modern
era.[17]

These classificatory systems all seem to be deficient. The first problem
with existing frameworks is one of terms. No uniform system of
categorization has yet been developed that can readily be applied to different
groups. It is obvious, in comparing the typological schemes of these
different authors, that there is lack of agreement of terms from one writer to
the next. The only category on which there seems to be general agreement is
that of *traditionalist/conservative. Modernist, reformist*, and *secularist*,
however, are each used by different authors to refer to completely different
tendencies.

Part of the confusion, it seems, is due to the fact that these authors work
within different disciplines and draw upon concepts and traditions within
those disciplines in developing their systems of classification. Another
source of divergence is the fact that they are concerned with different topics
(e.g., Islamic thought, Islam and politics, the confrontation between Islam
and the West), different time periods (premodern, modern), and different
specific problems (e.g., explaining the Islamic resurgence, showing the
historic roots of Islamic reformism). The result is that the categories of these
authors are not readily interchangeable and cannot simply be applied to new
groups, individuals, or tendencies.

A second problem lies in the content of categories, that is, the meanings
of the terms that are used and the phenomena to which they refer. In general,
the categories seem to need clearer definitions and labels. To label one
response toward modernization *reformist*, as opposed to *secularist* and
fundamentalist responses, for example, implies that the latter are not
reformers—which is debatable. Secularists, for example, could be seen
reforming through abandoning Islamic ways; likewise, fundamentalists seek a
reform of rejecting modernization and returning to Islam. The problem seems
to go beyond terminology to the content of the categories themselves,
including, for example, the significant question of whether there are different
sorts of reformers operating within Muslim contexts.

Part of the problem may be due to the fact that it is not yet clear what
subject is under consideration, what broader category is being discussed. What
do the different groups and individuals being studied have in common? What
is the proper light by which to look at them? Do they represent examples of
Islamic reform, Islamic thought, Islamic response to the modern world,
fundamental tendencies that have always existed within Islam, or Islamic
approaches to politics? This crucial question must be answered for any
comparative, typological scheme to be of value.

A third problem with existing frameworks is that they are all rather narrowly defined. The Da'wa, Islamic Way, and Progressive Islamicists, considered in their wholeness as living groups, are too rich, varied, and multifaceted for the categories that have been developed. This is partly because these systems oversimplify complex phenomena, focusing on one dimension and ignoring others. Some of the authors, for example, are narrowly concerned with Islam and politics. Only one of these Tunisian groups, however (Islamic Way), can properly be discussed as having the political realm as a primary focus. Others have classified Muslims according to their thought but again only one of the Tunisian groups (the Progressive Islamicists) has Islamic thought as its central concern. The Da'wa does not easily fit any of these typological schemes, since the group is primarily religious rather than political or speculative, being concerned to live true Islamic lives as individuals. Thus, it is difficult to discuss the three groups in comparison with each other, in terms of any of the existing frameworks.

There is also an overlap of tendencies between the groups and the various categories. The Da'wa, for example, are clearly not modernists (in Rahman's sense). Yet they have some significant elements of thought in common with al-Afghani, the founder of Islamic modernism. Furthermore, according to the various systems indicated above, they might be seen as conservative/ traditionalist (in that they hold to a traditional historical understanding of Islam) or fundamentalist (in that they are against the status quo and in favor of return to the "true Islam" of the origins). In some ways, they resemble, more than anything else, premodern reform movements like the Wahhabis.

Likewise, the Movement of the Islamic Way does not fit easily into existing categories. In Voll's scheme, for example, the Islamic Way is somewhat adaptationist and somewhat fundamentalist, fitting comfortably in neither category. It has tendencies in common with al-Afghani and 'Abduh, the Muslim Brotherhood, and a score of other individuals and groups, making it especially complex and difficult to label.

One can discuss these groups in terms of available categories, in other words, only if prepared to look at them with a limited focus that will of necessity obscure salient characteristics of each group.[18] The basic difficulties posed by these classification systems seem to be two: (1) the difficulty of comparative study and the process of classification and (2) the difference between *experience-distant* and *experience-near* concepts, or between deductively generated and inductively generated academic constructs.

The problem that Clifford Geertz labels the "pigeonhole disease"—the overvaluation of classificatory modes of thought (1968, 23)—seems to characterize the works cited above. These authors share a deductivist approach. They all begin with set categories (assuming the existence of different styles, positions, or tendencies) and then use these categories in discussions of their chosen topics (e.g., Islam and politics). Occasionally, they give broad-stroke examples of cases typical of the categories; but such examples seem meant to illustrate the categories, not to flesh them out or define them precisely. None of the authors, in other words, attempts to establish the existence of their categories empirically or to demonstrate why they have chosen the labels they have or why they have included various individuals and groups together in the same category. The underlying assumption of most of these authors appears to be that diverse Islamic phenomena have been adequately reduced to a limited number of types. To one who is evaluating classificatory systems from the perspective of experience with living groups, however, they appear to denature the material.[19] This classificatory problem—and the resultant denaturing of the material being studied—results from the fact that historians, political scientists, Islamicists, and comparative religionists, tend to approach the study of Islam in the modern world from a somewhat distant vantage point (e.g., through texts, rather than through personal involvement with the groups themselves) and at a general level (i.e., dealing with Islamic groups in the modern world rather than with a particular group in one locale). They see Islam, that is, from above, as opposed to the anthropological view from below (Gellner 1981, 99). It may also be due to the fact that in a deductivist approach one is looking to *find* what is believed to be there rather than looking to *discover* what the data might reveal. Because of this stance, it is only natural that the concepts employed to describe these groups are experience-distant.[20]

What seems to be needed at this point, to balance some of the weaknesses of the deductivist, classificatory approach to the study of modern Islamic phenomena, is more firsthand study of particular groups and individuals, the goal being to present them in terms of scholarly concepts that are informed by, and sensitive to, experience-near ones.

This study is an effort to capture the essence—to "explicate context and world" (Rabinow and Sullivan 1979, 13)—of three Islamic groups. The attempt has been to understand and present these three Tunisian groups in their own terms as much as possible, that is, in terms of concepts and tendencies that seem to be significant to, and characteristic of, the groups, rather than look at them simply from the viewpoint of available academic constructs.

In other words, this is an effort to describe the groups with concepts that are *meaning-adequate*. To be meaning-adequate, concepts must "retain an intelligible connection with the meaningful intentions of the actors in the situation" (Berger and Kellner 1981, 40). This does not mean that all of the ideal types by which we characterize the social world (e.g., *Islamic reform group*) are equally experience-near. It does, however, mean that the individuals whose activities are being interpreted should be able to recognize their world in our social-scientific delineation of it. If my analysis is meaning-adequate, in other words, members of each group should be able to agree that my depiction of their group is accurate.

One benefit of such an approach is that it should be possible to generate a classificatory system that represents the phenomena more adequately than do existing frameworks. In attempting to let these Tunisian groups speak for themselves, it may be that salient features, dynamics, or impulses will come to light that would be obscured by employing existing frameworks for comparison.

This is especially significant in light of the fact that the most important question of comparative study has to do with the definition of the unity within which the phenomena under study will be compared. How, in other words, are they fundamentally alike? Within what common heading should their differences be looked at? My conclusion is that these Tunisian groups represent three different but complementary approaches to Islamic reform. I summarize the salient points of contrast between the Da'wa, Movement of the Islamic Way, and Progressive Islamicists, considered as reform groups in Table 10.2.

This information can be simplified in terms of a contrast between the groups on the dimension of the focus or reform orientation of each group (see Figure 10.1).

This characterization, it seems to me, best captures the essential difference within similarity that exists between the three groups and best allows for the comparison of the groups as whole groups. The three groups all define themselves as Islamic reform groups. All have as their goal the building of an authentic Islamic society. All agree that "God sends to this Umma every one hundred years those who renew its religion" and that the renewal of Muslim society is the ultimate goal for which they are striving. Where they differ is on the question of how the society should be renewed—having chosen different foci, emphases, and realms of activity, in their efforts to bring about true and lasting reform.

The Da'wa is convinced that if a Muslim becomes personally upright, he will think and act rightly. Those in the Islamic Way are certain, on the other hand, that if a Muslim holds to comprehensive, socially active Islam, he will in the process be living rightly as a Muslim and thinking rightly. The Progressive Islamicists, finally, believe that in coming to think rightly (e.g., to rightly understand and articulate the fundamentals of Islam), a Muslim will naturally act effectively, and live appropriately as an individual. Those in each group live as Muslim individuals, take action in the social realm, and think; but each group approaches these three realms through a primary emphasis upon one of them.

Table 10.2 The Da'wa, Islamic Way, and Progressive Islamicists Considered as
          Reform Groups

Characteristic	Da'wa	Islamic Way	Progressive Islamicists
Focus	personal uprightness	social action	thought
Perceived decadence of	Muslim individuals	Muslim society	Islamic thought
Perceived solution	Call individuals to the true Islamic life	Rebuild Islamic society	Restructure Islamic thought
Key reform concept	*taslih*	*tajdid*	*tashih*
Means of working	individual by individual ("calling")	participation in the political process ("struggling")	questioning the fundamentals of Islam ("thinking")

Figure 10.1 Dimensions of Focus or Reform Orientations

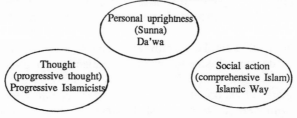

■ Notes

1. This comparison of the three groups is not meant to imply that they are of equal weight, either numerically, or in terms of political or religious impact. For further details and discussion, see Magnuson 1987.

2. The Da'wa has groups worldwide as a result of members traveling abroad for the purpose of extending the "call" to the life of faith.

3. These were given by al-Jurshi, who moved from this early group, through the Islamic movement, and finally to the Progressive Islamicists.

4. Their thinking at this point was influenced by the Muslim Brothers to the East (e.g., Sayyid and Muhammad Qutb, Hassan al-Banna, and al-Mawdudi).

5. This discussion of the Da'wa is based on participant observation and interviews with Da'wa members.

6. This leads the Da'wa to an apolitical stance for which they are often criticized by other Islamic reform groups (it being said that they possess a "church Islam," separating religion from politics). They root this noninvolvement (like all that they do) in the model of Muhammad. Da'wa members point out that the Prophet spent thirteen years in Mecca, teaching religion and right belief before the Hegira to Medina and the bringing of the

judgments of God in the areas of politics, economics, culture, and societal life. Similarly, Tunisian Muslims, lacking Islamic belief and practice, need to be taught the basics of Islam before they can possibly understand or accept the judgments of God in areas of societal life.

7. Da'wa members strongly resist the line of reasoning that the essence of sunna lies only in the behavior and character of Muhammad (e.g., his way of thinking, of dealing with problems, and of relating to people). Rather, every aspect of his life (e.g., dress, eating, sleeping, washing) is exemplary; and one's love for Muhammad—and therefore for God—is demonstrated by the degree to which one follows the Prophet's model in every area of life. Correspondingly, the focus and call of the Da'wa are *back* to the age of the Prophet. They have a clear model of the true Islamic life and society in the life and society of Muhammad and the Companions. The quest of the Da'wa is for a timeless faith, rooted in an exemplary first period, which is good for all times and which they believe can be recreated in its most significant details.

8. Wearing, for example, various kinds of head coverings including turbans, long-sleeved garments that reach to or below the knees, with pants worn underneath, and long beards. Da'wa women wear the *hijab*, "a veil [*khimar*] covering the whole head and neck but not the face, and a gown reaching to the ankles and wrists, with nothing showing from beneath it but the face and the two hands" (al-Qasir 1982, 36), as do the women of the Islamic Way. The symbolic statement being made by the *hijab*, however, differs between these two groups. For the Da'wa, it indicates living as an upright woman, according to the plain teaching of Islam.

9. In many urban Tunisian families, men and women may visit together in the same room and even eat together. In rural areas, which are more conservative, men and women are generally separate through the course of normal daily activities; but they are not strictly kept from seeing and talking to each other. The separation, in the traditional case, is due more to custom and the nature of things than to explicit belief about the way things should be.

10. In regard to their goal of righting themselves during, for example, their outings to call others to Islam, I have also heard Da'wa members use the term *tajdid*, (renewal). This is a different use of *tajdid* than by the Movement of the Islamic Way, who use it with regard to social activism and renewing the Islamic life of the society. In the framework of the Da'wa's reform activity, *tajdid* is part of the broader work of *taslih*, with the focus of bringing about personal uprightness (for further discussion of *tajdid* more broadly in Islamic history, see Voll 1983).

11. It is unclear whether he has in mind the Islamic state that presumably existed in Tunisia and fell either during colonialism or with the post-Independence Tunisian regime or whether he is referring to the fall of the Caliphate.

12. From the time of the declaration of November 7, 1987 and the removal of Bourguiba, the rhetoric of the movement regarding the ben Ali regime has been remarkably positive. The movement has clearly regarded this change as an opportunity to move beyond an adversarial relationship with the regime and to press their claims for full legal recognition as a political party. In January 1990 Ghannouchi in Paris withdrew his approval of ben Ali, but the movement did not follow suit.

13. The rest of this discussion of the Progressive Islamicists, except where otherwise noted, is based on interviews with al-Jurshi, another key leader of the group and a leader of the LTOH discussed in Chapter 2.

14. Another word used in common with the Islamic Way is *rebuilding*; but again, the emphasis of the Progressive Islamicists is on rebuilding Islamic thought on new foundations (Krishan 1982, 9).

15. Note that his modernism includes Christian Westernizers and Muslim secularists.

16. Note that Badawi includes five different categories rather than four, two of which—*Islamic reform* and *revivalist*—seem to correspond with the terms listed in category 4.

17. The four styles that he specifies vary somewhat from the systems of classification used by the other authors. His adaptationist category seems to include what other writers have separated as *secularist* and *modernist*. The most notable difference is the inclusion of the category *individualist*, which is the emphasis on the more personal and individual aspects of Islam (and includes, for example, the Sufi tradition, the Shi'a imamate, and Mahdism.)

18. Richard P. Mitchell's comparison of the Egyptian Brotherhood and 'Abduh (1969, 323–327) provides another good example of this overlapping of categories and tendencies within and between groups, indicating that a categorization such as *traditionalist–secularist–modernist–fundamentalist* may obscure significant points of similarity and differences between groups and individuals.

19. As Voll has pointed out, "The great movements of Islamic revival have been classified and reclassified by scholars until much of their spirit is lost from view" (1982b, 110).

20. According to Geertz, "an experience-near concept is, roughly, one that someone—a patient, a subject, in our case an informant—might himself naturally and effortlessly use to define what he or his fellows see, feel, think, imagine, and so on, and which he would readily understand when similarly applied by others. An experience-distant concept is one that specialists of one sort or another—an analyst, an experimenter, an ethnographer, even a priest or an ideologist—employ to forward their scientific, philosophical, or practical aims" (1983, 57).

11

The Islamicist Movement and November 7

Elbaki Hermassi

Islamicism takes its contours from the society in which it appears. There is something specific and even unique in the Tunisian Islamicist movement and in particular in its capacity to conform to local reality no matter how discouraging it may be. In the closed societies of the *hanbali* tradition, there is extremist, sectarian Islamicism. But in an open, acculturated society, Islamicism is more worldly, oriented toward modernity and pluralism. Tunisia is a country with a century and a half of reformist tradition, since Kheireddine. It is completely normal that its Islamicism be impregnated with that reformist tradition and shaped in the context of a long-lived national movement and a free labor movement.

The Islamicist movement thrived on the ideological looseness of the post-Independence state and has had the capacity to attract many of those left behind by economic growth, or—to talk like Max Weber—the proletarian intelligentsia who despair of the nationalist and socialist discourse. Yet the movement could not avoid coming under the influence of the environment in which it had developed, namely, a society that has been the recipient of one-and-a-half centuries of successive reforms (Hermassi 1989). However, none of these factors alone has been able to explain the structure or the evolution of the Tunisian Islamicist movement.

A conceptual effort toward modernism, shaping the movement into an avant-garde party able to face the underground as well as the broad daylight of public life and at last dictating the choice of a more convincing—and more and more convinced—tendency toward a legalistic strategy: this is the main feature of the Tunisian Islamicist movement, which turns Tunisia into a laboratory where the main questions asked are, What are the chances for the incorporation of Islam into the power structure? and How could this incorporation take place in a modern and democratic way?

The present flexibility of Islam in Tunisia is the outcome of a long and complex evolution, itself stamped by three preparatory phases. First, during the pre-1978 period, the group that was active in mosques, focusing on devotions and doctrinal questions, was indistinguishable from the Muslim Brotherhood in Egypt. It suffered from the same social conservatism and the same intellectual and political limitations. Between 1979 and 1984 there was a second period of intense interaction with other ideological currents within the country, encouraged not only by the necessity of creating a wave of solidarity for the leaders of the movement, then in jail, but also by the egalitarian discourse proffered by the Iranian revolution in its beginnings. This is how the fundamentalist discourse took on a progressive aspect, both within the university and also within the trade unions. Leaving the mosques, the movement became political and acquired organizational notions and operational concepts that had hitherto been the monopoly and the prerogative of left-wing protest movements. However, the apprenticeship of this objective Leninism was softened by the interaction of Islamicist leaders with other groups that are the carriers of democratic values, such as the MDS and the LTDH, as well as by their association with the newspaper *al-Ray*.

The third phase goes from August 1984, when the founding members of the MTI left prison, to the succession of November 7, 1987, which marks the end of the revolutionary impetus of the movement and the beginning of its present political phase (the fourth phase). The movement began converting itself to the local environment; and to mark this conversion a certain number of measures were taken: acceptance of the republican order and recognition of the Constitution and of the principles of intellectual and political pluralism. It was precisely this adaptation that hastened the movement's repression, as had already occurred when it requested legal status as a political party in June 1980 and its leaders (sixty-five members) were sent to prison. Yet never before was the distance from other Islamicist movements, such as the Muslim Brotherhood in Egypt and the Islamic revolution in Iran, so pronounced. The movement no longer sought to spread Islam but instead applied to become a political party that accepted the rules of the game of the republican regime, as shown by its numerous speeches against the use of violence and in favor of a common action with other legalized partners and a total respect for legal rules.

However, neither the doctrinal evolution nor other concessions made to the Tunisian national space or to political and ideological pluralism were ultimately able to change the course of the confrontation that was being prepared behind the scenes of public debate. On the public side, the press, which enjoyed relative freedom in the 1980s, conducted a continuous debate on these issues and demonstrated the protracted conflict between the MTI and the militant laicism of left-wing movements. The latter did not miss an opportunity to show the contradictions apparent in the Islamicists' discourse and the weaknesses of their doctrines. The changes that have been the most difficult to deny, such as their break with classical Islamicist positions and their decision to rely—like all the other partners—on the judgement of the electorate were for their adversaries considerations of a purely tactical nature.

For the Left (as distinguished from parties, such as the MDS, that have a more subtle and more political attitude), Islamicism in the 1980s presented a dangerous and even formidable competitor. After long years of struggle against Bourguiba's authoritarianism, the Left had to suffer the rise of an opposition that not only held another discourse—considered obscurantist—but also invested the traditional ground of the Left, namely, the university and the trade unions. As a result, the Left appeared to face a choice between an "upstart" and anachronistic force on the one hand and a worn-out but modernist regime on the other; it chose to become the defender and apostle of Bourguibism, that is, to defend the conquests of the republican regime and bar the way to rising "obscurantism."

Behind the scenes of slogans and debates, the regime of President Bourguiba in 1987 was preparing a brutal return to repression and to its natural consequence, the radicalization of the Islamicist movement and the escalation toward violence. How can such an excessive repressive movement be accounted for in the spring and summer of 1987, and how can the MTI's choice of legalistic strategy be reconciled with its decision to create an underground security force?

The regime committed two grave errors, first by refusing the entry of the MTI into the club of legally recognized political parties at a time when the movement courted such membership (*Le Monde* September 18, 1987). Admitting the MTI onto the political scene and even into Parliament would have amounted to forcing it to become publicly responsible, obliging it to define and defend a program that is ultimately highly unpopular with Tunisians. Above all, it would have clearly established the limits of the MTI's audience. In preventing the Islamicists from expressing themselves freely, Bourguiba underestimated the political maturity of Tunisians.

The other great error made by the authorities was to call for the death penalty against the Islamicist militants. There was no lack of charges against them—sedition, defamation of the president, membership in an illegal association—that could have justified long jail sentences without shocking public sensitivities or blackening Tunisia's reputation. Bourguiba, however, preferred strong medicine and therefore ran the risk of offering new martyrs to the Islamicists.

Although weakened and persecuted, the MTI remained an organization that represented a danger for those in power. Officially, 1,270 Islamicist militants were arrested, tried, and sentenced to up to eight years of prison throughout the whole country between March and the end of August 1987. The unofficial figure is close to 3,000. Despite police raids, house searches and torture during this period, the MTI was able to organize seventy to eighty political demonstrations. Before the movement of arrests started, it had been estimated that the highly structured MTI network of militants organized five to six thousand people, more than half of them still running free. Out of the five leaders of the MTI political bureau, only one was arrested. During the two years of its existence the movement had become more extreme. Its organizational skills and its success in infiltrating the civil service and controlling the university—by force or persuasion—were obvious signs of power. No other movement has ever challenged the regime on a national scale and with so much force.

Behind this relentlessness was the obstinacy of the old anticlerical leader to free Tunisia from any kind of revival of religion. Bourguiba seemed to consider such a comeback as a personal revenge against his attempts to shape Tunisia along the lines of nineteenth-century positivist ideals and of triumphant laicity. "The eradication of the Islamicist poison," he said, "will be the last service I'll render Tunisia." The campaign of repression was launched, however, at a moment when the state was going through a crisis— as though, indeed, it was a question of covering up deficiencies and hiding the delinquency of the ruling classes. It was at the same time an opportunity for several courtiers to maneuver for power, and they therefore had the utmost interest in exaggerating the importance of the "Islamicist danger."

Repression was worse than a crime, it was a mistake (in Tallyrand's formula); it did more to reinforce than to weaken the Islamicist organization. Although the campaign was able to dismantle almost entirely the whole organizational level corresponding to intermediate leadership, most of the leaders, apart from Rachid Ghannouchi, were able to escape. Moreover, since 1984, this symbolical and educated leadership had been strengthened by technicians, engineers, computer scientists and pharmacists, that is, by officials and executives without any initiation into religious matters but ready to serve the movement as technicians, especially in the underground struggle. Security members were astounded when, using search warrants, they encountered all the technical and electronic arsenal available to the movement as though the fundamentalists wanted to show those who doubted that they were capable of mastering the most advanced technology. (It may well be imagined that those who ran them to the ground asked themselves questions like, If Khomeini has been able to take over power by means of simple cassettes, what then about people who make use of computers, videos, telecommunication media, and even mobile broadcasting equipment—whose different parts had been imported secretly and mounted on the spot?) The MTI had been the first opposition movement to stand up to Bourguiba. There were many Tunisians during that fatal summer who began to feel that something had changed and that Tunisia would never again be the same.

It is in this context that the National Salvation movement, led by Zine Labidine ben Ali to stop the country from further drifting, appeared on November 7, 1987. Earlier on, ben Ali had been the defender of a realistic concept of national security that consisted in dismantling the apparatus and networks of Islamicists but also in resisting to the last the reopening of the trial of men who had already been sentenced and, especially, the imposition of a death sentence on their leaders. However, his initiative proved to be not alone, as former party militia members were apparently preparing their own move, probably with foreign help; and the underground branch of the MTI had decided to break with the legalistic strategy as a counterstroke to Bourguiba's relentlessness and to have recourse to arms to attempt to depose the head of state. There is very little information on this incident; not only the spokesmen of the new regime but also those of the MTI have deliberately tried to minimize it, considering it as a leftover from the old regime. According to several MTI leaders, it had been a matter of self-defense, because at that time they considered themselves threatened with physical elimination. A move somehow inspired by Sudan would have permitted them to depose Bourguiba and to constitute a government of national union open to all political parties. The plot by the military nucleus of the movement, revealed on November 4, three days before the change took place, would have been "embarrassing for President ben Ali as well as for ourselves" (Interview with Ghannouchi).

November 7, which was to open a new era for Tunisia and the Maghrib in general, had two main beneficiaries from the strictly political point of view: ben Ali's forces and the Islamicists. Between the new leaders and the MTI a new relationship was created, marked by realism and some common concern but also by crucial differences, notably on the subject of security. From the very beginning, the new regime adopted a new style and approach that were soon to change the outline of the political scene. One of the outstanding features of this new style was the will to achieve national reconciliation by establishing an ideological truce and ending all expressions of symbolical violence against the Islamic and Arab character of the Tunisian population. At the level of the political elite, reconciliation took the forms of the National Pact of November 1988, which sanctioned the basic political consensus between all its partners. Another feature of ben Ali's reform strategy was to begin the process of democratization; and a third, still at its beginnings, to get the country back to work.

Reconciliation over Islam and the Islamicists required a three-sided approach: the rehabilitation and reaffirmation of Islam as the religion of the nation; a more conciliatory attitude toward what was, for the first time, considered to be a more moderate form of Islamicism; and finally a firmer attitude—but this time at the legal and not the repressive level—toward any form of subversion in the name of Islam.

The attitude adopted by the MTI leaders toward President ben Ali was clear-cut and spontaneous: they considered the action of November 7 as a "historical event." They went even further: "If the political world has discovered in this action the response to the people's aspiration for a change, our movement sees in it, moreover, a divine act meant to save the country from civil war created and sustained by the former president." For the first time the MTI addressed the head of state to indicate that it was entirely ready "to turn over a new leaf concerning the past, to establish a dialogue with you without any reservations or complexes, to support the country's stability and security and to help achieve the contents of your appeal of November 7" (*Maghreb*, September 23, 1988).

The regime, for its part, gradually undertook to unfreeze the situation: Islamicist militants were freed from prison, negotiations were opened with their leaders, and different signs of appeasement became apparent mainly at the cultural level. The regime, however, did not appear to be ready to go any further and resisted the idea of allowing the Islamicists to constitute a political party. A dialogue was opened up with the moderates in order to create a "space" of activities, but the shadow of extremism and the security nucleus continued to haunt the relations. Moreover, the fear of seeing too-great concessions made to Islam and the Islamicists led certain laicizing intellectuals and some political parties to require of the authorities that they put clear limits to their appeasement. These limits, in turn, set to prevent the Islamicists' access to the political arena, were the subject of statements by Ghannouchi—more particularly of an interview to the newspaper *al-Sabah* that has attracted particular attention. All of the issues raised during negotiations with the state representatives, as well as those discussed with the left-wing opposition, were broached in the statements. First, the specific features of Tunisian fundamentalism were emphasized. Tunisian Islamicists have established, with other opposition movements and parties, "relationships of work, cooperation and solidarity which have stood the test; . . . this indicates that the relationships between the Islamicists and their opponents have a distinct and quasi-unique character within the Arab–Muslim world" (1988b). This formative experience, as well as the conceptual preparation undertaken since the beginning, enabled the movement to resist "the isolation of clandestinity and of monopoly: the hardships which our movement has had to suffer could only reinforce our determination to work within a legal framework, because the environment of isolation and clandestinity is not of a nature which would favor the evolution of thinking . . . it is more likely to favor violence and the will to break" (1988b).

More surprising is the attitude taken toward the security group; this is one of the thorniest problems in the state–MTI relationship. But it is also a delicate problem within the movement itself, since those who had decided to organize and undertake action at the risk of their lives did it only to save the movement's leadership—more particularly, Ghannouchi's neck. However, it was difficult for Ghannouchi both to defend the choice of democratic legality and the attempt to integrate his movement within the pluralistic tide and to convince the head of state of his movement's "right" to have recourse to emergency measures, including military means, in case of a political impasse. As a result, after some long thought, he decided that "these measures are not part of the movement's orientations, in spite of the exceptional circumstances surrounding them; therefore, these measures are not binding on the movement, but concern the law" (1988b). He took the opportunity to state that the MTI had adopted the following principles: (1) refusal of violence and its causes; (2) adoption of the democratic approach in its political activities; and (3) commitment not to organize within the army and the security forces.

Finally, concerning the status of women, the sheikh added a useful correction to conventional attitudes. Having for a long time considered the Code of Personal Status as part of a campaign of forced and alienating Westernization, this same code was now considered to be "a body of choices and decisions which are part of different schools of Islamist thought." The code is an example of *ijtihad* (interpretation) and represents a positive element; care should, however, be taken not to make something sacred out of it, since, like anything that is accomplished by humans, the code needs to be reevaluated from time to time as necessary, without its essence being called into question.

These clarifications were deemed sufficient for authorities to invite the MTI to take part in the formulation of the National Pact in September 1988 and, later, to appoint Sheikh Mourou as a member of the Higher Islamic Council. But the obstacle course was not over. The law on political parties includes a section providing that "no party is entitled to make reference, either in its principles, its objectives, its action or its program, to religion, to language, to race or to region." This legal stratagem is aimed almost exclusively at barring the way to the MTI and embodies the convergence of interest of the dominant political party (the RCD) and the left-wing parties— both threatened by the rise of a new power and both determined to defend Bourguiba's bequest against an opponent charged with double dealing and subversive discourse.

The authorities, thus, did not stop probing the intentions of the fundamentalists, because the apprehensions they raised were real and could not be done away with in one move. The MTI proved, however, to be a partner difficult to disarm: if the legislation on parties forbids any reference to religion, "it does not matter, we shall give up anything that threatens to raise problems in the organization of political life in this country." The movement also changed its name from the Movement of the Islamic Way to the Renaissance party, a fairly conciliatory denomination that contains nothing provocative nor any tutelary or exclusive claim. This, they hoped, would set them right and in conformity with the law on political parties. The choice of a name also reflected their desire to become reconciled with the Tunisian intelligentsia by accepting the same descent and the same roots, namely, those of the Renaissance from Kheireddine in the nineteenth century to Abdulaziz Thaalbi, Tahar Haddad, and Tahar ben Achour, as summarized in the text of the National Pact.

It was, however, the decision to hold early parliamentary elections on April 2, 1989 that played a decisive role in the relationship between the authorities and the Islamicists. While they showed the undeniable electoral vitality of the nation, the elections also proved to be counterproductive in that any Islamicist success in the field paradoxically would both generate general public protest and make the legitimizing process more uncertain. At first, the Islamicists showed no particular interest in the elections, since, for political and psychological reasons, they were preoccupied by the search for legal recognition for their party. Thus, Maitre Abdelfattah Mourou said, "Our party has no wish to be present at the forthcoming parliamentary elections. We must first of all normalize and legalize our situation. . . . Our party is not out to change anything in the present political balance; we will be satisfied with two to fifteen seats in the National Assembly during the three forthcoming parliamentary elections. . . . But even though we may not be running, our voices will be present and count for about 30% of the votes" (*Réalités*, January 27, 1989). It became evident that the Renaissance party was seeking to deal as tactfully as possible with the executive. The movement did not want to display undue haste or exert any pressure that would have upset the authorities. On February 7, 1989, the movement considered the moment opportune to submit a request to the Ministry of the Interior for authorizing the party. Ghannouchi said that if his movement obtained legal status, it would not take part in the election, so as not to embarrass President ben Ali but that without any progress in legalization, the movement would have to have an indirect part in the elections by lending support to the lists of Independents.

But once the elections had taken place, none of the participants was satisfied with their outcome. All of the 141 seats were won by RCD candidates, who proved to be effective campaigners, with not inconsiderable experience with the electoral machinery and relying on the good will of an administration that was always only too ready to support the party in power. This behavior was particularly marked in the rural areas where *omdas* and the heads of party cells are the real bosses. Although electoral manipulations were denounced by various participants, nothing was able to compromise the sure victory of the RCD. The opposition parties were throttled. Even Ahmed Mestiri's MDS, which in President Bourguiba's time had been the strongest opposition party, was to obtain a mere 3.76 percent of total votes. The Islamicist movement, however, paradoxically emerged as the country's second-largest political force, since it was able to account for 17.75 percent of all the votes. In Tunis itself and its outskirts, as well as in the larger towns of the country, it exceeded this percentage and in any case was able to score higher than all of the opposition parties together.

The polarization of political life resulting from the elections—as well as their short-term impact—calls for certain analytical remarks. First, it is the political groups with an organization structure and networks, such as the RCD and the Renaissance, who win elections; opposition parties that are weak and scattered are condemned to be losers, however correct their positions may be. Second, by refusing the idea of a common electoral front, the MDS hastened its own erosion and that of other small political parties, as well as sharpening the political crisis—even though their own political program was widely taken up and applied by President ben Ali and his team. Furthermore, many Independent voters preferred to vote "useful" in favor of the RCD when confronted with the uneasiness created by the Independents' campaign speeches.

Third, the electoral code assured the RCD's victory. If the election had been proportional representation, the Islamicists could have won twenty-four seats and the MDS two or three seats. This would have constituted a break in the all-too-unanimous behavior of the regime and given more credibility to Tunisia's political pluralism (cf. Rafaa ben Achour in *al-Sabah*, April 6, 1989). Finally, the success of the Islamists hastens polarization and ultimately militates against them:

> The Islamicist leaders were able to canvass everywhere actively, showing a real interest in the socio-economic problems of the constituencies where they had candidates, while at the same time pursuing their own campaign themes. This was done in such a way that the party in power was often forced on the defensive against these skillful speakers who found responsiveness in their audience. Indeed, the whole Islamicist strategy consisted of a sensible discourse meant to reassure the authorities without frightening the population's fears of radicalism. This is how, during the entire campaign, for instance, they avoided explicitly calling for a revision of the Code of Personal Status, which is the most literal legislation for women in the entire Maghrib. That ultimately they are aiming at power, nobody would doubt that. At present, however, they endeavor to compromise with Mr. ben Ali and not to go it alone. (*Le Monde*, April 5, 1989).

In reality, the situation is more complex. Government circles could have wished the Islamicists to have abstained voluntarily from electoral participation, at least this time. Among the opposition, Mestiri agreed to the participation of the Islamicists—but as an electoral base for his own party, as had happened during the 1981 elections. But the government did not make enough concessions (in particular by offering amnesty), and the opposition did not understand that their *protégés* had become a force in their own right. Neither one had an exact notion of the pressures and the impatience of the

militant base of the fundamentalists. And it was these pressures that led the
leaders to take part in the elections in conditions that were less than ideal and
to win enough votes to alienate all the other partners. The Renaissance
Independents raked in many votes and drew on at least three sources. First of
all, traditional Islam was represented by Sheikh Mohamed Lakhoua or Ali
Lasram, both descendants of conservative families where the imamate, or
magistrature, was passed from father to son:

> This type of Islam, with its traditional garments and somehow dusty
> discourse, does not try either to seduce or to attack, but only to say the
> "truth" as, for instance, on the inferiority of women in religious matters
> within society, on the separation between religion and the state, which
> is a heresy, or the reference (more subtle where Sheikh Lasram is
> concerned) to the *shura* which "in Islam is the real democracy." (*Jeune
> Afrique*, April 12, 1989)

Second, praising a more liberal and open Islam are modern notables from
the bar like Maitre Hila, or businessmen like Radhi Kchok, unafraid to
develop a less conventional discourse. Hila even went as far as to regret that
there was no female Islamicist candidate, "since men and women are equals."
Finally, the third type of Islamicist candidate is the radical militant,
untarnished and uncompromising, spokesman of the *mustadhafin*
(underprivileged). As the leading candidate for the independents in Sfax,
Maitre Abdelaziz Loukil wrote, in his book entitled *Excerpts from the
Prophet's Conduct*, that the law "has transgressed the right to divorce and to
polygamy, which are sacred rights in Islam" (cited in *Jeune Afrique*, April
12, 1989). When these spokesmen of the poor addressed a meeting at Al-
Hadika, a popular quarter of the capital, "an increasing tension could easily be
felt, and the young, often coming in large numbers to these meetings,
chanted slogans" (*Jeune Afrique*, April 6, 1989).

This general mobilization upset the authorities and in the last days
before the election led the RCD into launching an aggressive campaign
against the Independents, exaggerating the danger so as to frighten and
influence public opinion. Tension built up; and the other political parties, as
well as the intelligentsia in general, became frankly hostile (cf. Mohammed
Mouaada in *al-Mustaqbil*, April 8, 1989). Following the elections, the
president proposed a bill of general amnesty in favor of all those who had
been sentenced for their opinions or their affiliations. At the same time, the
last members of the clandestine group (called the Security Group) were
released. Thus, the Islamicists consider themselves as being restored to their
human rights; but they are still not at the point of obtaining their political
rights. On July 23, 1989 the Tunisian president set the bar even higher than
before: "Nothing justifies the creation of a group as long as it has not defined
the type of society it commends, clarified its position toward a certain

number of civilizational issues and committed itself to respect the equality of rights and duties of citizens, men and women, as well as the principle of toleration and of the liberty of conscience."

To deal with the problem, there are many scenarios. The first is to be excluded out of hand: it is the scenario of confrontation. While there are Tunisian circles who fear Islamicism and indeed fear any ideologization of local culture, hate and fear must not hide the memory that confrontation is a logic that was tried by the previous regime and failed. If confrontation remains improbable and repression becomes unlikely after the political opening and electoral success of the Islamicists, certain voices can even be heard arguing for the opportuneness of recognizing the party. This was the case of the president of the Constitutional Law Association, for whom "there exists no logical or legal reason to exclude a political current of a Muslim nature . . . and I think that is would be politically wise to encourage its public participation and to resist all forms of secret activities" (*Maghreb*, May 12, 1989). Others have adopted the same attitude because they consider legalization the best means of weakening the movement; they feel that this type of structure will not resist the open air for long. As with all of the legally recognized parties, the Islamicist party will be torn and weakened by its own contradictions. For still others, legalization will be the best means of comforting the moderate wing, whose ambition tends not so much to changing society as to participating in politics (*Réalités*, January 27, 1989).

Another scenario is ideal, that of bypassing simple recognition in the juridical sense. The Islamicists give too much importance to the notion of an official seal of approval, as if a piece of paper would change deeper realities. In fact, the real recognition of Islamicism comes with the restructuring of the political system—for example, through the formation of a new presidential party. The RCD is powerful in the rural sector and the Islamicist movement in the urban sector. There are therefore some two million modern urban and semiurban Tunisians who are outside of either organization and who support the new regime. A third party would create the political system capable of discussion and debate and allow for the luxury of recognizing the Islamicist movement. This solution, however, is not for the immediate future.

Yet it is most likely that for quite some time to come the Islamicists will have to accept a de facto existence and a mode of conflictual participation, as everything seems to indicate that the regime is ready to take advantage of the fear raised by the Islamicists within the liberal opposition and the privileged circles to legitimize its control of power and its reticence to accept a political game that would be entirely open (cf. Leveau 1989).

This is not an ideal solution; it is even a costly one both for the movement itself (because without a civic existence, the leadership faction that opted for pluralism is in danger of being contested or even eliminated by extremists) and for the regime (because de facto recognition is often accompanied by surveillance and police).

Tunisia is a laboratory country with the opportunity of taking some chances that could be useful for its own future and for the rest of the Arab world. One such venture would be that of institutionalizing political Islam to show that one can be both Muslim and democratic.

12

The New Strategy of the Movement of the Islamic Way: Manipulation or Expression of Political Culture?

Abdelkader Zghal

From the beginning of the 1980s, it became evident that the "Tunisian Muslim Brothers" were not repeating all the political slogans of the Egyptian Muslim Brothers, who were the first to enunciate the general demand of all the Islamic militants, "*Al-Islam din wa-dawla.*" The literal translation of this political slogan, "Islam is both religion and state," indicates a rejection of the distinction between religious and state affairs. The Tunisian MTI adopted this new concept of politics, expressed for the first time by the founder of the Egyptian Muslim Brothers Association, Hassan al-Banna, but rejected his stand on the concept of democracy and on the role of political parties. Instead, the MTI joined the position of the leader of the Sudanese Muslim Brothers, Hassan al-Turabi, on the legitimacy of the political parties, including the Communist party, in a Muslim community. This was a real progress for the Islamicists, compared to the political stand of al-Banna.

However, there should be no confusion about the meaning of the political position of the Islamicist militants in Tunisia and Sudan. For them, democracy and political pluralism are not values in themselves. The goal is still *Al-Islam din-wa-dawla*, that is, the fusion of polity and religion and the strict application by the state of the religious law, or Shari'a. Political democracy and multipartism are for them just a less costly means than armed struggle of putting pressure on the political decisionmakers and the first step in conquering the state machinery. The final goal is not a state under the laws of a constitution voted by the representatives of the citizens but an Islamic state following the precepts of the motto, *Al-Islam dastourouna* ("Islam is our constitution").

The Sudanese Muslim Brothers' participation in the government of the bloody dictator Jaafar al-Numeiri in order to apply the laws of the Shari'a shows the priorities of values for some Islamicists who claim to be attached to the idea of a political democracy. However, the Tunisian leaders went further in their general demand for political democracy. After the overthrow of Bourguiba on November 7, 1987, and the liberation of almost all the Islamicist political prisoners, the language of the Islamicist leaders changed quite rapidly and put the Tunisian Islamicists in the vanguard of the political movements of Islam. The issue at hand concerning the new strategy of the Tunisian Islamicist movement is whether it is a mere manipulation of public opinion in order to be legally recognized as a political party or whether the new standpoint is the reflection of the roots of the movement in civilian society and the Tunisian political culture.

The thesis developed in this chapter is that manipulation is an inappropriate explanation of the Islamicists' strategy in the sense that the truth is not the most relevant criterion for situating political actors. Instead, the interpretation proposed puts the new strategy of the MTI in the context of the social conditions of production and the general framework of the speeches and activities of the Islamicist militants. The current political mobilization of Islam has been analyzed in two ways: orientalists or neo-orientalist scholars essentially ask to what extent the militant action of the Islamicists is the reactivation of the Muslim tradition, the reenactment of a drama whose scenery and costumes change with the historic periods but whose scenario always stays the same. Political scientists rather focus on the analysis of present political stakes. Their studies are in general limited to a single country and their investigations deal essentially with the socioprofessional origins and the political viewpoints of the Islamicist militants. These studies have already produced a huge amount of empirical data and interpretations that deserve to be confronted and better integrated in a theoretical debate about the formation of the social and political movements. It does not seem that this theoretical debate is really engaged beyond the classical controversy between "culturalists" and "structuralists."

The interpretation that will be defended in this chapter is that the study of the Islamicist phenomenon must place the social movement neither in the nonhistorical temporality of the orientalists nor in the empirical temporality of the political scientist. The true historical framework of the Islamicist phenomenon is decolonization and the construction of modern nation–states. The Islamicist phenomenon is a component of the ideology and the dynamics of nationalist movements and can be interpreted as an outgrowth or offshoot of the national liberation movements and a reaction to the institutionalization of these movements in the context of a nation–state. If one accepts this hypothesis, one must admit that what made the unity and the diversity of the nationalist movements such as the Egyptian Wafd and the Tunisian Neo-Destour has also reproduced the unity and diversity of the Egyptian and Tunisian Islamicist movements. Al-Banna, founder of the Egyptian Muslim Brothers is, so to speak, the illegitimate son of Saad Zaghlul just as Rachid

Ghannouchi, the leader of the MTI, is the illegitimate son of Habib Bourguiba.

■ Ghannouchi and Bourguiba

Along with all the other nationalist leaders, Bourguiba shared the European idea that each nation or cultural community should be ruled by its nationals. The criterion of national belonging is above all cultural. Nationals speak the same language and are, in principle, socialized in the same culture, in the anthropological sense. Nationalism is a phenomenon of politicization of the cultural dimension, a political mobilization of the culture. The task of nationalism is to impose an automatic cultural homogenization between the governing and the governed. The state model that mobilized the passion of the nationalists—the nation–state—limits itself to one principle, namely, that political legitimacy is above all cultural. The nation–state means the nondifferentiation between the cultural and the political. The cultural is the foundation of the political, and the latter is at the service of the cultural. The role of the state, according to the nationalists, is first of all to safeguard and develop the national culture; on a practical level, the nationalists are always asked to resolve the tension between efforts to safeguard the culture inherited from the past and the will to modernize this culture in order to acquire the wealth and the power necessary for the defense of national independence. Each political community organized under the model of a nation–state has managed this tension according its specific conditions.

Tunisia is, in the Arab world, the nation–state that, under the rule of Bourguiba, has been the most radical in its will to modernize cultural practices even at the expense of a large part of the public who remain tied to their own traditions. The Islamic movement is the product and the expression of this resistance to the modernization policy of Bourguiba, a policy perceived as a mechanism of submission and alienation to the West. To this part of the public, Bourguiba through his reforms repudiated the ideology of the nationalist movement, whose principal demand was the preservation of the national culture against a colonial policy that aimed at marginalizing the national language and culture. The Islamicists saw Tunisian society caught up in a process of Westernization of customs not even achieved during the colonial times. The program of the Islamicists is to oppose this process of Westernization on behalf of the national culture and more specifically on behalf of Islam.

However, just as the interpretation of the notion of national culture and subsequent classification of social practices into legitimate or illegitimate behaviors have been the subject of political conflict among nationalist militants, the interpretation of Islam and subsequent classification of social

practices into orthodox or heterodox behaviors was and still remains a subject
of political conflict among the different tendencies of Islamicist militants.
According to Ghannouchi—and on this point his analysis is accurate—there
are, in Tunisian society and within the MTI, three modes of practice of the
Muslim religion: (1) traditional practices including the participation in
religious brotherhoods, (2) behaviors influenced by the Salafist movement
and the ideology of the Egyptian Muslim Brothers, and (3) rational religious
behavior that gives precedence to reason in the interpretation of holy texts.
What Ghannouchi did not say was that Bourguiba, although imbued with the
political culture of the Third French Republic, was not an atheist intellectual
in the precise sense of the term but a Muslim in favor of a rational
interpretation of Islam. Unlike Attaturk in Turkey, his political project did
not seek to detach the Tunisians from the Muslim religion but rather to
reconcile Islam with certain values of modernity. The strategy of the direction
of the MTI, on the contrary, was to deal carefully and tactically with
traditional Islam, to adapt Salafist Islam to the Tunisian context, and to
impose limits on the interpretations of Islam according to rational thought in
order to reconcile Islam with the values of modernity. Thus, in a text written
in 1984, Ghannouchi criticized the defenders of the rational religious
behaviors—(al-tadayun al-aqlani)—who dared liken the banning of polygamy
to a "liberating asset."

The question then is, What happened to the MTI to lead Ghannouchi to
state, after Bourguiba's fall, that the law forbidding polygamy was the
expression of an *ijtihad*, or legitimate interpretation of the holy texts,
contradicting his statements of 1984? This declaration was the prelude and
probably the precondition to a tacit recognition of the movement by the
government and to the participation of one of their representatives in the
elaboration of the National Pact. But did they sign this pact—which made the
Code of Personal Status promulgated by Bourguiba one of the foundations of
the Tunisian Republic—solely in the purpose of participating legally in
political competition?

Indeed, the leaders of the MTI went further than expected in their
acknowledgment of the values of modernity in the universal sense.
Abdelfattah Mourou, the second leader of the movement, defied Muslim
opinion almost entirely when he told the French magazine *Le Point* that he
would not mind having Salman Rushdie's book *Satanic Verses* freely
circulate in the Muslim countries, at the very moment when several
thousands of Muslims were demonstrating against the publication of a book
that ridiculed the Prophet and his fellows. This declaration, undoubtedly
provocative to the traditional Islam, as well as to Salafist Islam, was
published in Tunisian newspapers without apparently producing any real
uproar within the MTI. The book by Salman Rushdie remains, of course,
banned in Tunisia as in the other Muslim countries.

However, the provocative nature of Mourou's declaration should not be overstated. Above all, it has been perceived as a specific position limited to the political level in order to show the autonomy of the MTI in relation to the regime of Khomeini. In fact it is Ghannouchi who is perceived as the spokesman and the theoretician of the movement. The legitimization of the law forbidding polygamy was first declared by Ghannouchi, in another political statement, but one that also bears on the interpretation of holy texts. It announces a shift in position very close if not the same as that of Muslims claiming the primacy of reason in the interpretation of the holy texts. Ghannouchi defended his new theoretical stand in a debate at the Islamic Center of Los Angeles on January 1, 1989, when U.S. and non-U.S. Muslims of different backgrounds participated. Some short passages deserve to be quoted in order to illustrate the nature and the scope of the changes in interpreting Islam related to the Salafist stand.

Addressing Americans of Muslim confession, Ghannouchi said:

Your duty as Muslims is to entrench yourself in this land, to assimilate the culture of your surrounding environment, to assimilate its language, its history and to consider yourself as faithful patriots. No one asks you to import the Arabic fashion of practicing religion—al-tadayun—or of the Gulf countries or of Tunisia. Your duty is to innovate your religious practice, to innovate a form of inter-action between Islam and the reality of your environment in order to produce something utterly new. We are asking you as Muslims living in a society that has reached the highest scientific level, to not imitate, reproduce the religious practices developed in under-developing environments. We ask you to be a new contribution to the Muslim notion to reform Muslim thought, and produce an evolved form of religious practice that will favor the evolution of underdeveloped Muslim populations. . . . You are living in a country closer to Islam than underdeveloped countries because here, a set of norms—sounan—divine in the universe and in society is well respected. (1989a)

In answering a question about the relationship between Islam and democracy, Ghannouchi defended the principle of citizenship in Muslim states independent of the religious adherence: "If we suppose there to be Christians and Jews, they are citizens in the Islamic state with only few restrictions concerning religion as in the case of the head of state whose function is to apply the [state] religion. However we have known in Muslim history a large number of Christian and Jewish ministers" (1989a).

To a question regarding the place of woman in the MTI, Ghannouchi answered by recalling an incident that occurred during a meeting of the Central Committee of the movement, the authority intermediate between the political bureau and the congress, where for the first time two women took part in this political decisionmaking body. A member of the committee took the floor to protest against the women's attendance, saying that the principle of their participation in the work of the committee should be discussed and settled by a *fatwa*—a legal opinion. According to this member, a commission should be created from the beginning to give an authoritative judgment on the principle of participation of women at the level of political authority. One of the women took the floor to say: "If men set up a commission to judge the legality of women's participation in the political life, I wonder why women do not set up a commission to pass the same judgment on the political role of men. If Islam came for men as well as for women, I do not see any reason why a commission should give the right to authorize or forbid the political action of one of the two sexes" (1989c). According to Ghannouchi, after the intervention of this woman, the problem of women's participation was no longer the subject of debate.

The set of these politicoreligious standpoints of Ghannouchi and of Mourou are built on a tension between two, apparently contradictory notions of politics: *religious* and *liberal–consitutional*.

The religious conception gives the head of state the function of applying the religion, according to the sayings of Ghannouchi. He did not specify on what basis of reasoning the head of state is supposed to interpret the holy texts. Ghannouchi changed his mind in regard to the law forbidding polygamy. The new interpretation of this Qur'anic text on polygamy is undoubtedly the result of the political change since November 7, 1987 with Bourguiba's overthrow. It was as the leader of the MTI that Ghannouchi legitimized the law forbidding polygamy. Putting the head of state in charge of the "application of the religion" means that religion is subjected to politics. In the absence of institutional and financial independence of the ulema (religious scholars) "Islam is both religion and state" can only mean the submission of religion to politics, including the possibility of changing religious men into political men.

The liberal–constitutional conception, coexisting with the first, takes into account the notion of citizenship and the set of values that are the foundation of the principle of the of human rights such as equality between the sexes, freedom of information and the press, and equality before the law independent of the religious convictions of the citizens. It is this same conception of politics that was defended in the slogans and declarations of the nationalist parties in the period from the 1920s until Independence. The nationalist strategies were to place the colonial powers in a difficult situation in asking them to respect their own values and to apply the principles of their government within the colonies.

One cannot say that the nationalists did not believe at this time in Western values. But they were, above all, nationalists. The foundation of their claims was that the state should be ruled by political men who spoke the language of the country and shared the culture of the society. Democracy was conceived as a byproduct of the sovereignty of the nation understood as a community sharing the same history and the same culture. Thus during the period of confrontation between the nationalists and the colonial powers, the national culture with its different components (history, language, religion) became the real subject of the political struggle. During this period Bourguiba defended the wearing of the veil against the first Tunisian women who claimed the right to appear in public without it. He pushed the defense of Islam even up to the point of declaring as heretics the Tunisians who had willingly acquired French citizenship. As a consequence, they were deprived of the right to be buried in Muslim cemeteries.

This position of Bourguiba can be compared to that of Ghannouchi at Los Angeles when he addressed U.S. Muslim citizens, asking them to be faithful to their country and to assimilate its language and its culture and to not live isolated and withdrawn into the Muslim community. Bourguiba, as a nationalist, used to politicize the cultural—more specifically the religious— within the perspective of the conquest of political power. Ghannouchi, as the leader of the MTI, distinguished between the notions of citizenship and religion in order to give an image of his movement different from that of Khomeini. Ghannouchi is, in the end, the illegitimate son of Bourguiba, as Bourguiba was the illegitimate son of the Third and Fourth French Republics. However, both are above all the products of Tunisian civil society, well entrenched within the long tradition of exchange between the two shores of the Mediterranean and continuing the reformist tradition of political men such as Kheireddine and of the ulema such as Tahar ben Achour.

■ Ghannouchi and the New Social Periphery

Bourguiba acquired from the beginning of the 1930s the status of spokesman of the nationalist movement. He expressed specifically the concerns and expectations of the new social periphery created by the changes introduced by colonization. The geographical basis of this social periphery is in general urban and semiurban. The nationalist militants of rural origins are, most of the time, educated people, which was exceptional in a rural environment, or people whose professional activity would continuously put them in touch with the urban environment. This social periphery has known a relative improvement of its standard of living while at the same time feeling a blockage in regard to social promotion. The socioprofessional recruitment of the social periphery came from the products of French schools and traditional education, craftsmen, and shopkeepers as well as qualified or semiqualified workmen in large industrial firms. Traditional elites of urban or rural origins were suspicious of the nationalist movement and more specifically of its radical tendency.

Independence consolidated and enlarged this social base while creating a new bourgeoisie composed of businessmen and technobureaucrats. However, the most spectacular change since the time of Independence has been twofold: (1) the urbanization of the countryside and the ruralization of the cities and (2) the expansion of the education network throughout the whole country, including the most remote rural regions from the urban centers. These changes produced a new social periphery coming essentially from the many graduates and school-leavers who have been blocked in their social promotion and from a large sector of the new petite bourgeoisie coming mainly from the rural or semiurban parts of the country and destabilized by the rapid changes and the new requirements of modernity and, as a result, downgraded in comparison to the new bourgeoisie. The conspicuous consumption of the latter and its slavish imitation not of Western values but of external manifestations of Western behavior are one of the factors that created the feeling of frustration of a large part of the new petite bourgeoisie and of the mass of educated people prone to unemployment or professional disqualification.

The feeling of frustration of the new social periphery could not express itself in terms of class struggle because of the broad diversity in the socioprofessional status of its members. They could express their frustration politically only through moral judgement that would delegitimize the existing political system. The political regime that came with Independence is perceived by the new social periphery as above all a system of corruption: it stands with the rich against the poor and favors the diffusion of Western values and culture against the national culture and values—in other words, a betrayal of the goals of the nationalist movement. The latter was born to defend the national culture and values—more specifically, Islam—against the encroachment of the Western colonial powers; yet the state, born of Independence, through its policy of modernization behaves as the successor of the colonial regime under the direction of nationals.

The delegitimization of the new Tunisian order extends to almost all the Arab and Muslim states. The defeat of the Arabs in 1967 strengthened the conviction of the betrayal of all the Arab countries. The only perspective of change perceived by a large part of the new periphery lies in a return to the foundations of the nationalist movement, that is, the submission of the political to the cultural and the elimination of difference between the culture of the governed and that of the governing, or society and state. The current ruling class is seen to be, as a whole, utterly Westernized and culturally detached from its social basis. Hence, the slogan *Al-Islam din wa-dawla*, which means that the whole culture is to be submitted or reduced to the religious—more specifically to a temporal interpretation of the religious presented as the only legitimate interpretation of Islam. Ghannouchi's path reveals *his* identification with the new social periphery and its tacit ideology, as well as *its* identification (a large part of it) with Ghannouchi and his explicit ideology. A comparison of the itineraries of Ghannouchi as the leader of the MTI and al-Banna as the founder of the Association of the Egyptian Muslim Brothers allows us to understand the originality of the MTI and its new strategy that places it, relative to other Islamic movements, in a vanguard position and in a modernist direction, just as the Destourian party of Bourguiba was in a similar relation to the other nationalist parties.

Ghannouchi was born in 1941, thirty-five years after al-Banna, a span of time equivalent to the distance between Tunisian and Egyptian independence. Both were teenagers at the time of their country's independence. Both were born in a modest social environment: Ghannouchi's father was a small peasant, al-Banna's a clock repairman.

Ghannouchi was born in an oasis, Al-Hama, 30 kilometers from Gabes, in a region close to the Libyan border. It is a deserted area compared with the coastal plains of the Sahel, from which many of the political elites (above all Bourguiba) came. The South of Tunisia was one of the most active centers of the Youssefist movement of dissidents from the Neo-Destour at the beginning of Independence, during the confrontation between Salah ben Youssef and Bourguiba and is well known for its attachment to Arabism. Ghannouchi was therefore born not only in a poor family but also in a region that felt deserted by the newly independent state. Ghannouchi was forced to leave primary school for two years because of the poverty of his family, but he returned to the more traditional school system of the Zitouna Mosque, whose instruction in Arabic did not prepare for higher education in Tunisia, because the latter was exclusively taught in French. From the beginning of Independence, Ghannouchi was in a position of objective marginalization, feeling that he was blocked in his desire to be socially promoted. He could support the Egyptian leader Abd al-Nasser against Bourguiba, confusing Arabism and Islamism, as many Tunisians did at this time. Ghannouchi was neither really politicized nor excessively concerned about religion. His main concern was to save enough money so to go to Egypt and keep studying in a country where university education was given in Arabic. In order to realize his project, Ghannouchi, without knowing it, followed the example set by al-Banna by starting his career as a teacher, in a primary school in the area of Gafsa. He eventually fulfilled his design and applied to the Agronomy School of the University of Cairo.

It was during his stay in Cairo that Ghannouchi's curiosity led him to listen to Radio Albania, which broadcast in Arabic to the Middle East. He even wrote to the station, which emitted a special ideology—a mix of Third World Marxism with a millenarianist tonality combined with a constant criticism of the Soviet policy. This detail tells something about Ghannouchi's personality and more precisely his predisposition to revolutionary millenarianism. However, at that time Ghannouchi was not affiliated to any political party. He only thought of succeeding in his studies. In the meantime, the relationship between Tunisia and Egypt suddenly deteriorated and Ghannouchi found himself threatened with expulsion. Thus, Albania seemed to Ghannouchi the only available solution to keep up his studies. The future leader of the MTI was saved by a mere accident from being educated in a Marxist–Leninist university, however. In buying his plane ticket to Albania in a travel agency, he met by chance a Tunisian friend who was coming back from Syria and who advised him to go to Syria. The Syrian government was generous in giving scholarships to Tunisian students. At the end, he went to Damascus and graduated from Damascus University in Philosophy and Social Science.

In Syria, Ghannouchi was still a supporter of Abd al-Nasser and against the Ba'th party that provoked the failure of the union between Egypt and Syria. He even militated, for a while, in favor of the pro-Nasserist Socialist Union party. However, his political involvement was rather superficial. It was only after the defeat of 1967 that Ghannouchi felt utterly and psychologically destabilized and looked for a meaning and reason to this defeat. Since that date, his intermittent curiosity about religion and politics became the center of his reflection and concern. After the Arab defeat and his own psychological crisis, Ghannouchi let his beard grow—"like Castro," as he used to say. This last remark, along with his plans to continue his studies in Albania, show a certain sensitivity not to Marxism or communism but to the Third World revolutions that did not repudiate their national culture.

Ghannouchi, victim of Bourguiba's francophone policy, was naturally in favor of Nasser's Arabism and sensitive to the Third World revolutions. The defeat of the Arab states in 1967 convinced him that Islam was the only force of resistance able to oppose the policy of domination of the Western powers. However, like all the Tunisians of his generation, he was fascinated by the West. During his stay in Syria he visited several European countries, sometimes doing some work reserved for immigrants. At the end of his studies in Syria, he spent a year in Paris in order to prepare his doctorate on Muslim philosophy while working in the same conditions as an immigrant. At the end, it was neither in Tunis nor Cairo nor Damascus that Ghannouchi had his first experience as an Islamic militant but rather in Paris, as part of the Group al-Tabligh, which went around the poorer districts of immigrants in order to spread the word of God. This first experience of militantism followed a spirit similar to that of the discussions of al-Banna in the bars of Cairo as a student, with the difference that al-Banna knew little of the reality of the Western society, whereas Ghannouchi had lived and been a militant in the West.

The death of his mother while he was in Paris put an end to Ghannouchi's plan for a doctorate in Islamic philosophy. On his return to Tunis at the beginning of the 1970s, he was rapidly integrated in a group that organized discussions and studies in mosques. The participation of the youth in these circles rapidly exceeded the expectations of the supervisors. As the Left and the extreme Left were at this time the only poles of opposition that bothered the government, the group easily obtained authorization to publish a magazine, *al-Maarifa*. Two main themes dominated the direction of the first issues: a criticism of Westernization and a systematic attack of the Left and the communists all over the world. The criticism of the government policy was more than timid, again recalling the political orientation of the Egyptian Muslim Brothers at the time of al-Banna, which was more against the Wafd party than against Farouk. With the Iranian revolution and the rapid expansion of the base of Islamic militants, the orientation of the magazine changed completely. Ghannouchi suddenly found himself at the head of a political movement that he could not control, like al-Banna at the time of the assassination of Prime Minister Mahmud Nuqrashi. Al-Banna was assassinated by the secret police of King Farouk, whereas Ghannouchi escaped from a death sentence and execution because of Bourguiba's overthrow.

The parallels between al-Banna's and Ghannouchi's paths are instructive beyond the differences in the countries and periods. Both have a teaching background rather than that of a religious man. Nonetheless, they acquired the status of imam (al-Banna) and sheikh (Ghannouchi). Neither has enriched Muslim thought with an original work that could be considered a true *ijtihad* of modern times. Both are, above all, men of political action. They launched themselves into politics almost without realizing it and without being able to control the wave that pushed them to confront the state with its police and army, without having at their disposal stable, autonomous networks of support that would be recognized by the population, like the Shiite militants in Iran.

The differences between the two paths are equally meaningful. Despite their belonging to profoundly religious families, the two leaders did not have the same type of relationship with Islam. Al-Banna was always concerned about religion. Ghannouchi before the defeat of 1967 was not more active in religion than the majority of the Tunisian youth of the time. Like most everyone in the Maghrib, he respected the fast of the Ramadan more than the practice of the prayer. He visited the Great Mosque of the Zitouna of Tunis only after his final return from Paris, when he was thirty. Ghannouchi might have been a Marxist–Leninist militant if he had not had to leave primary school for two years and to attend the Zitouna system of Tunis instead of the high schools that led to the universities of Tunis and Paris.

Ghannouchi has a difficult relation with the West, as did the nationalists before Independence and even after. However, for Ghannouchi the fight for independence is not over yet. He used to say that he would like "to free himself from the hegemony of the Western culture as well as the Western way of life, in order to build a contemporary Islamic society that would dip into the Western culture without losing itself." To dip into the heart without losing oneself, this is the ambivalence of great thwarted passions—hence, the recurrent condemnation of Westernization and at the same time the terrible sentence from Los Angeles: "You are living in a country closer to Islam than that of the developing countries because here a set of divine norms in the universe and within the society is well respected." To be sure, the latter sentence will not be said spontaneously by Ghannouchi in a public lecture in Tunis. However, who would ask a politician to reproduce the same speech in front of different publics? What is important is that he expressed publicly this very positive image of U.S. society. One could say that this sentence was above all a message to the U.S. government via the Muslim population of Los Angeles. However, Ghannouchi knew that the tapes of his speeches would circulate quickly in Tunisia. He knew he would not be repudiated by his militant base due to the content of this speech. Inevitably, some militants would be shocked, as they were when he declared publicly in Tunis that the law forbidding polygamy was an *ijtihad*. Al-Banna and the other leaders of the Islamic movements did not dare to legitimize the ban on polygamy. The demand for polygamy is limited to a small number of old ulema educated at the Zitouna. This category of Muslims attached to the traditional concept of Islam does not represent the militant base of the MTI. The hard core of the militants is composed of intellectuals of the new social periphery, among whom several used to read the French newspaper *Le Monde*. As a politician seeking to keep control of his militants—as of his sympathizers—Ghannouchi is obliged to have different political speeches in order to keep his base and to make indispensable political alliances. He will certainly be considered as someone who has a double language, as Bourguiba did at the time of the struggle for national liberation. This should not be surprising since he is not a theologian like Ibn Taymiya, a predecessor of the Egyptian Muslim Brothers, but a politician who tries to expand his political base and reduce the opposition from his partners and opponents.

These contradictions are above all the expression of contradictions at the base, and to a certain extent throughout the whole, of Tunisian society. They are also, in a different way, the contradictions of nationalism that fought against the colonial regime while seeking to imitate the model of colonial society. The ambivalence of Ghannouchi's language is a reproduction of Bourguiba's language in the colonial era. Indeed, the social foundation of the MTI is structurally similar to that of Destour during the 1930s, with only a discrepancy of space and of socioprofessional categories. This gap is due to the changes that Tunisia has undergone over the last fifty years. Thus, the Sahel that had never generated any political elites has been the center of the nationalist protest and the active source of production of intellectuals and politicoadministrative authorities since the 1930s. Currently, it is in the deserted regions of the South, Center and Northwest that the revolutionary intellectuals of the secular Left, as of the religious Right, develop. Other areas produce their protesters, as in the past; but the leaders of the Islamicists and the leftists are currently coming from the disinherited regions of the country. The case of leftist and Islamicist female militants is special. They are everywhere in the position of another "social periphery," the one of gender hierarchy. Therefore, they come from all the social categories, more particularly from the top. All are not against Ghannouchi, but the most forceful opposition to Ghannouchi and to the MTI comes from the feminist militants.

Ghannouchi remains, at the end, a spokesman of the more or less Westernized new social periphery, fighting against the feeling of depersonalization and social marginalization. The path of Ghannouchi is a mirror that allows an understanding of this struggle and the contradictions of the ideology that are its underpinnings. The notion of manipulation as qualifying the new strategy of the MTI seems to be inappropriate to an understanding of the sociohistoric dynamics of this social movement.

_____ PART 4

REFORM AND
FOREIGN RELATIONS

13

Tunisian Foreign Policy: Continuity and Change Under Bourguiba and ben Ali

Mary-Jane Deeb
Ellen Laipson

S mall, Third World nations face certain constraints that to a significant degree determine the course of their foreign policies. They are vulnerable to external intervention, primarily by regional powers, because they are small and less capable of defending themselves; they are strongly affected by events occurring within the larger system of states to which they belong, which can have serious destabilizing consequences for their regimes; and finally, they are rarely, if ever, economically self-reliant and depend to some degree on more advanced nations to provide them with the consumer goods they lack and the technological assistance they need.

In order to protect their independence and territorial sovereignty, as well as the political and economic stability of their regimes, small, developing nations have to adopt certain strategies to regulate their foreign policies within the system of states to which they belong, as well as with nations on which they depend outside the system. As a result, the effect of domestic changes on foreign policy—unless very radical—is limited, the corrective trimming of reform has less meaning in foreign than in domestic relations, and established patterns of foreign affairs tend to be reaffirmed.

Situated midway between Algeria and Morocco to the west, and Libya and Egypt to the east, Tunisia has had to find ways to maintain its political independence and territorial sovereignty within a North African system of states dominated by major powers. It has also had to protect itself from the aggressions of a minor neighbor such as Libya. It has achieved this by means of a number of mutually reinforcing strategies. On the Maghribi level, there have been sustained efforts to expand the Maghrib system, so that Tunisia would not be pinched between the Moroccan–Algerian rivalry, to avoid political confrontations that might lead to military interventions by its two more powerful neighbors, and to engage as a mediator and arbitrator in regional conflicts that threaten regional stability.

On the international level, the security dimension of cooperation with Western countries has been the dominant concern of Tunisia since Independence. The need to protect territorial sovereignty has made it imperative to maintain close ties with major Western powers such as France and the United States. Whereas until the late 1970s its reliance on the West for protection was primarily as an off-shore deterrent to would-be invaders in the region, since 1980 the West has become the source of arms and military training to enable Tunisia to hold its own in case of a military confrontation with its neighbors.

To build a strong economy despite limited resources, Tunisia, after Independence, had to rely on assistance from nations outside the system. Although France became its principal trade partner, Bourguiba's strategy was to expand and diversify Tunisia's ties to include other nations of the Western world and to maintain those ties despite some domestic and regional opposition. President ben Ali has followed the same course in foreign policy since he came to power.

These are the two poles—the West, represented most importantly by the EC, and the Arab World, represented primarily by the Maghrib—that form the parameters of Tunisia's world and world role. These two poles can be viewed as alternative or competitive options, as it can be argued that increased cooperation among Maghrib states, as exemplified by the 1989 Arab Maghrib Union (UMA) treaty, reflected growing and common concern among its signatories about the economic threat from the West and the challenge of the unification of Europe's market in 1992. At the same time, the two regional systems have many connections; and for small states like Tunisia, association with both areas is complementary, mutually reinforcing, and provides a needed balance. This chapter examines, in depth, Tunisian foreign policy toward these two regional systems. It considers the importance of the past in shaping current policies and examines the current and prospective agenda for Tunisia's foreign policy.

■ Tunisia and the Maghrib: Strategies of Alliance

The regional system of states that emerged in North Africa in the early 1960s comprised Morocco, Tunisia, and the newly independent Algerian republic. This ménage à trois meant that Tunisia, the weakest member, would continuously be called on to take sides with one or the other of the two major powers. Such a position was politically untenable for Bourguiba, as it would have resulted in external pressure on Tunisia and even intervention in its internal affairs. A regional system of states in which there were more than three states offered more flexibility and potential for maneuverability.

Tunisia was consequently one of the first Arab states to recognize Mauritania's independence in 1960, a move calculated to increase the number of states in the region and alter the regional balance of power to give it more freedom of action. Tunisia's recognition caused serious tensions to develop in its relationship with Morocco, which had adamantly refused to recognize Mauritania's independence claiming it as part of Greater Morocco (Damis 1983b, 30–31). At the risk of antagonizing Morocco in the short run, Bourguiba was far-sighted enough to extend the boundaries of the Maghrib in order to diffuse a threat to Tunisia's political independence.

Tunisia's position on Mauritania was consistent throughout the past three decades. It played an important role in mediating between Morocco and Mauritania in 1969, when Morocco finally recognized Mauritania at the Islamic Summit in Rabat, diffusing one of the major regional conflicts in the region. The reasons for Morocco's recognition of Mauritania at that time were due to regional developments unrelated to Tunisian diplomacy, but Tunisia played an important role in facilitating Mauritania's inclusion in the regional system of states (Damis 1983a, 36).

In March 1983 Algeria and Tunisia signed a Treaty of Brotherhood and Concord, which emphasized national security and defense issues. In December of that year Mauritania was included in the alliance as well. The primary instigator in the inclusion of Mauritania appears to have been Algeria; but, according to the treaty, it would not have been possible to include Mauritania without the consent of both parties concerned. Thus, Tunisia had its own interests for having Mauritania join the treaty. An alliance that included more than one state offered more freedom of action and decisionmaking than a bilateral alliance dominated by Algeria. Bourguiba thus paved the way for Mauritania to become an integral part of North Africa; and its later inclusion in the UMA may be due, in part at least, to ben Ali's good offices.

Despite their stormy relationship, Tunisia has had an interest in preserving good relations with Libya as well as with Mauritania and in including Libya in the larger framework of the Maghrib. Its foreign policy was based on the same rationale as in the case of Mauritania. The larger the number of states within the Maghribi system the easier it became for Tunisia to maneuver politically and to avoid being dominated by any of the major regional powers.

Libya was included as a member of the Permanent Consultative

Committee of the Maghrib (CPCM) since its inception in 1964. The CPCM, which brought together Morocco, Algeria, Tunisia, and Libya, was an experiment in regional economic cooperation (Slim 1980, 241–252). When Qadhdhafi came to power, Libya was drawn into the Egyptian sphere of influence and away from the Maghrib. In March 1970 at the sixth conference of the economic ministers of the member states of the CPCM, Libya did not attend, partly because of Egyptian pressure (Deeb 1989a, 23). It was Habib Bourguiba, Jr. who was sent to Libya to try and bring Libya back into the Maghribi fold. Bourguiba Junior would say later that he had done all he could to convince the new Libyan regime "of the similar destiny that unites the four Maghrib countries" (FBIS-MEA, March 10, 1970, PT4), but to no avail.

The inclusion of Libya in the Maghrib was not only to enlarge that subsystem of states but to prevent it from falling under Egyptian influence. An Egyptian-dominated bloc on the eastern flank of the Maghrib was perceived as a grave threat to the security of Tunisia, Algeria, and Morocco, as it would upset the balance of power in the region. The Tripartite Agreement—the Tripoli Charter of December 1969—between Egypt, Sudan, and Libya did precisely that and brought Egyptian political influence to the very doorstep of the Maghrib. Tunisia's role was therefore that of the balancer between the Maghrib and Egypt, to prevent a change in the regional balance of power in favor of Egypt. In the late 1960s, however, Egypt was seen by Tunisia as balancing Algerian influence in North Africa.

Tunisian–Libyan relations fluctuated throughout the following two decades. In 1972 Bourguiba refused a union proposed by Qadhdhafi, but in 1974 he signed a merger agreement between the two countries to form the Arab Islamic Republic. The merger talks had begun in September 1973, with Bourguiba proposing a union between Tunisia, Algeria and Libya at the fourth nonaligned conference in Algiers. Those unity talks took place at a time when Egypt and Libya were having unity talks of their own and a union between the two countries was imminent. As in 1970, the Maghribi states tried to draw Libya away from Egypt by proposing a union to the west. Tunisia was again in the forefront of those negotiations and had Algerian support.

After the Arab–Israeli war of 1973 Algeria lost interest in the unity talks, presumably because it became convinced that Libyan–Egyptian relations had deteriorated to the extent that there was little danger the two states would merge any time soon. Bourguiba, on the other hand, was not convinced of the seriousness of the tension between Libya and Egypt and so preferred to pursue the union talks until January 1974 (Deeb, 1989a, 24–26).

Tunisia again played the role of balancer in North Africa, attempting to draw Libya away from Egypt, to ensure that the Maghrib was not weakened or dominated by an Egyptian-led bloc on its eastern flank.

The Brotherhood and Concord Treaty of March 1983, led by Algeria, also served Tunisia's interests vis-à-vis Libya. It offered Tunisia protection against Libya, which at the time was seen as becoming militarily threatening because of its aggressive role in Chad.

At the same time, there were signs that Tunisia resented Algeria's dominance of the bloc. In July 1987 Algerian president Chadli ben Jedid visited Tunisia and made a general statement lauding Algerian–Tunisian relations, which he said were based on cooperation and good neighborliness. Bourguiba interrupted him: "There is no change to this basis; there is nothing like what Abd al-Nasir did when he took Syria and formed the United Arab Republic. Let us cooperate, but each country should keep its own name, let us cooperate but with each country keeping its own name" (FBIS-MEA, July 8, 1987, PH1). This unprecedented interruption revealed Bourguiba's fear of Algeria's intentions in North Africa. He was drawing a parallel between the role that Algeria may have wanted to play in the Maghrib in the late 1980s and that of Egypt in the Mashriq in the late 1950s and early 1960s.

Tunisia played a very active role in the formation of the UMA, which was proclaimed in February 1989. Like Bourguiba, ben Ali continued to pursue a policy of expanding the Maghrib and of containing the conflicts within it. A Greater Maghrib consisting of five states that cooperated both economically and politically was of critical importance to Tunisia. It gave it greater political freedom to cooperate both with Libya and with Morocco with no interference from Algeria. It opened new markets for Tunisian goods and therefore reduced its dependency on the Libyan market. It also bolstered its bargaining position with the European Community, as we shall see later (Deeb, 1989b, 45).

■ Tunisia and the Maghrib:
Strategies, Negotiation, and Conflict Resolution

Libyan–Tunisian relations have been determined by factors other than the mere necessity of inclusion in a Greater Maghrib. Those two states have been the only two truly economically complementary members of the Maghrib. Libya has had a shortage of skilled and semiskilled labor throughout the post-Independence period. Tunisia, on the other hand, has had a serious unemployment problem, with a workforce that is one of the most skilled in North Africa. Libya, under Qadhdhafi, has often suffered from a shortage of many consumer goods that Tunisia could provide faster and more cheaply than any other state nearby. Tunisia also has tourist and recreational facilities that do not exist in Libya and that are sought after by Libyans bored with their drab and puritanical social environment.

This should have made for mutual interdependence and a fairly smooth relationship. But the two states do not need each other in quite the same way; consequently, one became more dependent and therefore weaker vis-à-vis the other. Libya, if need be, could always afford to hire workers from other parts of the world; it did not depend on Tunisian labor. Tunisia's unemployed, on the other hand, have very few alternatives to Libya; and although France and the Arab Gulf states provided some job opportunities, those labor markets became increasingly saturated in the 1980s. Furthermore, Libya's location so close to Tunisia made it easier for Tunisian men to work in Libya and visit their families back home frequently.

Libya could also afford to buy goods similar to those produced by Tunisians from other sources, even if that meant spending more on imports. Tunisians, on the other hand, had to compete on the world market to sell their agricultural and manufactured goods elsewhere. Finally, Libya could decide to close its borders and prevent its population from traveling to Tunisia for holidays or recreation, thus denying Tunisia's tourist sector some revenue. In this sector, however, Tunisia does not rely too heavily on Libyan tourism: it was just an additional bonus.

The relation between the two states has been unequal for yet another reason. Libya's military forces are much greater and better equipped than those of Tunisia, and Qadhdhafi has been willing to use military force to get his point across. Traditionally, Tunisia relied on France and, to a lesser extent, Algeria to provide protection from external aggression. However, it was not always available when needed.

For those reasons, Libyan–Tunisian relations have not been as smooth as one would have expected them to be; and Tunisia has suffered from the vicissitudes of Libya's changing policies. Its attitude has always been conciliatory, because its relationship to Libya is very important for its economy and domestic stability and for a regional balance of power.

The continental shelf was a major bone of contention between Libya and Tunisia, especially after 1974, when Qadhdhafi turned it into a major political issue in order to pressure Tunisia into a union that Tunis no longer wanted. For Tunisia, the underwater oil reserves of the continental shelf represented an important potential source of revenues. Tunisia saw a way out of the dispute through arbitration rather than through confrontation. It proposed on a number of occasions to submit the matter to the International Court of Justice at the Hague. In September 1977 Tunisia negotiated with Libya a Special Agreement to that effect, and a year later the problem was finally brought to the International Court (Herman 1984, 825–858). Although Tunisia was able to negotiate only the first part of the Libyan–Tunisian agreement, this case illustrates Tunisia's style in foreign policy, which is that of negotiation rather than confrontation—of settling outstanding differences peacefully, without upsetting the applecart.

The applecart at that time was Tunisia's economic ties to Libya. It had very important trade agreements with its neighbor; and there was a large Tunisian workforce in Libya. Throughout the second half of the 1970s the Tunisian economy flourished in large part because of those economic ties to Libya.

But in January 1980, sixty armed men entered Gafsa, a small southwestern town in Tunisia, attacked its army barracks and its police station, and took control of the town. The insurgency was put down after four days of armed clashes with the Tunisian armed forces. Libya had apparently trained and armed the attackers and masterminded the plot, but Algeria was also implicated (*Le Monde*, January 31, 1980, 1, 8). There is as yet no completely satisfactory explanation of the Gafsa affair. Libya may have been motivated to undertake such an action by Bourguiba's continued rejection of a merger between the two states, the latest offers having taken place a year earlier. Algeria's support for the attack was to punish Tunisia for its pro-Moroccan stand on the Western Sahara.

Tunisia's vulnerability to external pressures was highlighted by the Gafsa attack. The Tunisian government asked for French assistance, which, when it arrived, consisted primarily of two Transall French military transport planes and some logistic support to reestablish order in Gafsa. Morocco also provided some aid to Tunisia in the form of two army helicopters and a transport aircraft (FBIS-MEA, February 4, 1980, PI9). Tunisia also brought up the case before the League of Arab States and the Organization of African Unity, who, without specifically condemning Libya, offered to mediate between the two countries instead (Nelson 1987, 257). It was thus that Tunisia dealt with one of the most serious crises in its relation with Libya.

By March 1982 Libya and Tunisia had reestablished diplomatic relations. For the next three years Tunisia did business with Libya "as usual" until the summer of 1985, when Libya again attempted to destabilize Tunisia by expelling thirty-five thousand Tunisian workers from Libya. Relations were broken, and the matter was again brought up before the League of Arab

States. Tunisia could do little else except expel some three hundred Libyan officials and residents from Tunisia in retaliation.

Since ben Ali came to power in November 1987, Libyan–Tunisian relations have improved markedly. Libya immediately began repaying millions of dollars of frozen Tunisian assets and inviting back tens of thousands of Tunisian workers (Laipson 1987, 28–29). Borders were opened between the two countries and an estimated one million Libyans have visited Tunisia since relations were restored (*Washington Post*, October 30, 1988, A43). Numerous trade and labor agreements were signed between them and as members of the UMA. Tunisia is finally no longer under any pressure to set up a bilateral union with Libya.

Tunisian–Algerian relations have also been, at times, less than amicable. In 1962 a plot to assassinate Bourguiba was uncovered in which the newly independent Government of Algeria was implicated. As early, therefore, as the first year of Algerian independence there was tension between the two countries, a tension based on the wish of Algerian leaders to influence Tunisian politics and the fear on the part of Tunisia of becoming dominated by Algeria.

Tunisia's policy toward Algeria, therefore, has been primarily conciliatory, preferring to negotiate and give in rather than confront. Tunisia has also relied on the regional balance of power to keep Algeria's interest focused elsewhere.

The Borne (Marker) 23 border agreement between Algeria and Tunisia demonstrates Tunisia's preference for negotiation over confrontation. That agreement recognized Algeria's sovereignty over a territory that Tunisians considered their own. Between 1966 and 1970, Tunisia attempted to negotiate with its neighbor to retain its hold on the territory. Eventually, however, Prime Minister Bahi Ladgham signed away Tunisia's rights over the land in 1970 in order to avoid confrontation with Algeria at a time when Libya, Egypt, and Sudan had formed a bloc on Tunisia's eastern borders and were perceived as a grave threat to Tunisia's security (Neziha 1975).

In January 1974, when Libya and Tunisia signed the Djerba Accord, Algeria put political pressure on Tunisia to break the merger (Interview with Tunisian government official, 1986). Tunisia fabricated an explanation that the merger had been a spur-of-the-moment idea concocted by Qadhdhafi and Tunisian foreign minister Masmudi and that when Bourguiba had realized the implications of the merger, he had immediately moved to stop the process. This was a face-saving device to conceal the fact that Algeria could influence Tunisia's foreign policy so significantly.

In 1980, while both Libya and Algeria were implicated in the attack on

Gafsa, which is located close to the Algerian borders, Tunisian government releases blamed only Libya, preferring again to explain away Algerian complicity. The reports at the time stated that "The authorities are now convinced that Libya is fully responsible for the attack and that the commandos who launched it enjoyed Algeria's complicity—but not the complicity of Algeria's central government" (*Le Monde*, January 31, 1980, 1, 8).

Tunisia's preferred policy of negotiation, mediation, and conflict resolution was also apparent in its relations with Morocco. Although Bourguiba and Hassan II have shared the same views on a number of foreign policy issues—particularly those regarding the Arab world and the West— they have also had their disagreements. At the onset of the Western Sahara conflict, Tunisia favored partition of the region between Mauritania and Morocco, a position that antagonized Algeria. Tunisia's position then shifted gradually away from one of support for Morocco to one of neutrality. Although it is not unreasonable to suspect Algerian pressure behind this change in position, Tunisia did try throughout the late 1970s and early 1980s to mediate the dispute between Morocco and Algeria; and it may very well be that a position of neutrality on the conflict was necessary if Tunisia was to be an effective mediator.

Mediation was not successful, and in 1982 Tunisia joined other members of the OAU to block Algeria's efforts to gain recognition for a delegation of the Saharan Arab Democratic Republic to attend the OAU Summit meetings. That pleased Morocco but antagonized Algeria. In November 1984, however, when the vote for seating the Sahraouis at the OAU summit meeting came up again, Tunisia did not oppose it. As a result of the near-unanimous vote in favor of the Sahraoui position, Morocco withdrew from the OAU (Pondi 1988, 147).

This change again in Tunisia's stand, from one of support for Morocco's position to one of neutrality, may have been due to two major factors. The first was Tunisia's membership, since 1983, in the Brotherhood and Concord Alliance with Algeria and Mauritania. As member of that alliance, Tunisia could not openly oppose Algeria in the OAU, especially in a situation in which it was clear that Algeria was going to have its way. Another reason was the Moroccan–Libyan alliance (the Arab–African Union) that had taken place a few months earlier in August 1984, which was a counterbloc to Tunisia's own alliance with Algeria. The union introduced a new element of tension in Tunisian–Moroccan relations: under the terms of the agreement, if an armed conflict broke out between Tunisia and Libya, Morocco was bound to support Libya in the confrontation. Although this did not happen, the possibility of its occurring may have deterred Tunisia from supporting Morocco's position at the OAU that year.

Since the Maghrib Union was formed in 1989, however, all members have agreed to a referendum on the Sahara to determine its fate. The Sahara conflict is therefore no longer a significant issue in Moroccan–Tunisian relations.

■ **Relations with the West Under Bourguiba:**
  Strategy of Cooperation

At Independence in 1956, President Habib Bourguiba pledged his new nation's support for the West. In many ways, Bourguiba was perhaps the most pro-Western of his Arab contemporaries. Despite post-Independence tensions with France due primarily to Tunisia's support of Algerian nationalism and its postcolonial economic policies, Bourguiba remained oriented to France as the key cultural and commercial outlet for his country and depended on French largesse (and self-interest) as the underpinning of his national security strategy. He allowed France to maintain limited military presence in the northern city of Bizerte, arguing that such military alliances need not compromise national independence. Tunisia placed less emphasis than other new Third World nations on the development of a self-sufficient national defense force, relying instead on Western assurances to help defend its independence and territorial integrity from outside threats. Investments in national defense as a percentage of national spending were considerably lower than for many other new nations, and the military was actively used in statebuilding activities. (Tunisia's defense spending has been in the range of 1.4 percent of GNP, the lowest in the region.)

Two issues soured relations with France in the early post-Independence years and may have accelerated the process of Tunisia's outreach to other Western partners and friends. First was Tunisia's very concrete support (in arms, territory, and political assistance) to the Algerians locked in a bloody independence struggle with France. In 1958 France bombed a Tunisian border village used by Algerian guerrillas. This contributed to mounting domestic opposition to French military presence, and in 1961 a thousand Tunisians lost their lives during attacks they launched against the French base in Bizerte, which was subsequently phased out. In 1964 Tunisia announced new economic policies that expropriated lands and economic enterprises remaining in French hands, prompting the French to retaliate by canceling commercial agreements. The net effect of these rather serious postcolonial struggles was to sharpen Tunisia's sense of interdependence with France and to stimulate diversification of relations with the West. Italy, West Germany, and the United States became other important outlets for Tunisia's pro-Western interests.

■ **Emergence of the European Community:**
Strategy of Seeking Trade and Aid

While Tunisia's concept of the West in the immediate post-Independence period was less EC-focused than today's, Tunisia was in the forefront of Arab and Mediterranean countries in recognizing the importance of the European integration movement. This derives from the close links between Tunisia's security interests and economic growth and from the dependence of its prospects for growth on trade relationships. Tunisia has engaged the EC in negotiations over preferential trade arrangements since the early 1960s (Zartman 1971). Tunisia's economic planners also realized the importance of creating cadres of EC technocrats, equipped to deal with the complicated supranational economic policymaking of the EC.

The EC was created in 1958, only two years after France ended its protectorate relationships with Tunisia and Morocco and while France was in the grips of its Algerian crisis, the colonial war closest to Europe's borders and interests. The French struggled over the very concept of a supranational European institution; but once the debate was resolved and they opted for membership, they pushed the organization to define its relations with, and responsibilities toward, former colonies. Tunisia and its two francophone Maghrib neighbors were the countries most affected by the EC and most capable of affecting, for better or worse, the economies of the southern EC countries. France succeeded in overcoming German and Italian resistance in particular in introducing into the Treaty of Rome a commitment to preferential treatment of former colonies and allowing a preservation of special postcolonial relationships. At the same time, the Treaty of Rome stated that association agreements would be "characterized by reciprocal rights and obligations"; and EC members other than France sought a balance between trade concessions the francophone Arab states of the southern Mediterranean would make to them and the aid and trade benefits extended to Maghribi economies and products.

Association with the EC, for former colonies, was defined as open-ended, did not envision full membership (as did association agreements with Greece, Turkey, and Spain, for example), and combined both aid and trade commitments. Over time, categories of agreements with non–EC states created in an ad hoc fashion fell into certain patterns. Of these, the Maghrib states were eventually linked with four other Arab Mediterranean states (Egypt, Jordan, Lebanon, Syria) into a cluster of seven parallel cooperation agreements signed in 1976 and 1977 (Commission of the European Communities 1982). These agreements were generally posited on principles of "balance of mutual advantages" rather than on the more precise and demanding concept of reciprocity. They provided trade preferences in industrial and agricultural products, financial and technical cooperation, labor cooperation, and creation of joint institutions on the basis of strict parity. Tunisia's category of association with the EC can be viewed as lying between those premised on eventual full membership (in which the concept of reciprocity is enshrined) and those of the poorer Lome Convention states (now numbering sixty-six in Africa, the Caribbean, and the Pacific, whose agreements with the EC are focused more on aid and asymmetric relationships).

By the late 1970s, in part at Italy's urging, the EC sought to define its Mediterranean policy, in order to harmonize its policies and tariff concessions to the Mediterranean "third countries" (i.e., non–EC states). The EC realized that its ad hoc arrangements with individual countries required a new look. It sought ways to equalize its trade relations with its various Mediterranean partners—to reduce imbalances and inequities that resulted from the EC's Common Agricultural Policy (CAP), which was designed to support and protect EC producers.

As a resource-poor state, Tunisia was dependent on the EC as a source of both raw materials and finished products. The proximity of the growing European market was of key importance in structuring Tunisia's exports and service and tourism sectors. Thus, despite the political attachment of the Bourguiba regime to the United States and the preeminence of the United States as an aid donor in the 1960s and 1970s, the EC even in its infant days was of greater value and potential to Tunisia. Its efforts to achieve associate status were delayed from 1964 to 1967 by internal EC disagreements over Tunisia's agricultural exports and over whether Tunisia alone or all Maghrib countries should be negotiating. While the EC worked out its differences, Tunisia succeeded in finalizing bilateral treaties of cooperation and commerce with both France and Italy. In the case of the former, this was significant, as it marked a return to more cordial relations after the stresses of the early 1960s.

Negotiations with the EC proceeded for two years, culminating in an association agreement signed in 1969. The agreement provided for industrial products to enter the EC with extensive preferences (i.e., treated as if they were made in Europe), while olive oil, citrus, and some other agricultural goods could enter the EC with more limited preferences. Other products were not covered by the 1969 agreement. At the beginning, Tunisia benefited from tariff concessions on fruits and vegetables, while other key products (such as cork and wine) were not covered, leading to immediate interest in amending or modifying the agreement. On both sides of the Mediterranean, the parties had to adjust to the newly defined relationship, and both sharpened their expectations and hopes for the future of trade and aid ties.

In 1976 a second and expanded agreement was signed between Tunisia and the EC, then the EC of the Nine, enlarged beyond the original Six. Its commercial terms provided for Tunisian industrial exports to enter the EC unimpeded, provided they were manufactured wholly in Tunisia. Agricultural products not produced in the EC could also enter duty-free. But in the crucial textile sector, voluntary restraint agreements (VRAs) were accepted by Tunisia, thus limiting trousers and cotton fabrics in specific EC markets. Similarly, agricultural products that competed with EC produce faced restrictions; and the enlargement of the EC in 1981 to include Greece and the admission of Portugal and Spain in 1986 caused a serious erosion in the preferential arrangements extended to Tunisia and other Maghrib states.

Tunisia's embrace of Maghribi integration and greater economic coordination also finds resonance in its relations with the EC. Historically, the EC has sought to avoid promoting competition among the Maghrib states and has tried to treat equitably each of France's three former colonies, which are the closest and demographically most significant of any Third World countries with special historic ties to the EC. The 1976 agreement cites "the importance of promoting regional cooperation between Tunisia and other States," and its protocols define products originating in Tunisia with the words "When products wholly obtained in Algeria, in Morocco or in the Community undergo working or processing in Tunisia, they shall be considered as having been wholly obtained in Tunisia" (*Official Journal of the European Communities*, 21:L265, September 27, 1978) and other similar provisions.

Tunisia's trade and export policies are heavily oriented to the EC, which, at the end of the Bourguiba era, was the destination of 79 percent of its exports and the source of 69 percent of its imports. Tunisia's dependence on trade with the EC has been the highest of any Maghrib state. A few examples amply illustrate the importance of the EC to Tunisia's impressive economic growth in the 1970s: in 1970 the value of Tunisian textile exports to the EC was $1 million; by 1976, the value had jumped to $100 million. Growth in overall Tunisian exports to the EC has continued in the 1980s: from $1.12 billion in 1980 to $1.78 billion in 1988.

■ **The ben Ali Era:**
  Strategy of Change Within Continuity

For most Western countries, the accession to power of ben Ali in November 1987 was a relief, after several years of increasingly gloomy predictions about Tunisia's fate. It is striking that a 1986 Harvard University study looking comparatively at several dozen Third World countries cited Tunisia as the most probable case of serious instability following the demise of its authoritarian ruler (Betts and Huntington, 1985/1986). By the early 1980s, the extent of Bourguiba's pro-Western attitude was no longer sitting well with the Tunisian public or the younger political elite. Although they continued to seek educational and employment opportunities in Europe and the United States, a more assertively pro-Arab awareness emerged. This new attitude could be seen as supplementing, rather than replacing, the established rapport with the West (Perkins 1986, 163). But with the decline of Bourguiba and the concurrent decline of Tunisia's national self-confidence, these attitudes developed a sharper anti-Western dimension. The Israeli raid against PLO headquarters in a suburb of Tunis in October 1985 was a catalyst that deepened resentment toward the United States. Although Bourguiba did not allow initial U.S. support for Israel's raid to sour official U.S.–Tunisian ties permanently, for many Tunisians, the U.S. reaction to the incident (initially praising Israel for its blow to terrorism, only a day later balancing that praise with concern for the territorial integrity and security of Tunisia) contributed to disillusionment with the West. The assassination by Israeli commandos of PLO deputy Abu Jihad in mid-1988 furthered this process and is considered a pivotal event in constructing the context of ben Ali's foreign policy.

In his first address to the diplomatic corps after taking power November 7, 1987, President ben Ali spoke of continuity in Tunisia's foreign policy and promised to uphold all international commitments. At the same time, he emphasized Tunisia's interest in bolstering the ties of solidarity with the Arab, Muslim, African, and Mediterranean groups to which it belongs. The long-term goal of Maghrib unity was also endorsed warmly as a high priority of the new government. In a press conference on November 10, 1987, Prime Minister Hedi Baccouche also stressed continuity in foreign policy, arguing that "our basic options in this regard are premised on a long-term strategic point of view aimed at guaranteeing the security of Tunisia and its independence" (FBIS-NEA, November 11, 1987). Baccouche named, in particular, France, Italy, and the United States as countries that were supportive during the transition and with which Tunisia sought to deepen cooperation.

These words of assurance were welcomed in Western capitals, and Tunisia's Western partners generally received the changes of 1987 and early 1988 with enthusiasm and relief. Western relations with Tunisia quickly improved from the sluggish level of discourse of the late Bourguiba era, and there has been a noticeably higher level of energy and vigor in diplomatic exchanges with Tunisia. New appointments in ministry positions were well received, as was the symbolism of naming to a few of Tunisia's embassies in Western capitals former dissidents or prominent persons who had fallen out of favor in the Bourguiba court.

At the same time, some Western diplomats have expressed concerns about what they consider a change in emphasis in Tunisia's external relations away from the West. They perceive that ben Ali has a different agenda than his predecessor, one that focuses Tunisia's horizons and political ambitions on its immediate neighborhood, the Maghrib. According to this view, Tunisia today is rediscovering its Arab and Islamic heritage, one that was repressed to a certain degree under Bourguiba's modern secularist philosophy. Ben Ali has thus adapted his foreign policy in its public articulation to a new Tunisian self-image, all the while retaining the important political and material links to key Western countries.

The security dimension of cooperation with Western countries is important to consider. In the short run, Tunisia wants to continue to receive military aid, training, and equipment, from France and the United States in particular. But the cumulative toll of the decade of the 1980s, including the shock of the Libyan-backed raid against Gafsa, problems with internal unrest, the two Israeli raids (1985 and 1988), the 1986 U.S. raid against Libya, and subsequent changes in Tunisian–Libyan relations combine to suggest new thinking within Tunisian security circles about longer-term strategy. Ben Ali is thought to be concerned about the erosion of popular support for the security policies of the past and to be making careful adjustments to take these altered assumptions into account. The lesson of Gafsa was to develop domestic capabilities for defense, not rely so heavily on the off-shore security guarantees of great powers. The legacy of the Israeli raids and the U.S. attack on Libya has had a corrosive effect psychologically although operationally, it has not yet diminished Tunisian desire to work with the United States in modernizing Tunisian defenses.

Concerns are strongest among French-speaking countries that have always considered francophonie as a durable bond. President ben Ali, for example, spoke in Arabic when he was received at the Elysee Palace in 1988, a fact that the Tunisian press (*Le Renouveau*, March 26, 1989) lauded as a sign that the new era had raised the place of "our religion and our language." Arabization of the education system (which began under Prime Minister Mzali in the early 1980s) may sow the seeds for the next generation to be less Europe-oriented. The French, in particular, express some concerns about a dilution of cultural commitment to francophonie. But some Tunisians are skeptical that this still-controversial change in educational policy has much significance for foreign relations. Urban Tunisians (an increasing percentage of the total population) remain very Europe-focused; and French remains the language of opportunity for professionally minded youth, with English as a rapidly rising second. In fact, some argue that the contest is not Arabic versus European languages but French versus English. Some French specialists see the erosion of their special relationship with Tunisia not only in terms of Arabism but also in terms of new Tunisian interest in U.S. jobs and culture.

The employment incentives that keep Tunisia attached to Europe are part of the textural changes in Tunisian–Western relations. The positive and cooperative attitude of the immediate post-Independence period has been replaced with a more complex combination of factors and more ambivalent attitudes. On the one hand, upwardly mobile Tunisians know that schooling and professional opportunities in Europe enhance their long-term career prospects and have considerable status at home. On the other hand, there is resentment both against their own country and leadership for failing to provide more compelling reasons to stay home and against European societies that are increasingly hostile to migrant workers and to Third World professionals seeking visas.

The Tunisian government, for its part, has clear economic and security reasons to protect the rights of Tunisian workers in Europe, and this has contributed to a more defensive attitude towards the West. In the early post-Independence period, hard-working Tunisians were well received in Western cities and grew to count on European (especially French) goodwill toward their modernizing aspirations. Increasingly, however, with the ebbs and flows in European economic prosperity and the endless flow of labor from the southern and eastern periphery of the EC, the mood in Europe has shifted. This is exacerbated by high birthrates in the Arab world and failed economic policies that compel jobseekers to leave their Arab homes. Tunisia—by no means the worst offender in these demographic trends—is now more assertive in defending its interests regarding labor and immigration; and these are always sensitive and potentially contentious issues on the agenda with several European countries, France in particular.

■ **Creation of a Single-Market European Comunity: Tunisia's Two-Track Strategy**

Tunisian concerns about the creation of a single market in the EC are primarily economic but converge with some of the political changes noted above. There has been a tendency in Tunisia, as in the United States, to exaggerate the meaning of 1992—to emphasize the Fortress Europe dimension rather than the need to prepare for competition, which is what drew the Europeans themselves—slumping in the economic race against East Asia and the United States—to take the bold decision to complete economic integration by 1992. Official Tunisian pronouncements on 1992 in the late 1980s were somewhat more alarmist than the views in the business community, which has been more upbeat about overall Tunisian economic potential and projected stimulating opportunities and prospects for new investment as a result of 1992.

Tunisia will not be completely shut out of Europe after 1992; in fact, it has positioned itself more creatively and more aggressively than most other Mediterranean non–EC states to weather the blow. It has trained technocrats who are experts in the arcana of Brussels regulations, and its experience in the negotiations culminating in the 1969 and 1976 agreements provide a solid legal and practical foundation to its relations with the EC. The challenge of 1992 has stimulated and brought to the fore some of the real strengths of the relatively homogeneous, well-educated, technocratically oriented young Tunisian elite.

In planning for 1992, the Tunisian economic and diplomatic establishment is pursuing at least two tracks. One is to promote the idea of Tunisia as a platform from which non–EC countries can enter the EC, taking advantage of Tunisia's associative status and benefits. This was emphasized by Tunisian officials at the first meeting of the U.S.–Tunisian Joint Commission on Trade and Investment in December 1988. They argued that U.S. investors and businessmen should bring technology and capital to Tunisia, to generate manufactured goods that would enter the EC as Tunisian products. Tunisia has been promoting the platform concept, listing as advantages tax-free profits, unrestricted profit repatriation, customs-free imports for all equipment needed in production, and its flexible decentralization policies (Cheikh Rouhou 1988).

A second—and related—promotion scheme encourages partnerships based in Tunisia, in which Tunisian manufacturing enterprises would benefit from outside investment and technology and the jointly produced wares could compete in new markets, in the EC or elsewhere. For linguistic and logistical reasons, the promotion focus for such partnerships has been France and Italy, even encouraging a degree of friendly competition between them. (Italy has become very active not only as a trading partner but as an important source of concessional loans— five hundred million dollars for 1988–1993.) In theory, these partnerships are available for other Western countries, including the United States, and the ultimate destination of the goods, while most likely to be Europe, need not be limited to the EC. Eastern Europe, for example, is expected to be a growth market for Tunisia. There are presently countless of these partnerships in agricultural processing and manufactured goods; and there are occasional press stories that jointly owned or foreign-owned companies compete to the disadvantage of wholly Tunisian-owned ventures.

In February 1989 the Tunisian–EC cooperation council met in Brussels for its fourth ministerial-level meeting. It was the first such meeting since the change of government in Tunisia. Foreign Minister Abdulhamid Escheikh and his Spanish counterpart reviewed the bilateral agenda. In their official communiqué, the two sides reaffirmed the 1987 agreement to assure Tunisia forty-six thousand tons of exports in olive oil (with a commitment to reexamine the olive oil regime by June 1990 and work for a new protocol); noted Tunisia's request to suppress tariffs on cotton fabric, pointing out the need to raise the quality; encouraged promotion of more contact and partnerships between small and medium-sized businesses between EC states and Tunisia; and agreed to expand the exchange of information about technical matters relating to the single market and to intensify cooperation, contributing to the economic and social development of Tunisia (*Le Renouveau*, February 26, 1989). Tunisia's concerns with the EC relate mainly to textiles and its key agricultural exports: olive oil, wine, and citrus; and to it its eagerness not to miss the opportunity for new investment in manufactures. In its efforts, Tunisia is trying to make up for time lost in the 1980s when its attractiveness as a low-risk country for investment temporarily lost its sheen. The government now proudly points to its status as the lowest-risk country in Africa and the sixth-lowest in the Arab world (*Euromoney*, September 1988).

■ **Tunisia's Promotion of the Euro–Arab Dialogue:
Strategy of Multilateralism**

Tunisian interest in the EC in the 1970s and early 1980s was not limited to commercial and financial issues. Tunisia, long an activist in multilateral forums, was a promoter of the Euro–Arab dialogue created in 1975. The dialogue was suspended briefly after the Egyptian–Israeli peace treaty in 1979, and Tunisia was active in negotiations to get it back on track. In its new role as host of the Arab League, Tunisia has been the head of the Arab delegation (the dialogue convenes with two delegations, Arab and European, rather than national delegations, in order to allow the PLO to participate).

The emergence of the EC as a "superpower" in the late 1980s has some important and mostly positive considerations for countries like Tunisia. The European Political Cooperation (EPC) established in 1970 provides for close coordination of foreign policy among the Twelve. In recent years, this has emerged in more tangible form, and the EC has developed a troika system, assigning three of its members to take the lead on key issues. The troika of Spain, Greece, and Italy have been working on the Palestinian issue, much to the satisfaction of the Arab world. Tunisia has long favored a stronger European role in the Arab–Israeli peace process, to modify or counterbalance what has been viewed as the excessively pro-Israeli U.S. policy and to stimulate negotiations and the convening of an international peace conference. Since 1985 (when the EC formally targeted 1992 as the deadline for economic integration) the EPC has become a more effective mechanism.

In the ben Ali era, Tunisia continues to play an active role in the Euro–Arab dialogue, and Tunisian diplomat and Arab League head Chedli Klibi was reelected in 1989 to a third term. With Tunisia's refound confidence, newly elected parliament, and symbolic role as host of the Arab League, it can be an important player and gain further political access to EC political leaders. But Klibi resigned in 1990 as the league returned to Cairo.

The creation of the single market in Europe was a powerful force in bringing Maghrib leaders together in February 1989 to create the UMA. Tunisia historically has been in the forefront of the Maghrib integration movement, and has helped articulate the rationale for the UMA. The UMA both imitates the phenomenon of 1992 and defends North Africa from it. Maghribis believe, rhetorically at least, that the decision to come together and combine economic resources and know-how is the best means to both protect them from potential negative consequences of 1992 and to project the

Maghrib as a stronger and more attractive partner for the EC. Tunisian government officials and businessmen appear to be persuaded by this logic. In the short run, however, and until the difficult task of integrating the disparate economic systems of Morocco, Algeria, Tunisia, Mauritania, and Libya can be implemented, Tunisia is likely to pursue its relations with individual EC states bilaterally, to monitor its association agreement carefully, and to expand its economic activities in non–EC countries, including the United States, Eastern Europe, and the eastern Arab world.

■ Conclusion

The foreign policy of Tunisia in the 1990s may differ in tone and style from the politics of the Bourguiba era. Changes in foreign policy under ben Ali are driven both by internal factors (the domestic pressures that contributed to Bourguiba's removal from power) and external factors (the looming completion of the EC's single market, and changing intra-Maghrib dynamics). While President ben Ali and his cabinet are for the most part inheritors of the modernist, secular, Western-oriented values of post-Independence Tunisia, they can no longer assume that Tunisians of today, youth in particular, are satisfied with the political formulas of the past. Ben Ali faces a changing and, to a certain extent, unsettled and ill-defined domestic market. He must try to alter the packaging, if not the content, of his product to ensure and, if possible, increase its appeal.

The underlying premises of Tunisia's foreign policy remain to keep Western confidence in the nation's economic stability and potential and its political moderation. At the same time, Tunisia's leadership needs to demonstrate renewed commitment to its Arab roots and responsibilities and has become more active in Arab world politics. This reflects both Tunisia's efforts to emphasize its Arabism and the fact that the consensus within the Arab world has moved closer to Tunisia's position on regional issues.

Finding the right balance between the two main arenas of Tunisia's external relations—with the Maghrib and with the EC—will remain a challenge for Tunisia's leadership. Its ability to be effective in both regions will likely depend on maintaining the strategies that have worked since Independence: Tunisia can be expected to avoid confrontations, stress activism and mediation in regional and multilateral forums, and pursue preferential economic relations with its immediate neighbors. Tunisia's prospects for protecting and projecting its interests also depend on factors beyond the scope of this chapter. It is important to bear in mind that the quality and effectiveness of Tunisia's foreign policy will be profoundly affected by concurrent developments and the success of current reforms in the nation's educational system, internal political evolution, and economic fortunes.

Bibliography

Achour, Habib. 1989. *Ma Vie Politique et Syndicale*. Tunis: Alif.

Adelman, Irma, and Morris Cynthia Taft. 1976. *Society, Politics and Economic Development: A Quantitative Approach*. Baltimore: Johns Hopkins University Press.

Agence de Promotion Industrielle, n.d. *Small and Medium Industrial Firms and Decentralization*. internal document (in Arabic).

Ajami, Fouad. 1981. *The Arab Predicament*. Cambridge: Cambridge University Press.

Alaya, Hachemi. 1989. *L'economie tunisienne: Réalités et voies pour l'avenir*. Tunis: Afkar wa Ich-haar.

Aly, Abd al-Monein Said, and Manfred W. Wenner. 1982. "Modern Islamic Reform Movements: The Muslim Brotherhood in Contemporary Egypt." *Middle East Journal* 36(3): 36–361.

Amnesty International. 1984. *Torture in the Eighties*. New York: Amnesty International.

Anderson, Lisa. 1986. *The State and Social Transformation in Tunisia and Libya, 1830–1980*. Princeton: Princeton University Press.

———. 1990. "Political Pacts, Liberalism, and Democracy," *Government and Opposition*, 25(4)/26(1).

Appleby, G., W. Settle, and A. Showler. 1989. *Africa Emergency Locust/ Grasshopper Assistance (AELGA)*. Mid-term evalutation. Washington: Agency for International Development.

Arat, Yesim. 1989. *Politics and Big Business in Turkey: Janus-Faced Link to the State*. Typescript.

Arid Land Information Center. 1980. *Draft Environmental Profile (Phase 1) of the Republic of Tunisia*. Tucson: ALIC, University of Arizona.

Arntsen, A. 1976. *Women and Social Change in Tunisia*. Ph.D. Thesis, Georgetown University.

Asselain, J. C. 1971. "La reforme des structures commerciales en Tunisie depuis 1962." In *Les économies maghrébines: L'indépendence à l'épreuve du développement économique*. Paris: Centre de Recherches et d'Etudes sur les Sociétés Mediterranéennes/Centre National de Recherche Scientifique.

Auerbach, L. S. 1980. *Women's Domestic Power: A Study of Women's Roles in a Tunisian Town*. Ph.D. Thesis, University of Illinois at Champaign-Urbana.

Babai, Don. 1988. "The World Bank and the IMF: Rolling Back the State or

Backing Its Role?" In Raymond Vernon, ed., *The Promise of Privatization: A Challenge for American Foreign Policy*. New York: Council on Foreign Relations.

Badawi, M. A. Zaki. 1976. *The Reformers of Egypt*. London: Croom Helm.

Baklanoff, Eric, ed. 1976. *Mediterranean Europe and the Common Market: Studies of Economic Growth and Integration*. Alabama: University of Alabama Press.

Bale, M. D., and E. Lutz. "Price Distortions in Agriculture and Their Effects: An International Comparison," *American Journal of Agricultural Economics* 63(1).

Banque Centrale de Tunisie. 1988a. *Rapport Annuel 1987*. Tunis: Banque Centrale.

Banque Centrale de Tunisie. 1988b. *Budget Economique 1989*. Tunis: Banque Centrale.

Banque Centrale de Tunisie. 1989. *Statistiques Financieres*. Tunis: Banque Centrale.

Banque de Tunisie. 1988. *Rapport Annuel 1988*. Tunis: BT.

Banque Internationale et Arabe de la Tunisie. 1986. *Rapport Annuel 1985*. Tunis: BIAT.

Banque Internationale et Arabe de la Tunisie. 1988. *Rapport Annuel 1987*. Tunis: BIAT.

Barbour, Neville, ed. 1962. *A Survey of Northwest Africa (the Maghrib)*. 2d ed. London: Oxford University Press.

Batatu, Hanna. 1986. "State and Capitalism in Iraq: A Comment." *MERIP Reports* 16(5): MERIP.

Baumol, William J., ed. 1980. *Public and Private Enterprise in a Mixed Economy*. (Proceedings of a Conference held by the International Economics Association in Mexico City). London: Macmillan Press.

Bechri, Mohamed Z. 1989. "The Political Economy of Interest Rate Determination in Tunisia." In Mustafa K. Nabli and Jeffrey B. Nugent, eds., *The New Institutional Economics and Development Theory: Theory and Tunisian Case Studies*. Amsterdam: North Holland.

Belhassen, Suhayr. 1983. "Comment les Tunisiennes aujourd'hui vivent-elles leur liberté?" *Jeune Afrique Magazine* 30: 32–37.

Belhassen, Suhayr, and Francois Poli. 1989. "Comment travaille Ben Ali," *Jeune Afrique Magazine* 68: 28–35.

Bellin, Eva. 1991. *Civil Society Resurgent? State and Social Classes in Tunisia* Ph.D. dissertation, Princeton University.

ben Ali, Zine Labidine. 1989. Speech of July 23.

Bendix, Reinhard. 1977. *Max Weber: An Intellectual Portrait*. Berkeley: University of California Press.

ben Othmane, Mongi, and Mohtat Souissi. 1987. "Rentabilité et performances des banques commerciales tunisiennes." *Finances et developpement au Maghreb* 1(January): 45–49, 2(December): 66–70.

Bentley, Alfred. 1935. *Government and Social Pressure*.

Berger, Peter L., and Hansfried Kellner. 1981. *Sociology Reinterpreted: An Essay on Method and Vocation*. New York: Anchor/Doubleday.

Betts, Richard, and Samuel Huntington. 1985/1986. "Dead Dictators and Rioting Mobs: Does the Demise of Authoritarian Rulers Lead to Instability?" *International Security* 10(3): 112–146.

Binnendijk, Hans, ed. 1987. *Authoritarian Regimes in Transition*. Washington: State Department Foreign Service Institute.

Bohm, Peter. 1973. *Social Efficiency: A Concise Introduction to Welfare Economics*. New York: Macmillan.

Boulares, Habib. 1983. *L'Islam: La peur et l'espérance*. Paris: J.C. Lattes.

Brown, Leon Carl. 1964. "The Islamic Reformist Movement in North Africa." *Journal of Modern African Studies* 2(1): 55–63.

———. 1966. "The Role of Islam in Modern North Africa," In Brown, ed., *State and Society in Independent North Africa*. Washington: Middle East Institute.

———. 1974. *The Tunisia of Ahmad Bey, 1837–1855*. Princeton: Princeton University Press.

Burgat, Francois. 1988. *L'Islamisme au Maghreb*. Paris: Karthala.

Burling, Robbins. 1974. *The Passage of Power*. New York: Academic.

Buzelay, A. 1971. *Vérité des prix et services publics*. Paris: Librairie Generale de Droit at de Jurisprudence.

Camau, Michel. 1987. "Tunisie au présent: Une modernité au-dessus de tout soupcon?" In Camau, ed., *Tunisie au présent*. Paris: Editions du Centre National de la Recherche Scientifique.

Camau, Michel, Fadila Amrani, and Rafaa ben Achour. 1981. *Controle politique et régulations électorales en Tunisie*. Tunis: Centre d'etudes, de recherches, et de publications/Edisud.

Camau, Michel, et al. 1984. "L'Etat tunisien: De la tutelle au desengagment." *Maghreb–Machrek*, 103: 8–38.

Cazenave, P. and C. Morrisson. 1978. "Justice et Redistribution," *Economica*.

Central Tunisian Development Authority. 1986. *Des statistique, variéas rassemblias en voie de la puparation du Septime Plan quingueennel*. Tunis: CTDA. Typescripts.

Chaieb, Frej. 1987. "Les elections qui ont valeur de symbole." *Le Temps*, December 26.

Charmes, J. 1983. "La secteur non-structure en Tunisie." *Cahiers ORSTOM*, 19, Serie Sciences Humaines 1.

Chayanov, A. V. 1966. *The Theory of the Peasant Economy*. Ed. D. Thorner, B. Kerblay, and R. E. F. Smith. Homewood: IL: R. D. Irwin.

Cheikh Rouhou, Moncef. 1988. Presentation to US-Tunisian Joint Commission on Trade and Investment. Washington, DC, December 5.

Chekir, Hafida. 1974. "L'UTICA." Master's thesis, University of Tunis.

Chenery, Hollis, and Moises Syrquin. 1975. *Patterns of Development, 1950–1970*. New York: Oxford University Press.

Claisse, Alain, and Gerard Conac, eds. 1988. *Le grand Maghreb*. Paris: Economia.

Commission of the European Communities. 1982. *The European Community and the Arab World*. DE 38/1982. Brussels: EC Directorate for Information.

Coulton, Timothy J. 1986. *The Dilemma of Reform in the Soviet Union*. New York: Council of Foreign Relations.

Cowan, L. Gray. 1989. "Institutional Factors in Privatization," Washington, D.C.: USAID Office of Policy Development and Program Review, Bureau for Program and Policy Coordination.

Damis, John. 1983a. "Prospects for Unity/Disunity in North Africa." *American–Arab Affairs* 6: 34–37.

———. 1983b. *Conflict in Northwest Africa: The Western Sahara Dispute*. Stanford: Hoover Institution and Stanford University Press.

Davis, S. S. 1983. *Patience and Power: Women's Lives in a Moroccan Village*. Cambridge, Mass.: Schenkman Publishing Company.

Deeb, Mary-Jane. 1989a. "Inter-Maghribi Relations Since 1969: A Study of the Modalities of Unions and Mergers." *Middle East Journal* 43(1): 20–33.

————. 1989b. "The Arab Maghrib Union in the Context of Regional and International Politics." *Middle East Insight* 6(5): 42–46.

Dimassi, Hassine. 1983. "Accumulation du capital et répartition des revenues: Essai sur la réproduction de la formation sociale tunisienne post-coloniale: Fin des années 50–fin des annees 70." Ph.D. Dissertation, University of Tunis.

Durrani, L. H. 1976. "Employment of Women and Social Change, pp. 58-74. In R. Stone and J. Simmons, eds., *Change in Tunisia: Studies in the Social Sciences*. Albany, NY: State University of New York Press.

Duwaji, Ghazi. 1967. *Economic Development in Tunisia: The Impact and Course of Government Planning*. Special Studies in International Economics and Development. New York: Praeger.

Dynamac Corporation. 1988. *Results of the Mali Pesticide Testing Trials Against the Senegalese Grasshopper—Final Technical Report*. Washington: Agency for International Development.

Economist Intelligence Unit. 1989. *Tunisia: Country Profile 1988–1989*. London: EIU.

Edwards, Sebastian. 1987. "Sequencing Economic Liberalization in Developing Countries. *Finance and Development* 12: 9–12.

Entelis, John P. 1974. "Ideological Change and an Emerging Counter-Culture in Tunisian Politics." *Journal of Modern African Studies* 12: 543–568.

Esposito, John L. 1984. *Islam and Politics*. Syracuse, NY: Syracuse University Press.

FEWS. 1987. *1986 Grasshopper and Locust Infestations*. Washington: FEWS.

Field, Gary S. 1980. *Poverty, Inequality and Development*. New York: Cambridge University Press.

Friedman, Wolfgang, ed. 1974. *Public and Private Enterprise in a Mixed Economy*. New York: Columbia University Press.

Geertz, Clifford. 1968. *Islam Observed: Religious Development in Morocco and Indonesia*. Chicago: University of Chicago Press.

————. 1983. *Local Knowledge: Further Essays in Interpretive Anthropology*. New York: Basic Books.

Gellner, Ernest. 1981. *Muslim Society*. Cambridge: Cambridge University Press.

Gellner, Ernest, and John Waterbury, eds. 1973. *Patrons and Clients in Mediterranean Society*. London: Duckworth.

———— and J. C. Vatin, eds. *Islam et politique au Maghreb*. Paris: CNRS/CRESM.

Gerth Hans H., and C. Wright Mills, eds. 1958. *From Max Weber*. New York: Oxford.

Ghannouchi, Rachid. 1979a. "Al-thawra al-iraniyya thawra islamiyya" [The Iranian revolution is an Islamic revolution]. *al-Ma'rifa*, February 12. Also in *Maqalat* [Essays], by Ghannouchi. Paris: Dar al-karawan li'l-taba`a wa'l-nashr wa'ltawzi'.

————. 1979b. "Qada al-haraka al-islamiyya al-mu'asira: Al-Banna, al-Mawdudi, al-Khumayni" [The Leaders of the modern Islamic movement . . .]. *al-Ma'rifa*, April 1. Also in *Maqalat* [Essays], by Ghannouchi. Paris: Dar al-Karawan li'l-taba'a wa'l-nashr wa'ltawzi'.

————. 1979c. "Al-amal al-islami wa qutta' al-turuq" [The Islamic work and the thieves of the paths]. *al-Ma'rifa*, May 15. Also in *Maqalat* [Essays], by Ghannouchi. Paris: Dar al-karawan li'l-taba'a wa'l-nashr wa'ltawzi'.

————. 1979d. "Bi-madha tuqas munjazat sha'b?" [By what is the production of a people measured?]. *al-Ma'rifa*, November. Also in *Maqalat* [Essays], by Ghannouchi. Paris: Dar al-karawan li'l-taba'a wa'l-nashr wa'ltawzi'.

————— [Abu Ma'ad, pseud.]. 1979e. "Musanada al-thawra al-iraniyya wajib 'ala man?" [Support of the Iranian revolution is obligatory for whom?]. *al-Mujtama'* November 30, p. 7.

—————. 1979f. "Interview with Rashid al-Ghanushi." in Fathiya Balghith, al-haraka al-islamiyya fi tunis min khilal sahifat al-'amal" [The Islamic movement in Tunisia through the newspaper *Action*]. Thesis, School of Journalism, Tunis.

—————. 1980a. "Al-hujum 'ala afghanistan bidayat al-nihaya li- marhala isti'mariyya ukhra" [The attack on Afghanistan is the beginning of the end of another stage of colonialism]. *al-'Aman*, February 15. Also in *Maqalat* [Essays], by Ghannouchi. Paris: Dar al-karawan li'l-taba'a wa'l-nashr wa'ltawzi'.

—————. 1980b. "Al-alam al-islami wa'l-isti'mar al-hadith" [The Islamic world and the new colonialism]. *al-'Aman*, April 11. Also in *Maqalat* [Essays], by Ghannouchi. Paris: Dar al-karawan li'l-taba'a wa'l-nashr wa'ltawzi'.

—————. 1980c. "Al-taghrib wa hatmiyyat al-diktatturiyya" [Westernization and the inevitability of dictatorship]. *al-Qhuraba'*, September. Also in *Maqalat* [Essays], by Ghannouchi. Paris: Dar al-karawan li'l-taba'a wa'l-nashr wa'ltawazi'.

—————. 1981. *Al-haraka al-islamiyya wa'l-tahdith* [The Islamic movement and modernization]. Tunisian Islamic movement.

—————. 1984. *Maqalat*. (Essays). Paris: Dar al-Karawan li'l- taba`a wa'l-nashr wa'ltawazi'.

—————. 1988a. "Min auraq al-Ghanushi" [From the papers of Ghannouchi]. *al-Majalla*, July 13–19, pp. 22–26; July 20–26, pp. 30–33; July 28–August 3; August 4–10, pp. 34–37; August 10–16, pp. 32–35; August 17–23, pp. 24–26.

—————. 1988b. *al-Sabab*, March 19.

—————. 1989a. Speech of January 1, Islamic Center, Los Angeles, typescript.

—————. 1989b. "In Order To Avoid the Deadlock in Tunisia." Islamic Tendency Movement. Typescript.

Gharbi, Samir. 1986, 1987. "Tunisie: Que peut faire ben Ali?" and "L'homme nouveau en Tunisie." *Jeune Afrique* (October 14 and July 9).

Gouia, Ridha. 1987. "Regime d'accumulation et modes de dependence: Le cas de la Tunisie. Doctoral dissertation, University of Tunis.

Graaff, J. de V. 1970. *Les Fondements Theoriques de L'Economie du Bien Etre* Vol. 1. Paris: Dunod.

Green, Arnold. H. 1978. *The Tunisian Ulama, 1873–1915*. Leiden: E. J. Brill.

—————. n.d. "An Interest Group Analysis of Tunisia's State Enterprises." In M. K. Nabli and Jeffrey B. Nugent, eds., *The Institutional Economics and Development Theory and Applications to Tunisia*: North Holland. Forthcoming.

Haggard, Stephan, and Robert Kaufman. Forthcoming. *The Politics of Stabilization and Structural Adjustment*.

Hahn, Lorna. 1972. "Tunisian Political Reform: Procrastination and Progress." *Middle East Journal* 26: 405–414.

Haile-Mariam, Yacob, and Berhanu Mengistu. 1988. "Public Enterprises and the Privatisation Thesis in the Third World," *Third World Quarterly* 10(4): 1565–1587.

Hale, J. R. 1977. *Florence and the Medici: The Pattern of Control*. London: Thames and Hudson.

al-Hannachi, Salah Brik, and Abdessatar Grissa. 1987. "Les conditions prealables necessaires à la réussite de la privatisation." Presented at USAID privatization conference, Tunis.

al-Harmasi, Abd al-Latif. 1985. *al-Haraka al-islamiyya fi tunis* (The Islamic Movement in Tunisia). Tunis.

Herman, Lawrence L. 1984. "The Court Giveth and the Court Taketh Away: An Analysis of the Tunisia–Libya Continental Shelf Case." *International and Comparative Law Quarterly* 33(4): 825–858.

Hermassi, Elbaki. 1972. *Leadership and National Development in North Africa.* Berkeley: University of California Press.

———. 1984. "La société tunisienne au miroir islamiste." *Maghreb–Machreq* 103: (January) 39–56.

———. 1989. "Pouvoir-Islamicistes" *Réalités*, June 2, pp. 8–9..

———. n.d. *State, Development Policies, and Social Classes in Tunisia* (unpublished manuscript).

Hirshman, Albert O. 1963. *Journeys Toward Progress.* New York: Twentieth Century Fund.

———. 1970. *Exit, Voice, and Loyalty.* Cambridge: Harvard University Press.

———. 1978. *The Passions and the Interests.* Princeton: Princeton University Press.

Hopkins, Nicholas. 1977. "The Emergence of Class in a Tunisian Town," *International Journal of Middle East Studies* 8: 453–491.

———. 1978. "The Articulation of the Modes of Production: Tailoring in Tunisia," *American Ethnologist* 5(3): 468–483.

———. 1982. "Models in the Maghrib: Notes from Political Anthropolgy," *International Review of Modern Sociology* 12: 51–73.

———. *Testour ou La Transformation des Campagnes Magrebnies.* Tunis: CERES.

Hughes, Stephen. 1985. "Steady Pace in the Maghreb." *Banker*, December, 117–124.

Hunt, Chester L. 1966. *Social Aspects of Economic Development.* New York: McGraw-Hill.

Huntington, Samuel. 1969. *Political Order in Changing Societies.* New Haven: Yale.

Huxley, Frederick C. 1989. "Local History and National Leaders: A Case Study." Presented at the Tunisia Day Conference, School of Advanced International Studies, Johns Hopkins University, Washington.

Hyden. Goran. 1983. *No Shortcuts to Progress.* Berkeley: University of California Press.

Institut National de Statistique. 1979. *Récensement des Etablissements, Tunisie Entiere: 1976–1978.* Tunis: INS.

———. 1984. *Récensement géneral de la population et de l'habitat 30 mars, 1984.* Tunis: INS.

———. 1987. *Annuaire statistique de la Tunisie (1986–1987).* 31.

———. 1989. *Bulletin Mensuel de Statistique.* Tunis: Institut National de la Statistique.

Islamic Way, movement of. 1981. "Al-bayan al-ta'sisi li-haraka al-ittijah al-islami" [The foundational declaration of the Islamic Tendency movement]. *Magalat* [Essays], by Rachid Ghannouchi. Paris: Dar al-karawan li'l-taba'a wal'nashr wa'ltawzi'.

Jackson, Robert H., and Carl G. Rosberg. 1982. *Personal Rule in Black Africa.* Berkeley: University of California Press.

Jessua, Claude. 1968. *Couts sociaux, couts privés et optimum social.* Paris: Presses Universitaires de France.

al-Jurshi, Salah al-Din. 1983. "Limadha al-fikr al-islami al- mustaqbali?" [Why Futuristic Islamic Thought?]. *15*21*, January, 11–15.

———. 1984. "Akhta' sha'i'a 'an mustalah wa tayar" [Widespread errors of term and tendency]. *15*21*, 37–40.

Kapstein, Ethan B. 1989. "International Coordination of Banking Regulations." *International Organization* 43(2): 323–334.

al-Karm, Ahmed. 1989. "La strategie de libéralisation financière externe en Tunisie." Banque Centrale de Tunisie, Mimeo.

Karoui, N. 1982. "La Femme Tunisienne et la Phénomene 'Bureau': Etude Sociologique sur les Attitudes et Conduites des Jeunes Femmes Tunisiennes dans l'Adminstration de PTT." *Revue Tunisienne de Sciences Sociales* 70/71: 143–167.

Keller, Bill. 1990. "Gorbachev As Houdini." *New York Times*, February 5.

Khelil, Ismail. 1988a. Speech of March 23, Tunis: Banque Centrale.

———. 1988b. "La strategie de la réforme du systeme financière tunisien." Speech of 24 May. Banque Centrale de Tunisie, Tunis.

———. 1988c. Speech of October 4, Tunis: Banque Centrale.

———. 1989a. Speech of January 17, in Bahrein, Tunis: Banque Centrale.

———. 1989b. "Les nouveaux impératifs de la gestion bancaire." Speech of May 11. Banque Centrale de Tunisie, Tunis.

Khoury, H., C. S. Potter, H. Moore, and A. Messer. 1989. *Technical Mission Report for the Tunisia Locust Control Campaign, November 2–December 15, 1988.* Washington: AID/Office of Foreign Disaster Assistance.

Kolm, S. Ch. 1968. "Role Social Ambigu des Prix Publics," *Economie Applique*, Archives ISEA 2.

———. 1972. *Justice et Equite*, Paris: CNRS.

Krasner, Stephen. 1985. *Structural Conflict: The Third World Against Global Liberalism.* Berkeley: University of California Press.

Krishan, Ziyad. 1982. "Nahwa fahm taqaddumi li'l-islam" [Toward a progressive understanding of Islam]. *15*21*, November, pp. 9–13.

Laipson, Ellen B. 1987. *Tunisia After Bourguiba: Issues for U.S. Policy.* Congressional Research Service Report. Washington: Library of Congress.

Larif-Beatrix, Asma. 1987. "L'évolution de l'Etat tunisien," *Maghreb-Machrek* 116: 35–44 (April).

Larson, Barbara. 1986. *Rapport d'évaluation des impacts socioéconomiques dans le PPI de Garaat Ennaam.* Binghamton, NY: Institute for Development Anthropology.

———. 1987. *Rapport d'évaluation des impacts socioéconomiques dans le PPI de Bled Debbiche, Rohia.* Binghamton, NY: Institute for Development Anthropology.

Lecoq, M. 1988. *Les criquets du Sahel.* Montpellier, France: CILSS–DFPV.

Leeds, Roger. 1988. "Turkey: Rhetoric and Reality," In Raymond Vernon, ed., *The Promise of Privatization: A Challenge for American Foreign Policy.* New York: Council on Foreign Relations, Inc.

Leveau, Remy. 1989. "Tunisie: Equilibre interne et environnement arabe." *Maghreb–Machrek* 124(April): 4–17.

Magnuson, Douglas E. 1987. *Islamic Reform in Contemporary Tunisia: A Comparative Ethnographic Study.* Ann Arbor, MI: University Microfilms.

Mahjoub, Azzam. 1978. "Industrie et accumulation du capital en Tunisie depuis la fin du XVIIIéme siècle jusqu'à nos jours." Ph.D. dissertation, University of Grenoble II.

Mamou, Yves. 1988. *Une machine de pouvoir: La direction du trésor*. Paris: Editions La Decouverte.

Markham, James M. 1989. "Tunisia Is Pulling a Democratic Rabbit out of a Dictator's Hat." *New York Times*, April 10.

Marzouki, Moncef. 1989. "Winning Freedom." *Index on Censorship* (1): 23-25.

Mernissi, F. 1985. *Beyond the Veil: Male-Female Dynamics in a Muslim Society*. London: Al Saqi.

Mezoughi, Abdelaziz. 1988. "Revision structurelle au MTI." *Le Maghreb*, July 14, pp. 16–18.

Micaud, Charles, L. Carl Brown, and Clement H. Moore. 1964. *Tunisia: The Politics of Modernization*. New York: Praeger.

Migdal, Joel S. 1988. *Strong Societies and Weak States*. Princeton: Princeton University Press.

Mitchell, Richard P. 1969. *The Society of Muslim Brothers*. London: Oxford University Press.

Moore, Clement Henry. 1963. "Politics in a Tunisian Village." *Middle East Journal* 17: 527–540. Also in I. William Zartman, ed., (1973).

———. 1965. *Tunisia Since Independence*. Berkeley: University of Califoria Press.

———. 1970. *Politics in North Africa*. Boston: Little, Brown.

———. 1973. "Clientelist Ideology and Political Change: Fictitious Networks in Egypt and Tunisia." In Ernest Gellner and John Waterbury, eds., *Patrons and Clients in Mediterranean Society*. London: Duckworth.

———. 1988a. "Tunisia and Bourguibisme: Twenty Years of Crisis." *Third World Quarterly* 10(1): 176–190.

———. 1988b. "Islamic Banking: Financial and Political Intermediation in Arab Countries." *Orient* 29(1): 45–47.

Morrisson, Ch. 1968. *La Répartition des revenus dans les Pays du Tiers Monde*. Paris: Cujas.

Muru, 'Abd al-Fattah. 1979b. "Interview with 'Abd al-Fattah Muru." in Fathiya Balghith, *Al-haraka al-islamiyya fi tunis min khilal sahifat al-'amal*.

———. 1979a. "Liqa ma'a'l-shaykh 'Abd al-Fattah Muru" [A meeting with Shaykh 'Abd al-Fattah Muru]. *al-Ma'rifa*, March, pp. 21–25.

Mzali, Mohamed. 1987. *Lettre ouverte à Habib Bourguiba*. Paris: Alain Moreau.

al-Nasiri, al-Amin. 1988. "Arqam wa istintajat" [Numbers and inferences]. *Outrouhat*, March (special issue), pp. 21–24.

al-Nayfar, Ahmida. 1977a. "Al-Tariqun bi-'unf" [Those Striking with Violence]. *al-Ma'rifa*, 4(2), July, pp. 3–4.

———. 1977b. "Raj'iyun wa mu'asirun" [Reactionaries and Modernists]. *al-Ma'rifa*, 4(3): 3–4.

———. 1977c. "Da'uhu ya'innu" [Leave him groaning]. *al-Ma'rifa*, 4(4): pp. 3–5.

———. 1978a. "Al-khawf wa'l-intihar" [Fear and suicide]. *al-Ma'rifa*, 4(5), January, pp. 3–5.

———. 1978b. "Wa 'ada sutih" [And Sutih returned]. *al-Ma'rifa* 4(6), March, pp. 3–5.

Nelson, Harold D., ed. 1987. *Tunisia: A Country Study*. Washington: GPO.

Neziha, ben Yedder. 1975. "Le reglement pacifique des conflits maghrebins." Ph.D. dissertation, Memoire pour le D.E.S. de Droit Politique, University of Tunis.

Nicholas, Peter. 1988. *The World Bank's Lending for Adjustment*. Washington: World Bank.

O'Donnell, Guillermo, and Philippe Schmitter. 1986. *Transitions from Authoritarian Rule: Tentative Conclusions About Uncertain Democracies*. Baltimore: Johns Hopkins University Press.

Okun, Arthur M. 1982. *Egalite v.s. Efficacite: Comment Trouver l'Equilibre?* Paris: Economica.

Panitch, Leo. 1981. "Trade Unions and the Capitalist State." *New Left Review* 125.

Paul, Samuel. 1985. "Privatization and the Public Sector," *Finance and Development* 22(4): 42–45.

Pedgley, D. 1981. *Desert Locust Forecasting Manual*. London: Centre for Overseas Pest Research.

Pelletreau, Pamela. 1989. "Private Sector Development Through Public Sector Restructuring." Paper presented to the Tunisia Day Conference, Johns Hopkins University, Washington.

Perkins, Kenneth. 1986. *Tunisia: Crossroads of the Islamic and European Worlds*. Boulder: Westview.

Pipes, Daniel. 1983. *In the Path of God: Islam and Political Power*. New York: Basic Books.

Pirson, R. 1975. "L'Emancipation de la femme dans la société tunisienne contemporaine." *Population et Famille* 36(3): 129–153.

Pondi, Jean-Emmanuel. 1988. "Qadhafi and the Organization of African Unity." In René Lemarchand, ed., *The Green and the Black: Qadhafi's Policies in Africa*. Bloomington: Indiana University Press.

Posner, S. 1988. *Biologica, Diversity, and Tropical Forests in Tunisia*. Tunisia: USAID/Tunis.

Potter, C. S. 1988. *Draft Environmental Assessment of the Tunisia Locust Control Campaign*. Washington: AID/Science & Technology/Office for Agriculture.

al-Qasir, 'Abd al-Razzaq. 1982. "Haraka al-ittijah al-islami fi tunis: Mawqif al-khitab al-'ilmi wa'l-khitab al-suhufi" [The Movement of the Islamic Way in Tunisia: The position of the scientific message and the journalistic message]. Thesis, School of Journalism, University of Tunis III.

Rabinow, Paul, and William M. Sullivan. 1979. *Interpretive Social Sciences*. Berkeley: University of California Press.

Rahman, Fazlur. 1981. "Roots of Islamic Neo-Fundamentalism." In Philip H. Stoddard, D. Cuthell, and M. Sullivan, eds., *Change and the Muslim World*. Syracuse, NY: Syracuse University Press.

Reidinger, Richard B. 1981. *World Fertilizer Review Prospects to 1980–1981*. Foreign Agricultural Economic Report No. 115. Washington: U.S. Department of Agriculture.

Rejeb, M., and N. Krichene. 1983. *Evolution de la productivité et des salaires dans les secteurs public et privés*.

République Tunisienne. Ministère du Plan. 1986. *VII plan de développement économique et social (1987–1991)*. Tunis: Ministère du Plan.

———. 1989. *Statistiques financiéres*. Tunis: Banque Centrale.

République Tunisienne. Ministère du Plan. 1961. *Plan Triennal (1962-64)*. Tunis: Ministère du Plan.

République Tunisienne. Ministère de l'Industrie et du Connerce, Comité permanent technique du secteur des industries defabriction. 1986. *Préparation du VIIIe plan de developpement économique et social 1987–1991: Rapport de synthèse.* Tunis: Ministère de l'Industrie et du Commerce.

République Tunisienne. Ministère du Plan et des Finances. 1987. "Memorandum sur la situation et les perspectives de développement de l'economie tunisienne." Tunis: Ministére du Plan at des Finances, (January).

Riddell, Roger. 1987. *Foreign Aid Reconsidered.* Baltimore: Johns Hopkins University Press.

Romdhane, Mahmoud ben. 1981. "L'accumulation du capital et les classes sociales en Tunisie depuis l'indépendance." Doctoral diss., University of Tunis.

Romdhane, Mahmoud ben, and Pierre Signoles. 1982. "Les formes récentes de l'industrialization tunisienne, 1970–1980." *Geographie et developpement 5.*

Romdhane, Mahmoud ben, and Azzam Mahjoub. n.d. *Transformation économiques et changements sociaux en Tunisie.* Cairo: Le Forum du Tiers Monde.

RONCO Consulting Corporation. 1986. *Central Tunisia Rural Development Evaluation Report.* Washington: RONCO.

Rose, Peter S. 1987. *The Changing Structure of American Banking.* New York: Columbia University Press.

Rudebeck, Lars. 1967. *Party and People: A Study of Political Change in Tunisia.* Stockholm: Almqvist and Wiksell.

———. 1969. *Party and People.* New York: Praeger.

Rustow, Dankwart. 1970. "Transitions to Demoracy: Towards a Dynamic Model." *Comparative Politics* 2, no. 3 (April) 337–363..

Sadrin, Siham ben. 1983. "Al-Islam wa'l-'amal al-siyasi" [Islam and political action]. *al-Maghrib,* December 10, pp. 57–63; December 17, pp. 50–57; December 24, pp. 49–57.

Safra, Mongi. 1987. "Note sur le plan de redressement Tunisien de 1986." *Finances et développement au Maghreb* 1 (January): 63–68.

Saidane, Ezzedine. 1988. "Réflexion sur la dynamisation du marché monétaire." *Finances et développement au Maghreb* 4 (December).

Salem, Norma. 1984. *Habib Bourguiba, Islam, and the Creation of Tunisia.* London: Croom Helm.

Schmidt, Steffen W., James C. Scott, Carl Lande, and Laura Gausti. 1977. *Friends, Followers, and Factions.* Berkeley: University of California Press.

Scott, James C. 1972. *Comparative Political Corruption.* Englewood Cliffs, NJ: Prentice-Hall.

———. 1976. *The Moral Economy of the Peasant: Rebellion and Subsistence in Southeast Asia.* New Haven: Yale University Press.

———. 1977. "Political Clientelism: A Bibliographic Essay." In Steffen W. Schmidt, James C. Scott, Carl Lande, and Laura Gausti, *Friends, Followers, and Factions.* Berkeley: University of California Press.

Seddon, David. 1986. "Politics and the Price of Bread in Tunisia." In Alan Richards, ed., *Food, States, and Peasants: Analyses of the Agrarian Question in the Middle East.* Boulder: Westview.

Sharabi, Hisham. 1970. *Arab Intellectuals and the West: The Formative Years, 1875–1914.* Baltimore: Johns Hopkins University Press.

Showler, Allen. 1989a. "Report on FAO/Rome Desert Locust Research Conference." Typescript.

———. 1989b. *Scientific Protocol for Ecological Monitoring in Insecticide-Treated Regions of North Africa and the Sahel During Locust/Grasshopper Campaigns.* Washington: AID/Office of Foreign Disaster Assistance.

Showler, A., and K. Maynard. 1988. *Algeria Locust Control Operations Assessment, November 12–December 12, 1988*. Washington: AID/Office of Foreign Disaster Assistance.

Signoles, Pierre. 1984. *Régime d'accumulation et modes de dépendance: Le cas de la Tunisie*. Ph.D. dissertation, University of Paris I.

———. 1985. *L'espace Tunisien: Capitale et état-region*. 2 vols. Tours: Fascicule de Recherches 14.

Slim, Habib. 1980. "Le comité permanent consultatif du Maghreb entre le passé et l'avenir." *Revue Tunisiene de Droit*: 241–252.

———. 1982. "Elections, pluralisme contrôlé et démocratie 'intermédiare'," *Revue Tunisienne de Droit* 117–213.

Smith, Wilfred Cantwell. 1977. *Islam in Modern History*. Princeton: Princeton University press.

Société Tunisienne de Banque. 1987. *Rapport Annuel 1986*. Tunis: STB.

Souriau, Christiane, ed. 1981. *Le Maghreb musulman en 1979*. Paris: Centre National de Recherche Scientifique/Centre de Recherche et d'Etude sur les Sociétés MéditéranNéennes.

Springborg, Robert. 1989. *Mubarak's Egypt: Fragmentation of the Political Order*. Boulder: Westview.

Steedman, A., ed. 1988. *Locust Handbook*. 2d ed. London: Overseas Development Natural Resources Institute.

Steiner, J. L., J. C. Day, R. I. Pependick, R. E. Meyer, and A. R. Bertrand. 1988. "Improving and Sustaining Productivity in Dryland Regions of Developing Countries." *Advances in Soil Science* 8: 79–122.

Stoleru, Leonel. 1974. *Vaincre la Pauvreté dans les Pays Riches*. Paris: Flammarion.

Stone, Russell. 1982. "Tunisia: A Single Party System Holds Change in Abeyance." In I. William Zartman et al. 1982.

——— and Simmons, eds., 1976. *Change in Tunisia*. Albany: State University of New York Press.

Taamallah, L. 1981. "La Scolarisation et la Formation Professionelle des Femmes en Tunisie." *Revue Tunisienne des Sciences Sociales* 68/69: 107–127.

———. 1982. "Les Femmes et l'Emploi en Tunisie." *Revue Tunisienne de Sciences Sociales* 70/71: 143–166.

TAMS/CICP. 1989. *Programmatic environmental assessment for locust and grasshopper control in Africa and Asia*. TAMS Consultants Inc. and Consorte for International Crop Protection.

Tekeri, Bechir. 1981. *Du cheikh a l'omda: Institution locale traditionnelle et integration partisane*. Tunis: Imprimerie Officielle de la Republique Tunisienne.

Tessler, Mark, and Patricia Freeman. 1981. "Regime Orientation and Participant Citizenship in Developing Countries: Hypotheses and a Test with Longitudinal Data from Tunisia." *Western Political Quarterly* 23(4): 479–498 (December).

——— and L. Hawkins, 1979. "Acculturation, Socio-Economic Status and Attitude Change in Tunisia." *Journal of Modern African Studies* 17(4): 473–495 (December).

Tessler, Mark, J. Rogers, and D. Schneider. 1978. "Tunisian Attitudes Toward Women and Child Rearing," pp. 289-311. In J. Allman, ed. *Women's Status and Fertility in the Muslim World*. New York: Praeger Special Studies.

Tinberger, Jan. 1972. *Politique Economique et Optimum Social*. Paris: Economica.

Troin, Jean-Francois, ed. *Le Maghreb: Hommes et Espaces*. Paris: Colin.
United Nations Food and Agriculture Organization. 1985. *Food Aid in Figures*. Rome: FAO.
United Nations. Industrial Development Organization. 1986. *Industry and Development Report 1986*. Vienna: UNIDO.
United States. Agency for International Development. 1989. "Tunisia: A Strategis Option for the 90s." Typescript.
van Krieken, G. S. 1976. *Khayr Al-Din et la Tunisie*. Leiden: E. J. Brill.
Vanderlaan, G. 1980. "Equilibrium Under Rigid Prices with Compensation for the Consumers," *International Economic Review* 21(1): 63–73.
Vandewalle, Dirk. 1987. *Tunisia Reports 14, 15, 22*. Hanover: Institute of Current World Affairs (April, November).
———. 1988. "From the New State to the New Era: Toward a Second Republic in Tunisia." *Middle East Journal* 42: 602–620.
Vandevelde-Daillere, H. 1972. *Femmes Algeriennes à Travers la Condition Feminine dans la Constantinois Depuis L'Indépendance*. Alger: Office des Publications Universitaires.
Vatin, Jean-Claude. 1982. "Islam As an Alternative Political Language." In Ali Dessouki, ed., *Islamic Resurgency in the Arab World*. New York: Praeger.
Voll, John O. 1982a. *Islam: Continuity and Change in the Modern World*. Boulder: Westview.
———. 1982b. "Wahhabism and Mahdism: Alternative Styles of Islamic Renewals," *Arab Studies Quarterly* 4(1&2): 110–126.
———. 1983. "Renewal and Reform in Islamic History: Tajdid and Islah," In John Esposito, ed., *Voices of Resurgent Islam*, pp. 32–47. New York: Oxford University Press.
Waltz, Susan. 1982. "Antidotes for a Social Malaise: Alienation, Efficacy and Participation in Tunisia," *Comparative Politics* 14: 127–147.
Ware, Lewis B. 1984. "The Role of the Tunisian Military in the Post-Bourguiba Era," *Middle East Journal* 39: 27–47.
Waterbury, John. 1976. "Corruption, Political Stability, and Development: Comparative Evidence from Egypt and Morocco." *Government and Opposition* 11.
———. Forthcoming. *Twilight of the State Bourgeoisie*.
Wood, Robert. 1985. *From Marshall Plan to Debt Crisis: Foreign Debt and Development Choices in the World Economy*. Berkeley: University of California Press.
World Bank. 1988a. "Report and Recommendation of the President of the International Bank for Reconstruction and Development to the Executive Directors on a Proposed Structural Adjustment Loan in an Amount Equivalent to US $150 million to the Republic of Tunisia," Report No. P-4808-TUN, May 20, 1988, processed.
———. 1988b. *World Development Report 1988*. New York: Oxford University Press.
Zartman, I. William. 1967. "Political Pluralism in Morocco," *Government and Opposition* II, 4: 568–583 (fall), reprinted in Zartman, ed., 1973.
———. 1971. *The Politics of Trade Negotiations Between Africa and the EEC*. Princeton, NJ: Princeton University Press.
———. ed. 1973. *Man, State and Society in the Contemporary Maghreb*. New York: Praeger.

———. 1975. "The Elites of the Maghreb: A Review Article," *International Journal of Middle East Studies*, 6: 495–504.

———. 1982. "Political Elites in Arab North Africa: Origins, Behavior, and Prospects." In Zartman et al., 1982.

———. and Adeed Dawisha, eds., 1988. *Beyond Coercion: The Durability of the Arab States*. London: Croom Helm.

———. Mark A. Tessler, John P. Entelis, Russell A. Stone, Raymond A. Hinnebusch, and Shahrough Akhavi. 1982. *Political Elites in Arab North Africa*. New York: Longman, Inc.

Zghal, Abdelkader. 1967. *Modernisation de L'Agriculture et Populations Semi-Nomades*. The Hague: Mouton.

About the Contributors

I. William Zartman is professor of international politics and director of African studies at the Nitze School of Advanced International Studies, The Johns Hopkins University. He is also the president of the American Institute for Maghreb Studies and the Tangier American Legation Museum Society.

Susan Waltz is professor of international relations at the Florida International University.

Eva Bellin is assistant professor of comparative politics and Middle East studies at the Nitze School of Advanced International Studies, The Johns Hopkins University

Clement Henry Moore is professor of politics at the University of Texas, Austin.

Ridha Ferchiou is professor at the Institute of Finance and Development of the Arab Maghrib (IFID) in Tunis and former director of the Institute of Higher Commercial Studies (IHEC) of the University of Tunis.

Abdelsatar Grissa is professor of economics in the Faculty of the Economic Sciences of the University of Tunis.

Pamela Day Pelletreau is with the Agency for International Development in Tunisia.

Barbara K. Larson is associate professor of anthropology at the University of New Hampshire.

Christopher S. Potter is a fellow with the American Association for the Advancement of Sciences with the Agency for International Development.

Allan T. Showler is with the Agency for International Development, Bureau of Science and Technology, Office of Agriculture.

Douglas K. Magnuson teaches at the Bourguiba Institute of Modern Languages in Tunis.

Elbaki Hermassi is professor of political science at the University of Tunis.

Abdelkader Zghal is professor of sociology at the Center for Social and Economic Research and Studies (CERES) of the University of Tunis.

Mary-Jane Deeb is assistant professor of politics at the American University.

Ellen Laipson is with the congressional Research Service of the Library of Congress and has served on the policy planning staff of the Department of State.

Index

About the Book

L ike many countries at the end of the twentieth century, Tunisia is in the midst of a period of rapid change. The replacement of Life President Habib Bourguiba by Zine Labidine ben Ali in November 1987 opened the Tunisian political system to a wide agenda of reform. In the political sphere, the removal of Bourguiba allowed the possibility of a transition from single-party rule toward democracy. On the economic front, reforms demanded by internal conditions, as well as by external agencies, led to policies of structural adjustment and privatization. In contrast, in the area of social policy the demand for a regressive reform is being led by the proponents of the Movement of the Islamic Way, while the government has defended the existing codes, a legacy of an earlier reform movement under Bourguiba.

The interplay of reforms in these three areas, and the interaction of societal pressures and government policies, are the subjects of this study of the first two years of the ben Ali regime.

The SAIS African Studies Library
(available from Lynne Rienner Publishers)

Tunisia: The Political Economy of Reform, edited by I. William Zartman

Ghana: The Political Economy of Recovery, edited by Donald Rothchild

Europe and Africa: The New Phase, edited by I. William Zartman

Other SAIS Studies on Africa:

The Political Economy of Ethiopia (1990)

The Political Economy of Senegal Under Structural Adjustment (1990)

The Political Economy of Morocco (1987)

The Military in African Politics (1987)

The Political Economy of Kenya (1987)

The Political Economy of Cameroon (1986)

The OAU After Twenty Years (1984)

The Political Economy of Zimbabwe (1984)

The Political Economy of Ivory Coast (1984)

The Political Economy of Nigeria (1983)